Intentionality and the New Traditionalism

ALSO BY JOHN SHAWCROSS

With Mortal Voice: The Creation of Paradise Lost
Paradise Regain'd: "Worthy Not To Have Remain'd So Long Unsung"
A Milton Bibliography For the Years 1624–1700
Editor, The Complete Poetry of John Milton
Editor, The Complete Poetry of John Donne
Milton: The Critical Heritage, two volumes (1624–1732, 1732–1801)
Achievements of the Left Hand: Essays on Milton's Prose (with Michael Lieb)
Language and Style in Milton (with Ronald D. Emma)

Intentionality and the New Traditionalism

Some Liminal Means to Literary Revisionism

John T. Shawcross

The Pennsylvania State University Press
University Park, Pennsylvania

A version of chapter 1 appeared in *Genre* 18 (1985): 413–34, and chapter 8 was first printed in *Classic and Cavalier: Essays on Jonson and the Sons of Ben,* ed. Claude J. Summers and Ted-Larry Pebworth (Pittsburgh, Pa.: University of Pittsburgh Press, 1982), 193–214.

Ezra Pound's poem "The Pact," from *Personae,* is reprinted by permission of New Directions Pub. Corp. and Faber and Faber, Ltd. Copyright 1928 by Ezra Pound.

The stanza from Donald Hall's poem "Six Poets in Search of a Lawyer," in *Exiles and Marriages* (New York: Viking, 1955), is reprinted by permission of Donald Hall.

Library of Congress Cataloging-in-Publication Data

Shawcross, John T.
    Intentionality and the new traditionalism : some liminal means to literary revisionism / John T. Shawcross.

        p.   cm.
    Includes bibliographical references and index.
    ISBN 0-271-00758-3
    1. English literature—17th century—History and criticism—
Theory, etc. 2. English literature—History and criticism—Theory,
etc. 3. Intentionalism. 4. Literary form. I. Title.
PR431.S53 1991
820.9′004—dc20   90-20919
                                                      CIP

It is the policy of The Pennsylvania State University Press to use acid-free paper for the first printing of all clothbound books. Publications on uncoated stock satisfy the minimum requirements of American National Standard for Information Sciences—Permanence of Paper for Printed Library Materials, ANSI Z39.48–1984.

Contents

1

Introduction:
Literary Revisionism:
Definitions and Devices

hree matters concern me in this book: the system of literature delineated by literary genre; certain insufficiently used approaches to fuller understanding of authorial presence and craft (including genre); and limited readings of literary works and authors largely stemming from inattention to such approaches. While some current modish literary criticism still offers *the author dead / the reader born* as a first given, I eclectically maintain that what the author does and what the author intends to do are important issues for anyone interested in the creative process, as well as for a means to understanding a literary work, and that what the reader elicits from a literary work is a major factor in determining what the author does or does not do. The author's input and the reader's output are both, therefore, significant in evaluation. The text is an experience that the reader undergoes; it is an experience whose lineaments, however, have been laid out by the author. Poststructuralist criticism has not been concerned with evaluation; description, based on linguistic and affective analysis, seems to be the extent of interest most often. Evaluation of course will change from age to age, from person to person, from acquisition of little to more knowledge, but it is or should be a function of literary criticism.

In the poem "To the Learned Ingenious Author of *Licentia Poetica discuss'd*" (that is, to William Coward, a medical doctor, who was related to John Milton), published in 1709, John Gay made an important observation:

> The Vulgar Notion of Poetic fire,
> Is, *that laborious Art can ne'er aspire,*
>
> *Nor Constant Studies the bright Bays acquire,*
> *And that high Flights the unborn Bard receives,*
> *And only Nature the due Laurel gives. . . .* [1]

But he goes on to dispel this "Vulgar Notion" and to assert the need for "labor" in producing worthy writing and "Constant Studies" to make a poem successful. In more recent times, Ernst Fischer in *The Necessity of Art*[2] pointed out that

> Emotion for an artist is not everything; he must also know his trade and enjoy it, understand all the rules, skills, forms, and conventions whereby nature—the shrew—can be tamed and subjected to the contract of art. The passion that consumes the dilettante *serves* the true artist: the artist is not mauled by the beast, he tames it. (9)

Awareness that literature is much more than the result of inspiration only (the romantic fallacy—and much literary structuralism and deconstructionism has emerged from so-called Romantic poetry and its critics) leads inevitably to a concept of planning, organization, techniques and devices, and revision, a concept that must be preceded by some kind of intention on the author's part. While a germ of inspiration, whatever its form or source, will enter either to begin, to sustain, or to bring to fruition a piece of literature, the fact remains that labor is required. The inspiration may be a thought, a few lines of poetry, or an epiphany in James Joyce's sense, and out of this may come a finally completed work, the original perhaps transformed, perhaps not. Maybe even more likely, that thought, those few lines, that epiphany, will be tucked away in a file (or an old shoe box) to be used (yes, "used") as a different creative occasion arises. The literary item may come to be used like an extra piece of nicely grained wood that we have saved because it might come in handy someday, and now we have just the right occasion in fashioning a table top or in adapting it to those other materials that are being wrought into a shadow box. Like the product that has been fashioned out of the wood, the piece of literature resultant is polished, is perhaps altered in little ways in shape or coloration, is placed in a setting, or is allowed to stand unto itself.

Thus the piece of literature. The literary critic has the task of viewing it disembodied or in some context (that made by the author, say, in placing a poem in a collection of poems; that made by its existence as a part of the author's world and literary corpus or as a part of a literary world that it has now joined). What does that piece of literature say or do or create as experience? What has made the piece of literature what it is? One way of answering these questions is through one's reaction to it, although we should recognize that reactions may change with rereading, with added knowledge, with changed emotions, with external circumstances, and from reader to reader. The answer may lie in an analysis of the language, the pictures (or signs), the sounds. It may lie in the construction of the work, its internal ordering and parts, its total being, and its individual building blocks. But now the literary critic is starting to recognize that the text *qua* text does not supply everything of importance for literary criticism. The critic has begun to recognize that the literary work is not simply words in some kind of appearance on the page: the reader's apprehension of those words and that page are important, but so is the reader's awareness of the totality and its parts, and awareness of the words and the totality or parts depends on both the reader as individual and on what has been put into the work under scrutiny by the author.[3] Fischer talks of the origins of literature in magic; the author as a magician who builds illusions, who leads the eye and plants ideas in the mind, creates settings and calls into play possible audience experience, associations, attitudes. The piece of literature may be reviewed by its verbalizations, yes, but it has more than just words as part of those verbalizations: it has structures, ambiguities, pictures. Some of those verbalizations represent the reader's reactions; some, the author's actions. The piece of literature may be viewed by its affectation of the reader, but some of that is manipulated by the author, much as our current affective critics dismiss such authorial action. The piece of literature may be viewed by its authorial actions, and they imply some kind of intent. I believe that literature should be viewed from all three vantage points: the text, the reader's text, and the author's text. These three texts may have many congruencies, and they may have distinct elements or discrepancies. They are only theoretically distinct as texts. The critic's job—as reader—is to render all three texts in their interrelationships. At times the direction of understanding may go from the text to the reader's text to the author's text; at times it is reversed from the author's text to the reader's text to the text.

Two direct examples of my distinction of these texts will be helpful: one deals with authorial device and thence allusion, the other with authorial allusion and thence device. In Book II of John Milton's *Paradise Lost* Satan, moving through Hell to find exit to proceed to Earth and harass the new creatures of God, meets his daughter Sin and their son Death. Lines 648–70 read:

> Before the Gates there sat
> On either side a formidable shape;
> The one seem'd Woman to the waste, and fair,
> But ended foul in many a scaly fould
> Voluminous and vast, a Serpent arm'd
> With mortal sting. . . . The other shape,
> If shape it might be call'd that shape had none
> Distinguishable in member, joynt, or limb,
> Or substance might be call'd that shadow seem'd,
> For each seem'd either . . . [4]

That is the text, and it is nothing but words in some order and has nothing other than existence until it is read. A reader's reading of it, the reader's text, may range from a simple understanding of the words to an understanding that these shapes are Sin and Death, and on the basis of allegoric recognitions such a reading may perceive first the way in which Sin entices humankind—by engaging man in normal sensual attraction, only to become vileness once he has become one with her—and second how Death is indescribable in human terms. But "the other shape" is introduced at line 666, and that number for some readers will trigger a remembrance of the Beast of Revelation. Only the more sophisticated reader would be attuned to make the observation of "the other shape" and the line on which it is introduced because that reader has previously observed that placement of words and numerological relationships may lead to "hidden" significance. If we wish to label such a reader "the informed reader" or "the ideal reader" or "the implied reader," of course we may, but an insertion of external knowledge into the text has been made once the line location of "the other shape" takes on significance. To observe that "the one [who] seem'd Woman" appears in line 650 does not insert external knowledge because that placement and that numerological fact have no significance in themselves. The reader's observation and recollection of the number of the Beast of Revelation, thus equating Death and the Beast (and all it may represent hermeneutically), has been made possible by the author's placement of the phrase on line 666. I as reader know the potential allusion in the number 666, but when I read John Dryden's "Absalom and Achitophel" the allusion is of no importance, for his line 666 is "Our laws for such affronts have forfeits made." This author has not set up such a reader's text because he did not intend a reader's text involving this piece of external knowledge. In Milton's case it is his text—the authorial text—that has been created to make possible the reader's text. The "text" thus is the specific words as they appear on the page;[5] the "reader's text" is the understanding the reader derives from reading that text; the "author's text" is the text the author has provided for the reader to read, with all its potentialities. A specific reader's text may become congruent with the author's text or not; it may even become more than the author's text. But to deny the existence of an "author's text," one that is potential for the variety of readers who may read, is not logical. What the author's text thus emphasizes is the action of writing, the craft that the writer writing has produced. The text defines continuing authorial presence.

In the example of Death as the Beast of Revelation we have Milton employing a device (that is, an artistic contrivance, a graphic symbol or figure) to lead the reader to an allusion and all the connotative meaning that allusion will subtend. Although the observation about line 666 has been previously made,[6] critics seem not to have gone back to the allusion for its fuller significance for the text. The reader's text has, in other words, not yet been adequately close to the author's text. Revelation 13 talks of two beasts: "And I stood upon the sand of the sea, and saw a beast rise up out of the sea" (v. 1); "And I beheld another beast coming up out of the earth [v. 11]... and his number is Six hundred threescore and six" (v. 18). Sin is thus likened to the first beast, who appropriately enough in allegoric significance has "seven heads and ten horns." "And they worshipped the dragon [Satan] which gave power unto the beast: and they worshipped the beast, saying, Who is like unto the beast: who is able to make war with him" (v. 4). "And it was given unto him to make war with the saints, and to overcome them: and power was given him over all kindreds, and tongues, and nations. And all that dwell upon the earth shall worship him, whose names are not written in the book of life of the Lamb slain from the foundation of the world" (vv. 7–8). (Note, too, that the first beast comes from the sea, a female archetype, and the second from the earth, a male archetype, in the scheme of water/air : fire/earth. Further, of course, "Adam," which ultimately means "red" and was then used for the red earth of the Fertile Crescent, implies man as one made from the dust of the earth. Later in the poem Milton will parallel Eve with Sin and Adam with Death.) The author's text, as this example shows, may embody device and allusion, and indeed any allusion or device becomes evidence of the author's text.

The allusion to this passage from *Paradise Lost* in Joseph Conrad's *Heart of Darkness* illustrates the way in which allusion may become device. When Marlow visits the Company offices, he finds two women in the outer room who are knitting black wool feverishly. The younger introduces those who arrive, while the old one sits in her chair.

> Often far away from there I thought of these two, guarding the door of Darkness, knitting black wool as for a warm pall, one introducing, introducing continuously to the unknown, the other scrutinizing the cheery and foolish faces with unconcerned old eyes. *Ave!* Old knitter of black wool. *Morituri te salutant.* Not many of those she looked at ever saw her again—not half, by a long way.[7]

Only the recognition of the allusion to Sin and Death allows the reader to comprehend fully the meaning of "warm pall," of "the unknown," or the widespread identity of "the cheery and foolish faces," or why so many look at the old knitter only once. The Latin "we who are about to die salute you" becomes obvious. The allusion occurs only a few pages into the novel, but through it the aware reader will be quite sure that the heart of darkness is the hell within sinful and doomed humankind, why the river is described as "an immense snake uncoiled," why the ships are named "Nellie" and the "Golden Hind" (first of the frequent female symbols in the novel) and "Erebus" and "Terror." And now, reread, the last sentence of the third paragraph of the novel—"It was difficult to realize his [the Director of Companies'] work was not out there in the luminous estuary, but behind him, within the brooding gloom"—alludes to the opening proem of *Paradise Lost* I, 19–26:

> Instruct me, for Thou know'st; Thou from the first
> Wast present, and with mighty wings outspread
> Dove-like sátst brooding on the vast Abyss
> And mad'st it pregnant: What in me is dark
> Illumin, what is low raise and support;
> That to the highth of this great Argument
> I may assert Eternal Providence,
> And justifie the wayes of God to men.

The Director as God-figure and Kurtz as Satan-figure (particularly in the popular nineteenth-century view of Milton's Satan as hero) emerge as we proceed in a "fascination of the abomination— . . . the growing regrets, the longing to escape, the powerless disgust, the surrender, the hate." Marlow as reporter wonders at the end whether, had he "rendered Kurtz that justice which was his due," they all would have fallen.

The allusion is unconfined, calling up further allusions, rendering the text a different text, allowing the author's text to be uncovered by the reader: it has become a device to illuminate the novel, to put it into perspective. Aware, we read such lines as the following differently from their cursory meaning: "He [Kurtz] is a prodigy. . . . He is an emissary of pity, and science, and progress, and devil knows what else"; "He had taken a high seat amongst the devils of the land—I mean literally" (compare the opening of *Paradise Lost* II); " 'Oh, but I will wring your heart yet!' he cried at the invisible wilderness" (compare Satan's antiheroism and Milton's "darkness visible," I, 63); "I saw him clearly enough then. I shall see this eloquent phantom as long as I live, and I shall see her [the unnamed girl whose name is the last word Kurtz pronounces], too, a tragic and familiar Shade, resembling in this gesture another one, tragic also, and bedecked with powerless charms, stretching bare brown arms over the glitter of the infernal stream, the stream of darkness."

The upshot of the revisionism that I am advancing here by looking at the author's text can be seen in two poems either generally inadequately read or actually misread by inattention to what I call authorial presence.

John Donne's epigram "A licentious person"[8] —

> Thy sinnes and haires may no man equall call,
> For, as thy sinnes increase, thy haires doe fall —

as text says that a licentious person continues to sin as he grows old, contrasting in "increase" a quantitative upward movement (the sins accumulate) and in "fall" a physical downward movement (the hairs disappear). But the comparison establishes that the "increase" is not simply quantitative but physical, and that the "fall" is not simply physical but quantitative (that is, the fallen hairs accumulate but those that remain become fewer). The placement of the two nouns "sinnes" and "haires" within the two lines likewise sets up comparisons: in the first it is as if they are the same, being conjoined ("sinnes and haires"); in the second it is clear they also contrast, being separated ("thy sinnes increase," "thy haires doe fall" — but they are metrical equivalents). The reader's text is based upon his or her reading of this text and recognition of the wittiness in the verbalizations. Not all readers necessarily produce this same reader's text. Some may end their reaction at this point; others may wonder what sins are being called up as physical. The most obvious, since this is a licentious person, are sexual "sins," and then the reader understands that *no man* may call this person's sins and hairs equal, but that a *woman* may. And then the reader either reads aloud with a somewhat off-pronunciation or remembers an older commonplace pun that renders "hairs" as "whores" (sometimes by way of "hares"). The sexual sins, thus, increase and the whores with whom the "licentious person" sins fall physically as the sins occur. His hairs falling physically will finally yield baldness, of course, and another commonplace bit of lore, often employed in Elizabethan literature, was that baldness was caused by the "French disease," syphilis. The reader is thus led to the pun "hairs / heirs," whereby we see that the poet is saying that he begets few heirs since the partners of his sexual sins would act to exert generative control and perhaps his semen becomes less fertile as he ages. The reader's text is not the same reader's text we first described, this latter being the result of external knowledge, the reader's experience with other texts ("tradition"), and in turn the author's employment of external knowledge and tradition. The argument that the author did not employ such external knowledge and tradition—did not intend such a reader's text—cannot be defensible in this case because of its commonplaceness, and indeed the text itself, as in the placement of the nouns and the ensuing contrast/comparison and puns, must be put squarely with the author's intention and execution. The critic is needed from time to time to point out such craft and ambiguity of language, external knowledge, and tradition. The critic is less needed by the reader who is able to view these matters without help, although many readers are not. The deconstructionist, undoubtedly, would say the critic is not needed at all because everything that is significant is in the text: if other matter is not extracted by the reader, so be it. Any experience of the text, to some, is the only importance.

This is illogical: the text has no effect until someone puts such effect (meaning, whatever) into it. If that someone is the reader, the effect may be more or less the effect that the author has made possible. What I am arguing is that the effect may be also (and it is *also* that must be emphasized) a taking out from the text provided. The effect is a polysemous reading, combining what the author did or did not do, what the reader recognizes that the author did or did not do, and what the reader comes to experience by what is the text. What the reader comes to experience is neither "right" nor "wrong," nor "complete," for the only stable element is the text one reads (except that a text like Donne's "The Flea" may change because there is no acceptably authorial text). Unlike Julia Kristeva, I believe that the signifier is both a sign of recoverable intention and a means for a reader to produce meaning. The recoverable intention should not be a limitation within the text, nor should the produced meaning ignore the potentiality that the author has provided. A pun is an obvious example. When Milton's Eve, having eaten of the fruit in order to take on wisdom and knowledge with the Gods, apostrophizes "Sapience" (IX, 797), the text has no meaning or effect until the reader is one who knows that sapience means wisdom, and the undercutting pun is not experienced until the reader is one who also knows that the Latin root of the word means *to taste*. But it is the author who set up these meanings and effects in the words by the way in which he or she used them. Clearly this is an example that could evoke for some reader-response critics the informed reader, but such a term becomes a dodge.

Yet I am not urging a transcendent meaning. Indeed, once the text becomes for the reader a set of undifferentiated signs an aliveness has left it; the text becomes easily forgettable. The predictable television murder mystery is a double case in point: not only is there no effectual aliveness when we see it on rerun, but there was not much even in the first viewing because it is so cliché ridden. But this view of a fluid text should not lead us to ignore what is inside the text, what and who made the text as it is. Indeed Milton's lines at this point in his poem offer the critical problem we have been looking at: Is meaning inherent in the sign and to be elicited, or is the sign the source from which meaning comes according to the reader of that sign? The lines are:

> O Sovran, vertuous, precious of all Trees
> In Paradise, of operation blest
> To Sapience, hitherto obscur'd, infam'd,
> And thy fair Fruit let hang, as to no end
> Created.
>
> (IX, 795–99)

The fruit contains that sapience ("wisdom" achieved through tasting ["experience"]) given it by God, but it is meaningless, superfluous, ineffectual until it is made active by someone. The action of that someone may lead to more or less "sapience" as given the fruit by God. For that someone— Eve at this point in the narrative at least—the tree bearing the fruit is "Sovran" (surely that is *more* than God intended though one would, faithfully, say that God's prescience knew of this "meaning"), and as "sovran" it is the tree that is addressed as "thy," not God. "Sapience," supposedly "hitherto obscur'd, infam'd," neither of which was true, is made *less* than God intended, for Eve's attitude toward the tree and its fruit hardly seems "wise," or perceptive. (We should, of course, recognize the genital symbols here of the phallic tree and the testiculate hanging fruit—surely much more than God intended, but not Milton.) The tree and its fair fruit were created to an end *in potentia;* what is derived from it may coincide or not. My point is that the fruit was created, hung on the tree, and interdicted by their creator, just as Milton has hung *sapience* here with primary and secondary meanings as textual creator: the reader may elicit only "knowledge," perhaps also "knowledge through tasting," perhaps come to understand differing "sapiences" ("forbidden knowledge" at least), perhaps be able to psychologize (and extend) the personality that makes such experience "precious" and "vertuous" (both "good" and "powerful," if we know our Latin) when first undertaken or encountered only to be reversed by repeated action and changed circumstances. Indeed, the word "operation" after we have understood the genital and sexual symbolization may finally strike the reader as a loaded term: both action and rote action, and that which is ultimately the effect of an environment, not of a given stimulus, as Eve thinks of it now. The words are the text; my reading of it (if not others') is a reader's text; and at least most of this is the author's text. The important text is the reader's text, but let us recognize the author's text and the author's craft: it may lead us to additional readers' texts. If one of those reader's texts was not part of the author's text (that is, if we ever could determine such a thing), we should not be surprised: people often do and say things without conscious understanding, and still the effect can be significant. What we should critically realize is that at times the author does and says things with conscious understanding, and this can lead us to craft and evaluation.

The other poem I wish to discuss that is generally inadequately read or actually misread by inattention to authorial presence is Thomas Carew's "Secrecy Protested." It is a lyric in tetrameter couplets (with one effective, purposely defective line) depicting a dramatic situation in which the speaker of the poem assures his loved one that only through his death and examination of her picture in his heart will their love be known to the outside world:

> Fear not, dear love, that I'll reveal
> Those hours of pleasure we two steal;
> No eye shall see, nor yet the sun
> Descry, what thou and I have done.
> No ear shall hear our love, but we
> Silent as the night will be;
> The God of Love himself (whose dart
> Did first wound mine and then thy heart)
> Shall never know that we can tell
> What sweets in stol'n embraces dwell.
> This only means may find it out:
> If, when I die, physicians doubt
> What caus'd my death, and there to view
> Of all their judgments which was true,
> Rip up my heart, oh then, I fear,
> The world will see thy picture there.[9]

Understanding can move in the direction of text/reader's text/author's text, but there is at least one significant element in the poem that will not be derived thus except by the very knowing reader (critic), an element we can pursue to see the development of understanding as author's text/reader's text. In either case such an element proves the author's conscious action with intent for the poem, leading the knowing reader to examine the poem differently from the way that reader would deal with it as disembodied text. The author has derived the last five lines from the first four of John Donne's "The Dampe":

When I am dead, and Doctors know not why,
   And my friends curiositie
Will have me cut up to survay each part,
When they shall finde your Picture in my heart . . .

The author's text is clearly one that recognizes the intertextuality of the two poetic texts. The discussion of Carew's poem by C. F. Main and Peter Seng[10] has not apparently recognized the allusive imitation and has treated the poem as reader's text only. They write, for example, "Here, as in any other drama, there has been some antecedent action: the 'hours of pleasure' (line 2) that the lovers have stolen." But we, aware of the poetical context out of which Carew wrote, in expectation that his reader would recognize the source, will realize that the hours of pleasure have *not* yet been stolen. The second stanza of Donne's poem makes clear that the lady is still resisting, for she has not dared be brave and kill the enormous Giant Disdain, nor the enchantress Honor. She has made a conquest of the persona but she has not yet killed him or let him die (with sexual double entendre). The poet of Carew's poem is in like circumstances: the God of Love has wounded his and then her heart, but the verbs are futural or implied as futural—"I'll reveal," "shall see," "[shall] Descry," "shall hear," "will be," "Shall never know." "Steal" in the second line is a present: it can mean *are stealing* or *will steal when you succumb.* "Can tell" in line 9 sounds as if they already know, and "what thou and I have done" in line 4 is a present perfect, but read in context with the realization that intercourse has not yet taken place, as both the other verb tenses and the allusion to Donne's poem establish, the words make sense and say, in the first instance, "The God of Love himself shall never know after we have made love that we will be able to tell what sweets dwell in stolen embraces," and in the second, "No eye shall see nor even will the sun [Day's eye] descry what thou and I have done [in the past]" makes no sense: if they have had intercourse, he should have said something equating "No eye has seen what thou and I have done, and no eye shall see us in the future either." Perhaps a truly close reading would have made the reader aware of the situation, but the allusion to "The Dampe" makes it unavoidable. In balance with her giant Disdain and enchantress Honor, the speaker of Donne's poem says he could muster up his giants and witches, and he names Constancy and Secretness. In the Renaissance the cliché was that man was constant and woman fickle, that man was secret about his affairs and woman talkative. The title of Carew's poem thus states the avowal of the male (in truth or not) to maintain his customary charge of secrecy.

One does not discern, indeed critics have not discerned, this reading from the text *qua* text; rather it has been read as a poem in midstream of a sexual relationship, which thus causes Main and Seng to remark, "The reader never knows whether she continues to be worried or why the lovers must meet secretly." Read as a seduction poem before the occurrence the remark has little meaning. Indeed, reading the text too closely as text (with the pair as lovers in the past) seems also to lead them into reading line 6 as implying that the scene is night. The simile set up by "as" implies (or else the simile is tautological) that they will be as silent as the night even though it is daytime, when other people are up and about, giving more meaning to the reference to the sun (l. 3) than only the sun at dawn. If we read "No ear shall hear our love" only to mean that I will not talk about it to anyone, we have missed the situation and a particularly interesting sexual statement. The full line is, "No ear shall hear our love, but we / Silent as the night will be." That is, while we are making love we will be so silent that no one will hear us. Experience should lead no one to believe that, although as a seductive pitch to a perhaps virgin to steal embraces during daylight hours (in or near some generally peopled location perhaps), it may have the hoped-for effect. The lady in Donne's poem is the cold Petrarchan mistress with whom the speaker is in love; the picture in his heart is there because he, constant one, loves her. The lady in Carew's poem, as we see her through the speaker's words, seems not to be cold, but rather near submission; the picture in his heart may be there because he loves her, or, more probably, it may be just another ploy to win her over. It may be a version of the "I really love you" approach that many men have found successful, and it argues that he will be secret about the affair. His main contention, however, is that there are great sweets in stolen embraces, rather than in married or betrothed ones, and so of course secrecy should be maintained. In fact, though, it is he who probably requires secrecy more than she.

My reading of the poem will not be arrived at through text/reader's text, it appears, but only through author's text/reader's text. The author has specifically presented a clue to the "meaning" of his poem, its dramatic situation, and its "characters." The poem he has written is not the poem that the reader, simply picking up the poem as text, reads. The author is not dead, and without such authorial presence the reader is stillborn as far as that particular literary text is concerned. I have engaged in a kind of deconstructionist reading, but the view that only this text *qua* text matters is false: it is not the text of "Secrecy Protested." The intertextuality that exists for the poem makes it a different text, and as that different text it is to be compared and evaluated alongside other texts by other authors (for example, Donne's "The Dampe").

The disembodiment of a text from its associate texts is a main reason why evaluation does not proceed from deconstructed or strictly reader-based criticism, evaluation thus being decried. Ultimately, I suppose, the problem is that such literary critics do not like or appreciate *literature.* Their world is a purportedly linguistic and philosophic one; it has been a world of reaction against the excesses of the past (I hope, *past*), which saw literature as the means to biography, a history of ideas, a ferreting out of the inconsequential (to the piece of literature). It would seem that such excesses are indeed past and with their demise has begun a decline in the viability of such strictly poststructuralist and deconstructionist criticism. We move into new fads. Let us hope that literary criticism will retain the insights and approaches of these critical "systems," amalgamated with the insights and approaches of authorial presence, theories of genre, of form, of mythic substructs, and the like. Authorial presence does not mean that the author is a character in the piece of literature (or the narrative voice or lyric voice), or that anything derived from the text is necessarily congruent with the author's emotions or ideas. Authorial presence means that the author has fashioned a piece of literature, has set up the words (the lexical) in some arrangement (the syntactical) within a form (the morphological). It also means that the author has introduced a metaphoric process, which at times will be clued by the lexical, the syntactical, the morphological, and at times by externals like allusion or imitation or type.[11] Some recent literary criticism denies this authorial presence, looking only at the lexical, syntactical, and sometimes morphological as disembodied text. It treats a work of literature as a singular thing so that no external has significance; it, indeed, denies communication of any sort, for that predicates "meaning" (that is, preconceived meaning) and a double presence of communicant and communicatee. Such criticism, I suggest, is not concerned with literature.

One aspect of the morphological is genre, and genre predicates an author and an authorial presence, in turn implying meaning for the reader. It imports the syntactical and at times the lexical for the text.[12] One does not just sit down to write a poem and find that a sestina, with its rigid form, is produced. At some point—prior to writing or during writing—the involved form that is the sestina has become a conscious effort on the part of the author. There is a communication between the author and the reader, saying that the reader is to recognize the genre and raising the questions Why is the poem put into this form? What does this form add to the communication within its content? In what way does the text become a different text because of this form rather than another? Genre is thus a part of the discourse of literature, as well as another element in reader cognition.[13] Even the view of the sestina as only text must recognize the repetitions of words that come to take on (or should come to take on) differing lexical and syntactical meanings, and an immediate upshot of that is a linearity in the poem akin to a reader-response reading. But as the poem is reread (and one problem, it would seem, in both deconstructed texts and reader-based interpretations is that these readings appear to be built on a first and single reading of the text only, implying that further readings will be different, without residue from the previous reading or readings), the reader anticipates the spatiality of the poem, the modifications of verbal meaning within those repetitions, and a ranging of significance of the parts as linearity takes over again. Authorial presence is unavoidable, for the author has chosen to encapsulate the content within the generic form and the generic form has set up the linguistic features of the poem. Were the content of the poem cast instead in an unmetered and unpatterned form (with the line as poetic unit), its morphological, syntactical, and lexical properties would be entirely different, even when some verbal repetitions exist. What the author is doing in choosing a specific genre is communicating to the reader cognition of expectations: the reader is directed. The reader who knows what a sestina is reads it differently from the way the reader who does not reads it, at least initially. This second reader may come to read it somewhat as the first reader does by, ultimately, coming to understand what would be answers to the questions put just before.

The sestina is perhaps the most obvious, and in that the simplest, poetic genre proclaiming authorial presence, for it is basically form. That form defines and is defined by its characteristics. Its characteristics do not involve subject or attitudes, philosophy or emotion. A sestina is a verse form of six unrhymed six-line stanzas, with each stanza using the same terminal words arranged in varying (but fixed) patterns; a three-line envoi repeats the six words in medial and terminal positions. Variations on the sestina may create a different arrangement of words, employ words that rhyme (for example, Sir Philip Sidney's sestina from "Astrophil and Stella"), extend the number of stanzas (for example, Malcolm Lowry's "Sestina in a Cantina"), and the like, but such variations are all of form and the characteristics that define the form. "Why is the poem put into this form?" To challenge the author to create such a form and thus to ask evaluation of craft in creating the form. "What does this form add to the communication within its content?" Probably nothing in the case of the sestina, since it is not concerned with content. At most (because form and rigidities of form may create reader attitudes) it may suggest an appropriation of form because of a formal or serious content, or an incongruency of form, ironically raising the supposedly informal content or the somewhat trivial content (for example, Rudyard Kipling's "Sestina of the Tramp-Royal"). "In what way does the text become a different text because of this form rather than another?" Clearly by the forcing of content into a specific lexis and a specific morphology (syntactic properties would vary within each stanza and the envoi). A genre that did not impose lexical or morphological requirements would allow content greater freedom of substance and expression; a genre that is characterized by more than form would allow for communication between form and content.

"The only fully justified solution to the question of literary genres," writes Adrian Marino, "would be their definitions as types of creativity, identified within the very process of creation as the most specific attitude of the creative self."[14] The sestina, perhaps at the far side of the authorial spectrum of literary genres, thus helps lead to this definition of genre: (a) a literary piece of writing that takes on a form (or structure), (b) with various characteristics, (c) implying the author's attitude toward that piece of writing. By structure I mean a spatial form with perhaps some geometric properties, but not all genres necessarily set up a spatial form for all literary works within a category. Rather, a genre has a form that may be defined by movement within the work, metaphoric development, relationships of parts, or physical elements (like line length or stanzaic pattern). The defined form within that category of genre may vary in certain ways depending on the reader's re-formation of it in the process of reading, but it is the result of a process of creation on the part of the author. Of course, any literary work does have some kind of spatiality, even if that spatiality does not duplicate any other literary work's spatiality. Characteristics may involve such abstract elements as movement or physical elements as verbal patterns, or they may encompass subject, context, or focus. But genre does *not* imply an author's attitude toward that subject, context, or focus; it implies only the author's attitude toward the piece of writing. It is, in Marino's words, the "attitude of the *creative* self."

To look at it in another way, and in counterview to what has been the result of linguistic approaches to the text, genre as I define it works with *langue,* not with *parole;* as kin to *langue* it communicates what the form/structure is, what the characteristics (including subject, but not meaning, context, and focus) are, and what the basis for creative evaluation is: it is a system of literary communication. Genre defines the speech-act, but it is not the speech-act; the speech-act itself is akin to *parole.* Recognition of the genre will lead to the communication of content and meaning, by its direction of the reader, but will not itself supply that communication, which lies in the speech act (that is, in the *parole* that is the specific literary text).[15] The first stage of communication that genre sets up moves the reader into an arena of the text, an arena that has boundaries whereby experience with the text may, at first at least, be directed linearly or sequentially, implying closure. Experience with the text may also reveal simultaneities within its enclosed space. An aim of the author in his treatment of the genre may be (1) to remain within those boundaries and to cause the reader to remain within those boundaries; or (2) to create within those boundaries an unseemingly constant or (linearly, sequentially, spatially) ordered experience; or (3) to try to abandon all boundaries and thus any closure. Form/structure and characteristics will depend upon the author's understanding of these matters for the literary genre employed, the ability to conform to or to vary such matters, and the creative desire to duplicate, imitate, revise, amplify, or delete such matters from the piece of writing in that specific literary genre.[16] My remarks accord with Edward Stankiewicz's comment when we emphasize the first three words:

> Truly poetic texts, however, tend to assert their independence from concrete and practical contexts, and are recognized as such through the unity and density of their internal structure. Such works are generally marked by a maximal integration of their form and meaning, i.e., by the use of form for the structuring of meaning and by the dependence of meaning on the structured form.[17]

A related concept to genre is mode. Confusion has reigned because of a lack of distinction between the terms, because of an equation of mode with mood, and because of a substitution for mode of such forms as narration (the narrative mode) or drama (the dramatic mode), except that there is narrative mode and dramatic mode, or of such techniques as theme (the so-called thematic mode).[18] Mode implies an authorial attitude toward the content. Whether that attitude be in terms of acceptance of the content, condemnation, skepticism, or the like, the evidence of the literary work will point to such modal attitudes as comic, tragic, or satiric. Discernment of these modal attitudes depends largely on reader response, which may arise often from the language system defined by the work. Intertextuality, of course, becomes manifest. The mode derived by the reader may or may not agree with the authorial attitude toward content, but that authorial attitude is nonetheless available, even when confused. Mode has an effectual relation with many components of writing, including genre. There is logically, therefore, no such thing as a "thematic mode"; what is meant by the term, I imagine, is that the author has primarily developed the piece of writing by presentation of a theme and that the intention has primarily been to present a theme. There is also, therefore, a distinction between "narrative mode," meaning that the piece of literature is presented primarily through narrative (a definition I reject), and "narrative mode," meaning that the author views the content of the material as demanding on the part of the reader a sense of story ("plot" in structuralist distinction from "story" would be a better word), an awareness of narrative techniques ("plotting"), and a view of its organization around externalities involving happenings viewed at a distance (again, "plotting"). The modal aspect of the narratological thus invokes mimesis, description, and discourse; it is not mere narration. Modal evaluation would be based upon the author's achievement in communicating modal attitudes to the reader.[19]

An example always helps. John Crowe Ransom's "Piazza Piece"[20] is a sonnet (a subgenre) and thus of the genre lyric; but its mode is not lyric, it is narrative. It is of the narrative mode, not because it is telling a story (it is not telling a story), but because it demands that the reader recognize (1) the sense of story behind the theme of *der Tod und das Mädchen*, (2) the techniques of description through dialogue and of an implied linearity of time with something having occurred before the poem begins and something happening not long after the poem ends, and (3) its organization around the externality of Death wooing the lady, viewed by the author at a distance. It has a dramatic context in that two people speak without speech tags and no nonspeech lines are given, yet it is not an example of the dramatic genre or mode. It is important to recognize the mode of the poem, for that and its context and its genre so clearly express the authorial presence. It would seem as if Ransom purposely ranged over genre, context, and mode as a demonstration of his craft, his ability to move out of the rigidities while staying within boundaries. (The love sonnet of seduction of the Elizabethans is clearly intertextual with this poem.) The innocent reader—the student in the classroom, for example, who reads the poem without some guidance—recognizes the genre of the sonnet and the dramatic shape it takes, but is baffled by what it all means until prodded to a literal restatement of "dustcoat" (a "coat" made of "dust," not a "duster") and an explanation of the joltingly incongruous "roses . . . dying" and "Spectral singing." Even then, the theme does not necessarily emerge, or the narrative sense, until, prodded some more, the reader comes to perceive a narrative behind the poem and the authorial distance. The reader expects neither from the more usual sonnet or the lyric mode. The evaluation of the poem can have nothing to do with its "meaning," but everything to do with its craft. The content is both the "meaning" and the form; it is more complex and more meaningful because of the play of genre and mode.

My literary revisionism takes me back to view the author as a significant factor in the literature one reads. With genre one will stress the author's "package" wherein he places his "wares," but the "wares"—the content, the ideas, the emotions, the message—are the substance to be communicated. We expect the package and the wares to be unified; we expect in a poem a relationship between its metrical form and its thematic structure; and we know that some literature has been concerned with form at the expense of meaning. Poetic form has "a system of obligatory features (the so-called 'constants') which unify the entire poem . . . and a system of more or less optional variables (or so-called 'tendencies') which put into relief the diversity of its parts,"[21] and these are interdependent. But the content also partakes of these same interdependent components: it is a variation upon the known, it presents a different set of constants, perhaps, with a different set of tendencies, yielding a different focus, and all within a literary form reveling in its own constants and variables. The author's content works out of these sets of constants, highlighting, diminishing, foregrounding, skewing them to achieve a different angle of vision (that is, different from some other author's or some other work's); the author includes variables to illuminate those constants, to put them into perspective, to make them meaningful and different. And some of these variables I label devices; among these literary devices are structural principles, allusions, imitative elements, onomastics, and the persona (overt or hidden). In this book I shall present, first, some ideas about genre and mode that demand a rereading and reevaluation of various literary works, some of which are well known and usually differently read and evaluated. The "system" is not prescriptive: it is a means to read more deeply and meaningfully, and a means to evaluate those works particularly that have caused critical concern. Second, I shall turn attention to works or authors that have, I believe, been insufficiently understood and underevaluated because of the inattention to genre and to such devices. My conclusions about all these works— which I hope to persuade the reader at least to consider as cogent—will stress both craft and meaning: the "truly poetic texts" are those that unify craft and meaning, though we may, as readers, praise for this or exult for that.[22]

Genre and mode, and such "devices" as allusion and onomastics, are conscious entries into a literary work: they become liminal means to enter into that work, the threshold over which one may step to enter the world of the literary work. Its space is confined but may allow for extension and vistas beyond that space; it may also figure forth other rooms, and other rooms in other places furnished differently. Liminal existence, we should remark, presupposes an overt, conscious creation, both the threshold and that introduced by the threshold. As Donne punned, "We'll build in sonnets pretty roomes" ("The Canonization," 1. 32), for "stanza" etymologically denotes a "room." These limina are a constant reminder of the author's presence: the reader reading should never avoid the writer writing.

In the course of this book, the poem, the novel, and the play will be looked at, although the subject is most often the poem; the literary world will range over numerous periods and even some places, but the thrust is the British seventeenth century, with sallies into other literary worlds. The reasons are simple: I wish the ideas of this book not to be localized to a genre, a country, a period, for I think they are not; but my own literary interest lies strongly in poetry, particularly the poetry of that most amazing century, the seventeenth.

PART ONE
The Consideration of Genre

2

Poetic Genre and Its Implications

My approach to genre is not new; yet it is a more exacting application of the theory behind genre than has been observable in recent years.[1] As always in close definition there may seem to be some reductiveness in my remarks. I begin with the realization—I do not say and do not mean assumption—that authors in differing degrees write poetry as an act of writing, not as an overflow of emotion or cerebration only. The writing of a poem, as Kenneth Burke has defined it,[2] is a symbolic act. We the readers should accordingly emphasize both the symbol and the act, the signifier and the signified, in Saussurian terms. An emotion or a thought within a poem must almost always be recognized by the poet and "understood" *before* the author begins to write, that is, before he or she chooses the images and symbols and does the act of writing which will encase that emotion or thought. The author only seldom works out the emotion or thought in the process of writing the poem that we have, although parts of such organic composition may persist in the finished product.[3] Writing may develop the emotion or the thought and may produce additional or other symbols, of course, but there are initial understanding and choices. The poet is a maker in the Renaissance meaning of the term, an artificer in Joyce's meaning of that word. Surely no one today can envision Milton's writing *Paradise Lost* from line 1 to line 10,565 without, at some point well before completion, his having first carefully blocked out the total work, without reorganizations and revisions, without first having conceived of the long epic that he was to alter in ways suggested by the proems to Books I and IX. Again as Burke has observed, the interaction of images and ideas is a symbolic action. In the novel obvious examples are Laurence Sterne's *Tristram Shandy* or Thomas Pynchon's *Gravity's Rainbow*.

If one accepts this view of writing, it will follow that the use of a genre by a poet must occur for specific reasons: genre is but one of the symbols (signifiers) employed in the act of writing. It becomes a limen into the work, a threshold to aid the reader in entering the world which is that work. It just does not happen that one sits down and a villanelle comes into being. Perhaps a poem can emerge that, for want of a real category, gets called a lyric or a song, or, to change terminological category, a piece of free verse, but what that means is that, first, we do not have adequate definitions of lyric or song, and second, we do not have sufficient labels to cover all possible spatial units of poetic expression. The poet writing a villanelle must know what a villanelle is and must consciously go about producing one. The writer's use of the form will depend upon an understanding of what that form is and what its attributes are, and the writer may purposefully set about to alter those attributes or form. Thus genre as one of the symbols employed in the act of writing implies form and attributes (characteristics) and the author's attitude toward that genre and toward the specific act of writing. It is possible, of course, that an author is not aware of certain attributes of a genre, and frequently form and attributes are rejected or altered.

My terminology at this point may seem to be different from Burke's, although it is not ultimately. As suggested in chapter 1, by form I have meant a poem's configuration on the page and the elements which give it that configuration. But form may be created by abstract elements (such as "build," or, to use Burke's word, crescendo) and by physical elements (such as line length, stanzaic patterns, etc.). To Burke, form is symbolic action, the meaning of a poem emerging as the reader re-forms it in the process of reading. Thus the psychology of form is the psychology of the audience. The form of a poem may thus be created by syllogistic means, by qualitative means, by repetitions, by conventions, or by other more incidental elements (e.g., an image). Clearly another way of looking at form in Burke's terms is as structure, both physical and abstract, and as the elements that create those structures. Indeed Burke has said that structure and form are often synonymous. Accordingly, genre exemplifies the form of adjustment often peculiar to itself, what I would call a collocation of a form, certain attributes, and an authorial attitude toward a specific piece of writing, which collocation defines a category available to many authors. While the parties to that collocation may show differences from one appearance to another, they stay within a recognizable collocation that is different from other collocations though possibly identical in part. (Calling such a collocation a family metaphorizes relationships: recognizable similarities but individual differences for members of that family.)

To illustrate: Denise Levertov's "Obsessions"[4] is a villanelle even though certain earmarks are altered or seemingly disregarded. The villanelle is a verse form consisting of five three-line stanzas and one four-line stanza. Only two rhymes are used, and the first and last lines of the first stanza each appear three times more in successive stanzas. "Obsessions" has four three-line stanzas and one four-line stanza: variation one of the genre. It works with more than two rhymes, technically speaking, but there is a kind of adaptation of the concept of two rhymes in the poem. "Return" ends three lines, "burned," two lines, and "burning," one line; these constitute one rhyme word. "Land" is used twice; "hands," twice; these constitute a second rhyme word. These rhymes -*urn* and -*and* appear in the first and last lines of each stanza; together they are employed as one of the rhymes common to the villanelle. Here we have variation two, part one, for the more traditional villanelle used only one rhyme for the first and last lines of stanzas. But Levertov's employment of these two rhymes has been conditioned by that traditional pattern. The middle lines of stanzas in the traditional villanelle constituted the second rhyme. In "Obsessions" we find two loose rhymes: -*y* as in "city" and "monopoly"; and -*s* as in "images," "violence," "noticed," and "us"—variation two, part two. The third variation in "Obsessions" is that Levertov does not repeat lines, but she does repeat language though not in any rigid order; for example,

"Maybe it is true we have to return" (l. 1);
"as ghosts or criminals return?" (l. 4);
"in that place to which we will not return" (l. 13).

What do we gain from recognizing the genre of "Obsessions"? First, we recognize that Levertov was using a specific form, however differently, and that implies in itself a gap between the emotion or thought and its expression. The use of the form indicates that part of her intent was to write a poem in that form; that it is often different in execution demonstrates that she purposefully tried to vary the form. The use of rhyme is so subtly similar to the traditional pattern and impression that authorial intent is clear. In turn we are led to a second recognition, that is, that Levertov is using a specific form differently for comparison with the traditional form. As poet, as maker, as artificer, she wants her reader to pay attention to the craft of her poem, which is inadequately understood if we do not recognize its genre. We can evaluate what she has done only by setting the variation alongside the standard. For me the poem is a fine achievement in the villanelle, for its variations play subtly with what I know the villanelle has generally been, with an emphasis on similarities of sound and variations of meanings in words repeated. She has met the challenge of the rigidities of the villanelle by altering those rigidities while being conditioned by them. A major villanelle in traditional form is Dylan Thomas's "Do Not Go Gentle into That Good Night." There are two rhymes and expected repetitions of lines. The two poems should be compared to appreciate the subtle changes of sound and meaning that Levertov wrought against the changes of meaning that Thomas's repetitions of lines yield. We shall return to the Thomas poem shortly to consider the symbolism of its genre form and re-view the Levertov poem in that light.

Besides form, genre implies two other matters, which are not always unique for a genre or even distinctive; with form they constitute the definition of a specific genre. As given in chapter 1, these two other matters are characteristics (attributes), such as length, device, contexts, attitudes, and authorial attitude toward the act of writing; that is, toward the specific piece of literature being produced, not toward the subject and not involving the poet's personal attitudes or emotions or beliefs. The most difficult concept is this last; it is really what distinguishes genre from mode and is, I firmly believe, basic to valid evaluation of a piece of literature. The concept fits with what Burke has written in *The Philosophy of Literary Form* (90): the reading of a poem, which "is to be sympathetically reenacted," "resembles, though with a difference, the act of its maker, the resemblances being in the overlap between writer's and reader's situations, the difference being in the fact that these two situations are far from identical." The poem will attempt to encase the author's personal attitudes or emotions or beliefs, and out of reading it will come an attitude, an emotion, or a belief, although a poem's genre has nothing to do with those things.

The distinction from mode will make my point clear. While mode is built through the details of experience, it is the sum effect of those details that creates literary mode. By mode I mean the overall emotional quality of a literary work, and the mode is defined by that quality: it indicates an author's attitude toward the expected effect upon the reader. The difference between tragedy as genre and tragic mode is an easy example, or between comedy and comic mode, or, less easily, between verse satire and satiric mode.

The verse satire and the beast fable, for example, have totally different forms and thus are two different genres. But they are both satiric, that is, are of the same mode. Not many of the characteristics of the verse satire are observable in the beast fable, and the most obvious characteristic of the beast fable—the beasts that populate it—is absent from the verse satire; again we can conclude that two different genres are involved, though the mode is the same. The poet writing a verse satire is attempting to write a verse satire with the form and characteristics of a verse satire as the poet understands them. The generic concern involves how to present a balance between *laus* (praise) and *vituperatio* (blame) and what specific elements of narrative, personages, imagery, and so forth should be used to create this balance. Genre, I am arguing, implies the author's craft, not heartfelt emotions and beliefs; it says nothing about the effect expected, for which we must turn to mode. A satiric mode implies the author's imbalancing of *laus* and *vituperatio* according to the effect that author wants in the reader. The beast fable is not concerned with balance between *laus* and *vituperatio;* it does exhibit a critical attitude on the part of the author, and thus falls under the rubric of satiric mode. "Satire" implies its etymology from *satura,* a bowl filled with mixed fruits. Verse satire is a generally longer poem (though not exceedingly long); chronologically its early physical form in English was created by a series of two-line units, usually pentameters, with alternate rhyme spread over four lines or with each couplet rhyming (an adaptation from the Latin elegiac meter, although Roman satire used the hexameter); and these nonrhyming or rhyming couplets moved in time, place, subject, and treatment, gradually or dramatically, in a *linear* manner. The couplets were often only loosely tied to what preceded or followed, and the whole did not tie together in balances, parallels, or integrations, but rather remained a series of items that all related to the subject of praise or blame. One couplet led to another, and that to another, thus giving the poem a linear movement; early verse satires often saw the poetic presenter walking down a street or a church aisle or the like. In this way such a series of items (each demarked by a couplet or two) rendered the verse satire a *satura,* the poem being the bowl or container of the couplets or mixed fruits, each new couplet or pair of couplets functioning as another fruit added to the bowl.

The final lines of Sir Thomas Wyatt's verse satire (in terza rima, however, because of its source) written to his friend John Poyns and based on Luigi Alamanni's tenth satire illustrate this definition:

> I ame not now in Fraunce to judge the wyne,
>   With saffry sauce the delicates to fele;
> Nor yet in Spaigne where oon must him inclyne
>   Rather then to be, owtewerdly to seme.
> I meddill not with wittes that be so fyne,
> Nor Flaunders chiere letteth not my sight to deme
>   Of black and white, nor taketh my wit awaye
>   With bestlynes, they beestes do so esteme;
> Nor I ame not where Christe is geven in pray
>   For mony, poison and traison at Rome,
>   A commune practise used nyght and daie:
> But here I ame in Kent and Christendome
>   Emong the muses where I rede and ryme;
>   Where if thou list, my Poynz, for to come,
> Thou shalt be judge how I do spend my tyme.[5]

The subject of the poem is the vanity of the world, and the treatment of the poem is satiric, which word implies an overall attitude that the author wishes the reader to feel toward that subject. In praise Wyatt has commented on French wines; in criticism he has commented on Flemish drunkenness. While Christian belief is implied, Roman Catholic practices are impugned. In contrast with this vain and corrupt world, Wyatt is in retirement at his father's estate in Kent. Whether such retirement is commendable is left to Poyns to judge—or rather is left to the reader to judge. If the reader has been manipulated to think as the poet in the poem does, the reader will not frame his or her tongue to lie and cloak the truth with undeserving praise when men "lyst all vice for to retayne." Social reform in any active sense is clearly not part of this verse motive.

The contrast between Donne's first and fifth satires clarifies the distinction being made. In "Satire I" Donne balances the scholarly recluse with the worldly humorist; the poem takes the form of a *débat* between soul and body. In medieval dialogue (a form of débat) the soul always wins—naturally, and I think most people read Donne's first satire as a statement of the victory of intellect and truth and the defeat of desire and temptation. I suggest it be read again; there is no more victory here, or authorial siding with one or the other, than there is in "The Love Song of J. Alfred Prufrock," an ironic débat between the outer and the inner man, although the "reason" of the inner man has defeated the "emotion" of the outer man (mind prevails over body) as the poem ends. Donne's "Satire I" is thus a good example of the verse satire as genre (and we note the linear structure created by each new circumstance as the "characters" of the poem leave the house and walk along the street meeting various people); some critics have not agreed. Its mode is satiric, just as is Wyatt's poem, in that it raises questions in the reader of the worth of intellect and truth over against sensuality and sham; but we cannot accept the scholarly recluse of the poem as model (though some critics seem to), nor can we totally reject the drives of the worldly humorist as Donne represents him. Donne raises a critical question and exhibits a critical attitude. We all have both sides within us, and there is something to be said for each. In "Satires II" and "IV" the critical attitude directs us firmly to rejection of lawyers and courtiers, as depicted in those poems. But "Satire I" is in this regard ambiguous, and as such the poem seems to some to be less satiric. It is no less a verse satire than the others; it is rather a less successful example of satiric *mode* for those who want clear-cut authorial attitude communicated to them: it does not involve ridicule or social reformation.

On the other hand, Donne's "Satire V" is, for most people, a failure, and I assume that this occurs, not because it falters in any way as verse satire, but because modally the author becomes too dominant. The emotional quality of the poem is influenced strongly by the author's beliefs and attitudes toward his subject; the reader is too much directed, too little the judge. For Donne himself, it will be remembered, enters the poem as do Queen Elizabeth and Sir Thomas Egerton as real people, not simply as representations (as Beza is in "Satire IV") or as metaphors (as Coscus is in "Satire II"). The point is, the author's intention in satire should be to raise questions between those oppositions classifiable as vice or virtue, untruth or truth, ignorance or knowledge, blame or praise, and to direct the reader to consider those questions. The satirist traditionally sided with the moral position, and the reader was made to agree through exposure of the immoral position, particularly through humor or ridicule. But this siding creates the mode satiric, not the genre verse satire that raised the questions. An obvious example: Sir John Davies's gulling sonnets are satiric, but not verse satires.

Two contrasting examples from modern poetry will aid us here. Donald Hall's "Six Poets in Search of a Lawyer,"[6] written in rhyming couplets, gives us Finesse, Dullard, Bomb, Lucre, Mucker, and Scoundrel, one after the other, and all but the last are depicted through couplet added to couplet:

> *Dullard* be second, as he always will,
> From lack of brains as well as lack of skill.
> Expert in some, all dilettante in all
> The ways of making poems gasp and fall,
> He teaches at a junior college where
> He's recognized as Homer's son and heir.
> Respectable, brown-suited, it is he
> Who represents on forums poetry,
> And argues to protect the libeled Muse,
> Who'd tear his flimsy tongue out, could she choose.

The form that I have described as usual in the past for the verse satire is employed; various characteristics, like symbols and metaphors, length and structural units, appear; and the author is indeed writing a satire in basically traditional ways, although his ordered structure of ten lines to each poet except for Scoundrel (who gets but two) imposes a more contrastive form upon the poem than is usual. The approach is vituperative, but beneath that vituperation we can see what would be praised: Mucker's pose is "To talk of baseball rather than of Yeats"; Lucre "writes his poems now to suit his purse."

The genre chosen raises the questions of what makes good poetry, what makes a good poet—a version of the moral soul arguing—and what makes that kind of poetry or poet slip over into viciousness. But the mode describes the author's attitude toward his subject, and the effect (as in

Luigi Pirandello's play that supplies Hall's title) makes clear that any poet, the author included, is the subject. The authorial voice, being a poet's, is all six poets potentially upon occasion, and the self-criticism emerges as a satirization of a potential self. The author is also the lawyer arguing a brief for poetry and for him- or herself as poet. The author has dared write satiric verses on Scoundrel, and should henceforth be deaf, dumb, and blind, nullifying the senses so that he or she will hear no evil, speak no evil, or see no evil; henceforth, that is, the writer should not be poet. Of course, Hall is saying that the poet must engage evil and the way the poet engages anything is through the self. The feelings that the reader experiences after finishing the poem, that is, the mode, lead to these understandings rather than the fact that this is a verse satire in a rather close use of traditional form. Hall's poem itself indicates the way in which, like Bomb, a poet may steal from old Gone, and how like Mucker he or she exemplifies Freud's thesis of opposites: "feminism" masquerading as virility, inferiority complex masquerading as superiority complex.

Or take e. e. cummings's "Poem, or Beauty Hurts Mr. Vinal,"[7] a fine verse satire built on a series of items not, however, given as couplets or in metered lines. The questions of vice and virtue, untruth and truth, ignorance and knowledge, blame and praise in the world of advertising slogans are coterminous with the poem. cummings used the symbol of shit to describe those slogans, and this is one of his conscious decisions to make the poem a symbolic form appropriate to its genre. It is all part of his adaption of genre, but the mode—that is, the total effect of the piece—is not concerned with the craft but with the author's attitudes and the attitude that he expects in his reader, one of snickering humor over the punning meaning of bodily function we hear in "Just Add Hot Water And Serve—/ from every B.V.D.," which is not unlike the punning sexuality in such former television assaults as Cora's "Good to the last drop" or "Have it your way" at whatever fast-food spot you frequent.

Implications in my differentiation between genre and mode should be pointed out. First, the relater of the poem (whether "I" or some omniscient observer) is not to be considered the poet who has written the poem when we are talking about mode. Of course, poet X will produce something different from what poet Y would have on the same subject and in the same genre, and of course the poem reveals much about its maker. But Donne is not, emphatically not, the "I" of "Satire I," much as one wants to romanticize upon Jack Donne, the rake, and Dr. John Donne, the Dean of St. Paul's. The congruency in many readers' minds of the person who is the author and the poet as she or he appears in a specific work has frequently been the source of difficulty in understanding Burke's points about mythic images and primitive sacrificial acts, which lie behind ideas, and which in turn lie behind the sensory images used. We can appreciate the universality of Hall's satire if we approach it generically, that is, without consideration of the author as person but only with consideration of the author as maker. It then follows that the topic and thesis, generically, have universality; that modally the topic and thesis may have direct relationship with the author. The evaluation of the author's achievement within a genre partially depends upon universality; without it the work is ephemeral. Aside from the difficulty of reading Latin and accepting the conventional, the failure of Milton's Latin elegies for most readers is that they do not understand the universality of topics and theses in those poems but look only at biographical elements. Yet a study of form would alter such an appraisal drastically: were readers to approach them generically they would recognize the craft that has gone into them—although that craft was not always equally successful.[8]

John Dryden's "MacFlecknoe" elucidates my point about the universal (a term the new historicism would eliminate) and the personal. Many readers may think of the poem first as personal because we know about the author and the butt of his satire, but this is not the way uninformed readers would greet the poem—and some contemporary readers were uninformed. It is in the universal type depicted in the poem that its significance and persistence as a meaningful poem exists, as reading it with an undergraduate class will demonstrate. It achieves another level of meaning for us, knowing as much as we do about the experience behind the poem, but I would suggest too that it means more to the person who has read Richard Flecknoe's dreary poetry and Characters (as well as the plays of the poem's subject, Thomas Shadwell) than one who has not. Generically we should look at the poem; modally we may want to pursue the question of why the author has the attitude he has demonstrated toward his subject.

My remarks about genre stem from the regulative and prescriptive concepts of classical theory referred to in chapter 1, but I also urge that we must consider adaptation of those regulations and prescriptions or conscious alteration of them. If the poet is aware of these regulations and prescriptions and he or she chooses to use a specific genre, then it follows that the author is implying in some way those regulations and prescriptions, either by use or by avoidance. True, the author may not always be aware of all those concepts. Like anything else as time goes by, genre may be altered in various ways so that it does not have some of the earmarks of the past or it has different ones. And some genres have always been mixed. This kind of change within the definition of a genre may drop or adapt some of the regulations and prescriptions and may, in part at least, best be talked of descriptively.

If we understand the distinction I am making between genre and mode, we can return to the villanelle and the other matter besides form and characteristics that defines genre. The attitude of the author toward the villanelle implies the craft in producing that particular poem: for Thomas it is an exact duplication of the form, to be evaluated in terms of his success at the form; for Levertov it is a variation of the form within recognizable parameters, to be evaluated in terms of her success at such recognizable variation. Perhaps a most significant point in high evaluation of Thomas's work is that at times people seem not to have recognized that this is a villanelle—even those one would think would know what a villanelle is. It is clear that Stephen Dedalus is working out a special form of poem in James Joyce's *Portrait of the Artist as a Young Man,* even if the reader does not know the villanelle. We are aware of the repetitions and the rhyming and the attempts to make the repeated words function as different parts of speech and thus have somewhat different meanings. This unavoidable awareness of the poetic elements is at least part of the reason for the failure that most people have felt in the poem. Stephen tries his hand at the villanelle because it is so difficult to execute well: if he had been really successful, it would have been very significant for his poetic potential. Even failing at such a difficult genre is more praiseworthy, I assume Joyce is saying, than just putting words down "poetically" on paper as they come to you. Further, the Joycean illustration backs up my opening statements that writing is craft: although Stephen's poem is the result of an epiphany, it has been worked over and fashioned and planned and revised, with only bits of the seemingly "original" verbal reaction to Stephen's pangs of love remaining in the final form.

An important context of the villanelle lies in the etymology of the word. It derives from *villein,* a peasant of low-classed rank in feudal times; it was a rustic unaccompanied part-song in the style of a rustic dance. The dance relationship probably accounts for the patterned repetitions. It was a form of entertainment shoring the peasants against their hard life and turning their minds and bodies to a kind of escape. Did Levertov and Thomas realize this and its implications when they wrote? At least our knowledge suggests further poetic texture in Levertov's emphasis on the "black air of ashcan city," on "ghosts" and "criminal," on "dust" and "burning." Have "we" escaped, or must "we" return? Is life possible outside the city and without the city? Is life possible anymore back in a world of "the wide land," a nonurban world of latter-day peasants? Or is it all still directed by the feudal lords of the city's corporations? Can the land anymore be worked, or will there only now be "anguish" and hands "clenched in violence / under that sun"? The poem that we may have first read as personal has taken on cosmic proportions. The title, and it is a plural, refers now to humankind's constant hopes of improvement of its lot, and the clenched hands suggest that a human being is never able to beat the sun at its own game anymore than all the villeins of all historical time have been able to free themselves from the controls of the lords of the manor.

And what of Thomas's poem? While he bids farewell to his father with the admonition that human beings should not allow inevitable Death to have its sway without some resistance, the generic form he chooses makes clear his acknowledgment that Death is inexorable. It is an excellent example of the antiheroic that nevertheless knows that all antiheroic poses are ultimately ineffectual. Recognition of the genre helps us place the poem within its assumptions and contexts, both to enhance meaning and to effect its evaluation against others of its class. This is the kind of thing I mean by the word "genre" and why I think it is important to talk about genre.

To some this may sound sophistic. Although it might be conceded that literary critics have confounded genre and mode or have otherwise not truly paid attention to genre, still it may not seem to make that much difference. Well, there will be degrees of significance, but let me provide one more example that I think indicates significance. The significance arises because we read the poem one way when we do not pay attention to genre and quite a different way when we do.

Andrew Marvell's poem "Clorinda and Damon" is a dialogue, a kind of débat, though it seems to be treated critically only as a pastoral. One edition of Marvell's poems says, "This pastoral dialogue with its religious theme ... links up with other examples in form and with *Thyrsis and Dorinda* and *A Dialogue between the Resolved Soul and Created Pleasure* in theme."[9] My differences from this view will be clear as we proceed, although part of the point I would make is that both those additional poems are also read inadequately because their genre is not attended to. Marvell employs the characteristics of the dialogue or débat genre in the poem under discussion here by having Clorinda represent body, pleasure, sin, and woman, and Damon represent soul, virtue, faith, and man, but the resolution comes through Pan, who is both a goat-god with Satanic hints and the Great Shepherd Christ who tends his flocks and leads them to green pastures. Before the poem begins Damon has turned away from enticing things because he has met Great Pan, who now fills all Damon's songs. The conclusion of the medieval dialogue—removal from things of the flesh to contemplations of the soul—has already taken place within Damon. Marvell's poem asks, Well, what happens after that? The poem is concerned with the movement of Damon back to an appreciation of what Clorinda represents. Note in the middle of the poem his reference to

Clorinda's cave with a fountain therein: "Might a soul bathe there and be clean, / Or slake its drought?" he asks. The question is not answered except by the way the reader interprets the poem.

We probably recognize the double entendres in the poem without placing the genre; for example, we know what Damon really means when he says Clorinda's grass will wither and her flowers fade, for the word "deflowered" is common enough. It makes more understandable on the sexual, physical level the meaning of the next line: "Seize the short joys then, ere they vade." But have we seen that just as Clorinda has taken on the inspiration of the Great Shepherd Pan when she says, "Sweet must Pan sound in Damon's note," Damon has taken on the inspiration of the goatish Pan when he says, "Clorinda's voice might make [my song] sweet"? Clorinda's final line is thus newly significant: "Who would not in Pan's praises meet?" The resolution of this debate rests in the fusion of body and soul, just as in the fusion of the two natures of Pan. The fusion of woman and man is seen in the chorus's "Caves echo, and the fountains ring," for *caves* are female (because enclosures) and *fountains* are usually male (as active water). The natural imagery in the line, like the *flow'ry pastures* of the preceding line, echo, ring, or sing to heaven, uniting earth and heaven. The last two lines of the poem said by the chorus thus involve double meanings that I suspect most readers have not heard: "Sing then while he doth us inspire, / For all the world is our Pan's choir." It depends on where you are: does a goatish Pan inspire the body or does a Christ-like Pan inspire the soul? And does it make any difference?

The recognition of the genre of Marvell's poem helps us read it more thoroughly because we know what characteristics are being called up, and we know accordingly how his poem differs from others in the same genre: its time past the original "debate"; its fusion of the oppositions; and its use of genre to alter an understanding of content, since the content is contrastively dependent upon the usual content that is a characteristic in the definition of this specific genre. I cannot accept singling out "its religious theme" because its genre predicates such a theme. Perhaps most telling for us in recognizing the genre of the poem is the identification of the author's point of view toward his work. As a dialogue with a long history of the kind of characteristics it shows, the poem suggests that the subject matter and the various resolutions are little biographically generated, and so little biographically generated that we cannot conclude something about Marvell's beliefs and attitudes toward the ideas in the poem. His attitude toward his rendering of this genre, like that of Samuel Daniel in "Ulysses and the Siren," concurs with the authorial attitude associated with the genre dialogue: it is an exercise in argument. The achievement of Marvell's poem is the wittiness of the imagery and of the reversal of circumstances, while he is still using the trite arguments and imagery of other age-old débats. Comparison with Milton's employment of a débat between Comus and the Lady (in "A Mask") emphasizes the point. Milton has taken only an approximation of the form and some general characteristics, but those characteristics are exploded to give the content metaphysical importance as a rendering of the temptations of Jesus in the wilderness by Satan. The authorial attitude is totally different when we read Milton's own brand of socialism:

> If every just man that now pines with want
> Had but a moderate and beseeming share
> Of that which lewdly-pamper'd Luxury
> Now heaps upon som few with vast excess,
> Natures full blessings would be well dispens't
> In unsuperfluous eev'n proportion. . . .

Milton's is an attitude toward his content, an attitude missing from Marvell's poem.

Despite some emphasis on genre and generic studies in literature in recent years, or at least the lip service of such emphasis, the most pervasive attitude has been to disregard distinctions among literary genres, though few critics would admit to this disregard. This attitude arises from the current fear that all categories are despicable and that everything is the same anyway if we just take enough perspective. Still there is such a thing as literary genre and there are many literary genres and subgenres. They exist and they existed, and an author writes and wrote within this genre or that. The author wrote consciously within a genre to prove to her- or himself and to others that she or he could accomplish a poem in a specific genre. The author wrote consciously within a genre to communicate to readers the ideas or connotations that were attached to a specific genre because such ideas or connotations related to intended meaning. It was one of the symbols to be employed in the act of writing; it provided an entry into the work. And the author wrote consciously within a genre in order to transcend that genre, thereby achieving another level of evaluative comparison with other writers working within that same genre, and thereby also achieving further meaning for the literary work in terms of variations from the standard. We cannot, to use Burke's terminology, sympathetically reenact a poem or hope to come closer to the act of its maker until we recognize genre and understand it as one of the maker's means in creating form.

3

Shakespeare and the Tragic

I t seems clear, in our critically charged age, that literary criticism often uses language too loosely and thereby creates problems that do not really exist. One problem is the definition (and use) of genre as a literary term, for example, when tragedy, the subject of this chapter, is discussed. We have looked at verse satire and the satiric in chapter 2, and I will examine comedy and the comic in chapter 4. Genre, as we have seen, does not include affectiveness in its definition, yet tragedy as genre has been associated with the effect of a work on an audience. What has happened is that genre has been confounded with mode; tragedy has been confounded with the tragic. Case in point: *Paradise Lost* is an epic but its effect has been considered tragic or comedic. Unfortunately a few have gone further to call it a tragedy and to treat it as one with a tragic hero. (The history of criticism of *Paradise Lost* from John Dryden through recent studies of Satan evidences where that erroneous "requirement" leads us.) Its genre is epic, but its mode is tragic or comedic according to how it is read. It is not a tragedy or a comedy except that epic as a mixed genre includes tragedy and comedy. In discussing such plays of Shakespeare as *Romeo and Juliet, Hamlet, Othello, King Lear, Macbeth, Antony and Cleopatra,* and *Coriolanus,* the plays that I will look at here, critics have elicited both generic characteristics of tragedy and affective or modal characteristics of the tragic or the comedic, and confounded the two without distinction between genre and mode. In considering *Paradise Lost* tragic or comic what is being expressed is not generic form and formulas, with certain expectations for the piece of literature if it is indeed representative of a specific genre; rather it is a question of mode. It does not require any set pattern (for example, the movement through the potentially tragic to a new alignment of elements when the mode is to be comic), but it does not mean either that certain tragic or comic patterns may not emerge. At times brief patterns may contribute to the mode and point to it.

Tragedy as genre implies that there will be wasting of good in the process of driving out or confronting evil, the emphasis being upon the driving out of evil, however. The evil must be driven out because it is imperfect in the moral order of the universe. The tragedy comes to exist as punishment for sin in a moral universe in which such punishment is expected (or ironically and sentimentally exacted); frequently that sin is presented as a quality of thought or action in an antagonist. (The terms "good," "evil," and "sin" should be understood as general signs. They are the words employed in talking about older plays, though other forms of writing can be subject to the same generic concepts; modern tragedy will be seen to adapt these terms, and others, in the ensuing discussion. The contexts of tragedy that I summarize are not prescriptive but rather what analysis shows as the contexts surrounding that which is seen as tragedy or the tragic; no "laws" are involved.) The tragedy may center on a hero, who functions as a kind of scapegoat, driven by some *hamartia* (by which one means excess of some attribute, an imbalance in makeup) that becomes the source for a fall. As one whose position in a sociopolitical world makes what happens significant to that world, this hero represents the potential catastrophe for that world and each member of it. The influence of the morality play, of course, allows that the sociopolitical world may learn at least temporarily and thus avoid catastrophe; it may find the sin driven out for the time immediately after the play ends, and may thus achieve some element of rebirth of spirit, if not of materiality. At times, as in *Oedipus Rex*, the protagonist and the antagonist merge.

The movement of tragedy comes to a climax with the catastrophe; the vision moves only to that point for the hero and not beyond it.[1] The rhetorical climax may lie elsewhere, and the climax for the hero is the point at which a course of action is chosen. The latter climax is normally both the anagnorisis (recognition of error in action or judgment or self) and the peripeteia (reversal of the action). The structure of a tragedy centers on the tragic hero, who must decide a course of action—basically good or evil as in a morality. Complicity of choice exists when the action is "evil" but is the only means of ultimately achieving good. The structure of a tragedy does not schematize into a geometric edifice as in comedy: rather it is skewed and changeable around the figure of the hero, who is a kind of fulcrum around which the action, dialogue, and characterizations revolve. With the hero's decision of action the equilibrium is upset and the play moves forward to allow the catastrophe to take place. The action, dialogue, and characterizations have little meaning except as they impinge upon the central figure or figures. As opposed to comedy, tragedy is concerned with the individual, not with the group; with what is significant for the individual, not with social signification;[2] with individual decision—often emotional, often made in personal isolation—not with a mechanization of life as ritual and cycle; with the disorder of the play's world, not with some new order to be achieved.[3] The relationship of the hero of tragedy to the "sin" exposed is not the same as the rebuking of vice as in comedy; the effect of that sin on the hero, who traditionally is not an ordinary person, is not concerned with the reprehension of the sins and follies of the middle class, which is the staple of comedy. The sin or evil is, rather, the catalyst for heroic action.

Hamlet unquestionably illustrates the foregoing characteristics of tragedy. It is a well-structured play, with balances and parallels of action and characterizations, with the rhetorical climax in Act III, the climax for the hero in Act IV, Scene iv (as Fortinbras is observed crossing the plain), when Hamlet comes to conclude that "Rightly to be great is not to stir without great argument,"[4] and the catastrophic climax in Act V, Scene ii. Its patterns and tragic formulations agree with the preceding descriptions of tragedy, and its authorial point of view certainly seems to be that the tragic lies in the punishment meted out to a scapegoat for dealing with sin in a supposedly moral universe. As tragedy we expect Hamlet to show certain qualities and elements, and we get them. It is not a question of prescription: to be tragedy Hamlet would exhibit these qualities and elements, directly or in variation. It is a matter of description of this and other literary works and of the genre. But what is the overall and prevailing emotional quality of the work? What was the author's intent and the expected viewer reaction? The difficulties with the play for most critics and most players have arisen from feelings of closeness with the hero and with the actions on stage. And this flies against the supposed Aristotelian idea of catharsis: we are too involved. And we are too involved because Shakespeare himself seems to be involved, working out personal problems with the world of the theater, problems of personal sorrow as well as weltschmerz, problems of reality and its appearances. The play strikes one as being Shakespeare's most ontological, I suppose, because we catch him without the answers worked out or at least without the questions obscured. Hamlet–Shakespeare–the viewer must develop a moral philosophy that can weigh such questions as justice and mercy, capital punishment, the relationship between the end and the means; and he must examine the meaning of existence, the reason for existence, and, therefore, the concept of destiny. The answer that Hamlet seeks is love—primarily as faith—but nowhere does he really find it except in Horatio. The difficulties of the play for us may be summed up as the opposition between the view of taking arms against a sea of troubles and by opposing end them or the view of leading the life of courtier, scholar, and soldier in a supposedly equitable world of meekness and goodwill—the opposition between activism and passivity.

The mode of the play is thus tragic, not because of generic characteristics of tragedy, but because its effect is one of open-ended questions: we are not sure that the waste in driving out evil is justified because we are not really sure that the "happy" ending centering around Horatio's speech and Fortinbras's assumption of the throne is anything more than illusory; its effect is one with the imagery of disease and ulceration and excrement and decayed or decayable human parts; its effect nags us into thinking that self-sacrifice is not very worthwhile. In the throes of insurrection against evil in this world, activism may loom magnificent—"Rightly to be great is not to stir without great argument"—but in the new dawn of the world's rubble, did that insurrection achieve anything, really? I suspect that viewer reaction comes close to Shakespeare's personal feelings here and there as he wrote. The lack of all the ends' being tied and the concentration on the individual's attitudes—Shakespeare's or the viewer's—defines a major, though not generally acknowledged, perquisite of a tragic mode. And it is the nature of that mode that has been the crux of controversy over this play—not its proportions as tragedy. The play is not about a man who could not make up his mind: modally it is about the uncertainty any thinking individual will experience when she or he examines so-called truth only to find it evanescent and when she or he realizes that nothing is sure until it is past.[5]

What I argue is that tragedy as genre has a "closed" ending because the audience is concerned with the action to the point of the catastrophe, whereas comedy as genre has an "open" ending because we recognize continuance past that ending. But in contrast, tragic mode develops a sense of "open-endedness" because the questions on which the action exists are unsolved, whereas comic mode has given a sense that all the questions have been answered and all the loose ends tied up, a "closed-endedness."

We should leave off confounding tragedy, the genre, and tragic mode; if we did, we would see *Hamlet* the tragedy clearly. But further, we would be on better ground to discuss the cruxes of the play, an obvious one being humankind's attraction to "evil" and subsequent sin, humankind's wrestling within itself to extirpate that evil through a kind of split personality, and, for some like Hamlet, solution through destruction of that evil in hopes of mercy for self-sacrifice. The tragic mode of *Hamlet,* not its being a tragedy, explains why we stress Hamlet's psychological initiation into the world of base men in our discussions—it is Shakespeare's and our initiation renewed, of course—and this in turn, if the earth is only a sterile promontory with its phallic symbolism, constitutes the substance of that tragic mode.

What I am about, therefore, is to limit discussions of genre to generic characteristics, and to raise the question of mode, which must be separated from genre.[6] My remarks on *Hamlet* are not really new, but I think they separate the real questions from the specious ones, and they argue that those real questions depend upon the affective quality of the play, that is, viewer reaction. Viewer reaction may vary in certain ways from person to person, of course; my reaction to this play as viewer (reader) concludes that the mode is tragic because it fits the definition of tragic mode that I suggest. The questions of Hamlet's psychology and those of his relations with Ophelia and with his mother and with his father persist well after the play has ended; he may have decided to "stir" but he has not altered his uncertainties about his world and its inhabitants. The problems that the tragic mode has created for viewers (readers especially) is a result of the author's not being in full control of his material. Shakespeare has not, for the moment of final creation of the play, convinced himself of the validity of his vision (the status of drama and its actors is a clear case in point), and what emerges seems to have elements of retelling of a source (and sources) in some conflict with nonnarrative elements of both general and personal questions or problems, so that structure and form (the play's length is one sign of this lack of final artistic control) are not tightly presented as, say, they are in *Macbeth*. Perhaps he did not fully understand the influences—personal, psychological, ideological—that were paramount upon him as he wrote. And I think that only by acknowledging this kind of reaction to the author's creation are we in a position to evaluate the play adequately.

The point of this discussion can best be seen, I think, by comparison with appropriate entries in a work like the *Princeton Encyclopedia of Poetry and Poetics*. There is no entry for *mode* or *mood;* Orsini's inadequate discussion of *genre* begins by using the term *mode* to define it; and Dorius contributes to the kind of confusion of terms I am talking about in discussing tragedy. For example, as previously noted, he cites *Paradise Lost* among other works under *tragedy,* though he then makes clear that the rest of the entry will deal only with drama.[7]

The earlier *Romeo and Juliet* allows striking comparisons with what I have been suggesting about mode and about evaluation of the final creation. We know that this play is called a tragedy and has generally been so classified, but it has also been called a comedy—for example, see Harry Levin's discussion, in which he projects the theme into the spiritual achievement of ending the feud and of translating the dead lovers to a heaven reserved for earthly saints.[8] Further, *Romeo and Juliet* has seemed to be a comedy because of the balances of characters and actions—partially in terms enunciated by Henri Bergson in *Laughter.*[9] And it is comic or has a comic tone because of its puns and wit, such comic characters as Mercutio and the Nurse, the bawd of Plautine comedy, and its coarse language. But I think if we divide genre from mode we see *Romeo and*

Juliet as a tragedy, though less worthy of high evaluation than others of the genre, and as an uncontrolled mixture of tragic mode and comedic mode, the tragic mode being next to dismissible. My view of the play, it should be obvious, does not allow me to rate it very highly as a tragedy, although I rush to say that I find the poetry and the characterizations and the theatrical piece (for the most part) wonderful. As a drama written for the stage and produced on the stage, I rate it highly (although excisions, which are commonplace in productions since Shakespeare's time, are helpful).

As tragedy *Romeo and Juliet* shows a wasting of good in opposition to the evil of feud; there is no emphasis upon conscious driving out of evil, however, as we would expect of a tragedy. The tragedy of the deaths of Romeo and Juliet, as well as Mercutio's, Tybalt's, and Lady Montague's, is the punishment Verona must experience because of the sin of feud in this seemingly otherwise moral world. Romeo and Juliet as joint protagonists represent the potential catastrophe for many members of the world of Verona, should feud continue. The tragedy is implemented by their separate errors of judgment—secrecy, avengement of honor, acceptance of appearance as reality. But these are made errors through the circumstances of the feud rather than through the protagonists' decision over clear-cut issues as we would expect in an enlightening tragedy, and they are made errors through the ironic circumstances of chance and time. The characteristics of the play as well-wrought tragedy are thus made ambiguous; nevertheless it is generically a tragedy—since, unlike comedy, the potential tragedy is not avoided and no mechanized ritual of life is involved in that tragedy. I am not concerned that certain attributes of tragedy do not appear; genre should not be prescriptive. I am concerned that the action of the play rests so much on externals and coincidence; I am bothered that the issues raised are not pursued, and that much seems given over to creating a stage vehicle only.

The mode of *Romeo and Juliet* is something else again. The effect at its close passes as tragic, for we feel sentimentally sorry that the lovers have died, particularly because they have died through chance and bad luck. Despite the final lines on the evil of the feud,[10] we are not really bothered that they have died through the lack of *caritas* in men but that they have died so young and so haplessly. The tragic feeling is mawkish and does not last much after we have left the theater or closed the book. It does not pervade the whole play even though the Prologue has told us that the "star-cross'd lovers" will "take their life" through "the fearful passage of their death-mark'd love." One reason the tragic mode is so unconvincing is that the lovers' deaths, the source of the tragic mode, have not occurred on purpose as an opposition to the evil of Verona's world. Another is that there is little disorder in that world, which is almost totally bifurcated into adherents of Montague and adherents of Capulet. No ambiguities as in Hamlet's world exist. Escalus as observer of this world throws the play's comic balancing into relief: we recognize Mercutio and Paris, the Duke's kinsmen, as embodying the tendency of this world to be either Montague or Capulet. We see Friar Laurence (and his moral attitudes) balanced by the Nurse (and her contrastive moral attitudes). Neither abstention nor license is approvable. Nor the kind of death (Thanatos) that the friar and his church represent, nor the kind of life (Eros) that the Nurse and her occupation suggest. Such balancing is comedic when it is the backbone of a play, and it is not farfetched therefore to see in Friar John's, Peter's, and Escalus's names meaningful puns: *God is gracious* on the one hand, and sex is the *rock* upon which a religion may be built on the other, but the *ladder* by which one achieves God's hopes for humankind is a mean between them.

Therefore we can understand why the most frequent mode of the play is comedic. I am not referring to its comic effects, for they do not create mode alone. They may contribute, either directly or by inverse effect—though that is not the case here. Rather, these comic effects exist for their own worth as wit and horseplay. Although the sexuality of much of that wit and horseplay can be assigned as contrast with the romantic love of Romeo and Juliet, reducing their fanciful excesses, Shakespeare has not stressed any real error on the lovers' part in pursuing their romantic love; thus tragic mode does not establish itself. Instead we discover in the play a kind of stress on the community and the social significance of the feud. The outcome is a new order by the rebuking of feud and development of *caritas*. The play has been concerned with the sins and follies of men.

Alongside the sentimental tragic mode, then, exists a comedic mode.[11] What Shakespeare intended seems as ambiguous and points, it seems to me, to a lack of determined control—at which we should not be surprised in such an early play, a play for a practical stage and a definite audience. The authorial point of view is that the tragic lies in the punishment meted out to both innocent and guilty who are touched by sin in a supposedly moral universe. But the authorial intent would seem to be only the practical aim of producing a popular play, one with soap-opera affinities, one with entertaining features and surefire shticks. What *Romeo and Juliet* makes clear is that a play may generically be a tragedy but may not necessarily evidence tragic mode. We may enjoy it, but literary analysis leads elsewhere. We can make similar statements about other literary works. I think of a favorite play, Tennessee Williams's *Summer and Smoke*, which is generally cast as a failure. Here the mode is tragic; the work as tragedy falters.

We are aware of the interpretation of *Othello* as a play strongly influenced by the morality play: Man, Othello, is buffeted on the one side by evil, Iago, and on the other by good, Desdemona. The ironic imagery and the interplay of hypocrisy and self-deception and of innocence and honesty underscore this relationship. Yet the play has a decided tragic effect and does not elicit the nonemotional reaction that morality does. Whatever comic effects there are in puns and the gull Roderigo serve to etch the tragic outcomes being shaped. As the play ends we are not conscious of Iago as an allegoric or mythic figure, and we do not view the action as an inevitable part of the mortal condition. The effect arises from the considerations that constitute tragedy: the wastage of good, the exposure of sin in an otherwise supposedly moral universe, the centrality of the hero who misjudges and who does "turn the business of his soul / To such exsufflicate and blown surmises" as match Iago's inferences (rather, implications). We are not impressed by geometries in the play, though they exist strongly. The effect is open and continuing. The author's intent is clearly to establish the tragic.

The difficulty with *Othello* is its genre. Genre depends on analysis, and analysis points up the play's morality level, its ritualistic and mythic essence, and its balances. Here I think not only of Desdemona and Iago, but of Emilia and Cassio (whose actions have exactly opposite value in moral scales), and of the contrastive balancing of Iago and Roderigo and of Emilia and Bianca, and of the symmetries of action and plot movement. While there is a wasting of good, the emphasis is not upon the driving out of evil, which is not recognized until after the catastrophe. Indeed is evil driven out? Or only exposed? Othello is not a scapegoat, and he is representative both of the average human who can be hoodwinked by design and fall victim to jealousy and inferiority complex and of an allegoric or mythic figure. The latter condition makes him something other than the standard tragic hero. The anagnorisis on which the play's movement proceeds is false, another example of deception and the problem of appearance and reality. The play suggests that the authorial point of view in *Othello* focused on the inevitability of evil in this world—and such a view does not strengthen a classification of the play as tragedy. What I am suggesting is that *Othello* exhibits tragic mode and has thus been classified as tragedy, but that generically it involves neither tragedy nor comedy, being basically a morality. I simply do not want to evaluate *Othello* as a tragedy but as a morality, and as a morality it is not outshone by any other literary work. Such recognition of genre for *Othello* does not detract from but enhances our appreciation of this great literary work and of Shakespeare's craft.

Macbeth gives us another avenue for Shakespeare's exploration of tragedy and tragic mode. For while it, like *Othello*, is engaged in mythic material—Macbeth and Lady Macbeth as representatives of an infernal

Adam and Eve, fully Satanized, killing their Lord, ascending to his power, and avenged by one not of woman born—it remains a tragedy by genre. Shakespeare has not let his source dictate his form as he did in *Othello*. Both Macbeth and Lady Macbeth have the potentialities of good until emboldened to sin; it is their sinfulness that must be and is driven out—by remorse and by superior achievement—one internal, one external. The hero is driven by ambition (and envy and pride), as well as by the acceptance of appearances because ambition overcomes judgment. While Lady Macbeth can seemingly overcome the internal at first, she succumbs to internal forces later, representing one form of potential catastrophe for all who follow their path. (Her squeamishness about Duncan's reminder for her of her father, of course, psychologizes the real person beneath the outward bravado, and we are not surprised at her emotional breakdown when it comes.) While Macbeth has difficulty in overcoming his psychological anxieties, he succumbs only to external force later, representing the other form of potential catastrophe. It is through their decision to act that the tragedy proceeds. Although contrasts are made available in Banquo, Malcolm, and Macduff, it is Macbeth who gives them meaning; there is no geometric setup that does not have Macbeth as its focus. We are concerned with Macbeth and his wife in the play, not the people that they may represent; and accordingly the disorder of the play's world rather than the order commanded by Malcolm and Macduff holds our attention. What is different about *Macbeth* as tragedy, of course, is that the protagonists are not a hero in any commendable sense. The play becomes Shakespeare's exploration of the question of what is good and what is evil, perversely attacked by eliciting our compassion for evil figures. The progression from *Hamlet* to *Lear* to *Othello* to *Macbeth* and from *Macbeth* to *Antony and Cleopatra* is a literarily meaningful path.

The tragic mode of the play is curious, for we are compassionate toward Macbeth and Lady Macbeth and thus experience a tragic sense. But we also cannot forget their deeds; by the end of the play it is difficult to remember that they were not always committed to their current course of action. Still our pity is raised. I think Shakespeare was experimenting with modal controls—and he succeeds—to determine whether reaction is inherent in subject or in treatment. Well, that is what is wrong analytically with *Romeo and Juliet*. The tragic reaction is in the subject, and it does not hold up. In *Macbeth* it is the treatment that manipulates us, and this in spite of the mythic proportions of the Porter and of the derisiveness of Psalms 2, which hangs over any earthly king on his high hill in the eyes of God and through the miraculous action of His only begotten, symbolized in Macduff.

Differentiation between tragedy as genre and tragic mode is significant for our evaluation of *King Lear*, *Antony and Cleopatra*, and *Coriolanus*.

Lear is undoubtedly a tragedy and would seem to be in the tragic mode. Most people's reading or viewing of it certainly places it in this modal category. Whether we see the play as an examining of despair or of enlightening experiences leading to a regeneration of spirit, the mode is tragic. I do not agree that despair is the pervading attitude of the play since there is an achievement of good and a rejection of evil, and since there is a rise in hope as it concludes. But this rise in hope does not constitute a comedic mode as sometimes seems to be hinted. Lear has fallen before the play begins, as encased in the first scene with its sharp illogicalities. The play is about Lear's spiritual regeneration, and this regeneration expresses man's hope of conquering the evil and the inevitable in this world, such as Albany's reversal would also suggest. Hope may ultimately be tragic, but like Thomas in "Do Not Go Gentle into That Good Night" the person who hopes may be moved to try to give those hopes actuality, and as in Hamlet's situation that may be sufficient for any lifetime. But in any case mode is more than just the final lines of the play—witness *Romeo and Juliet* and *Hamlet*. The mode of *Lear* redirects us to see that responsibility and order take precedence for Shakespeare, at least at the time of writing, over abdication of one's duties for whatever reason and over an attitude of allowing things just to happen as they come along. Action, direct and definite, not passivity, even in the form of withdrawal—like Cordelia's, Kent's, or Edgar's—is necessary in this world. I cannot avoid a linkage in mind between the problems of *Hamlet* for Shakespeare as person and the solutions of *Lear*. But such a psychodynamic examination cannot be pursued here, although such a linkage, in fact, suggests that *Lear* was written earlier than 1606, perhaps 1605 or 1604, or better still 1603, as other evidence could support—closer, that is, to *Hamlet* and before *Othello*, and perhaps within the general period of *All's Well That Ends Well* and *Measure for Measure*.

Does not the tragic mode imbue every line of *Antony and Cleopatra*?

> Come, thou monarch of the vine,
> Plumpy Bacchus with pink eyne;
> In thy fats our cares be drown'd,
> With thy grapes our hairs be crown'd.
> Cup us till the world go round,
> Cup us till the world go round!
> (II, vii, 109–14)

But we understand the double entendres of sex and of escape, in the vine and the hairs and in the lost consciousness. Mardian, the eunuch, may answer Cleopatra's question about his having affections punningly:

> Not in deed, madam; for I can do nothing
> But what indeed is honest to be done.
> Yet have I fierce affections, and think
> What Venus did with Mars . . . ,
>
> (I, v, 15–18)

yet we recognize the serious intent in the lines—it is Antony and Cleopatra's giving in to their affections that has provoked the conditions that will lead to the catastrophe, and it is only by denial of being—by mutilation of one's life-creating force—that one can be "honest" (that is, chaste). The question posed by the play is the weighing of the value of a full life against repression—any and all kinds of repression. We are made to side with Antony and then with Cleopatra, so that their tragic love commands our reaction throughout. But though we reject the symbolic life of a Mardian, we know that the other extreme as exemplified by the title characters is not sufficiently controlled by wisdom to be totally commendable. And thereby lies the tragedy and the tragic mode. Do we not experience the tragic mode most because we want to be cupped till the world go round and to do what Venus did with Mars and simply brave the laughter of the other gods?

In *Antony and Cleopatra* I see Shakespeare moving well beyond himself in any other play by making us, the viewers, weigh the questions the title characters face and decide with them even though we recognize constantly the way that we are heading. The astronomical and expansive imagery complements this affective development, for we reject the limited and local and embrace the universal. The tragic mode, in other words, not only exists in this play for the audience to discern and feel, but it is so manipulated that we experience its effects and development upon us as we read or view.[12]

Artistically—and I think psychologically—the play distances itself from *Hamlet* and *Lear* and the "side" investigations of *Othello* and *Macbeth*. Where does one go after it? *Coriolanus* gives the answer—both backward and elsewhere, for the active pitting of oneself against the "wisdom" of acceptance of things as they are (not too dissimilar from Hamlet's dilemma) leads to questions that other plays have explored and to a path that seems to be on some other level while also being a dead end. Coriolanus, unlike Ibsen's Doctor Stockmann, does not learn that to stand alone is best, enemy of the people though he be. The tragic mode explores the problem of the individual who, while believing in his or her superiority, must have the external world acknowledge that superiority. Viewer reaction depends on whether we align ourselves with Coriolanus against the mass stupidity and mere presence of "the people" or with the mass against the elitists and despisers of "common man." This is an omnipresent problem in any kind of leadership, not just political. In either alignment the effect is tragic, for no one wins and there is loss for everyone. In a way, as in *Hamlet,* the tragic mode arises from the open-endedness of the play—except that Shakespeare's distance in this play allows us to acknowledge that even though we align ourselves with the mass, we know that Coriolanus's evaluation of them is too often unavoidably correct. The play, it seems to me, begins to explore again a strain begun with *Hamlet* that moved in one line of vision to the conclusions of *Antony and Cleopatra.* Now Shakespeare is moving into a different phase—one not answerable through archetypal views of humankind and history. But unfortunately he did not proceed along this path—or could not. Perhaps this is the reason for the turn to *Pericles, Cymbeline, The Winter's Tale,* and *The Tempest.* A dead end? The psychological reactions of closing in on age fifty? Or has the thought behind *Coriolanus* and *Timon of Athens,* rather, advanced Shakespeare to understand the acceptance of the world as it is, encompassing finally the forgiveness that Prospero learns and the innocence of Miranda's brave new world? Is not this philosophic substruct what sets these last tragicomedies[13] aside from even such well-made comedies as *A Midsummer Night's Dream* and *As You Like It?*

The matters that I have raised have, first, related to the meaning and differentiation of genre and mode, and specifically tragedy and tragic mode. The plays mentioned are tragedies, except, in my view, *Othello,* and should be evaluated alongside plays of their own genre. Awareness of genre obviates the classification of *Romeo and Juliet* as a comedy and argues that *Othello* be considered a morality and proposes that most other points of critical commentary are concerned with mode. For genre does not depend on viewer reaction. Second, the mode of the play may be subjective, since it depends on viewer reaction. Mode is important as a guide to what would appear to be authorial intent, and which in turn should lead to a clearer, expectedly more valid, view of the "meaning" of the play. The modal confusion of *Romeo and Juliet* is important to remark and is the cause of its alleged generic confusion. Third, mode may be labeled "tragic" but it can take various forms. It can derive its quality from a pervasive attitude felt by the viewer toward the protagonist or a leading character's fate; from a feeling of incompleteness and uncertainty; from a resistance emotionally to the intellectual attitude developed. The form of the mode is described by the sense of significance and meaning in the play that the viewer has, and, accordingly, that sense is created by the form that the mode takes. Surely this is a major reason why *Antony and Cleopatra* is so overwhelming: the form of the mode and the sense of the play develop for the viewer together. And fourth, although I may seem to be splitting hairs, these points seem to lie at the base of many critical controversies as I read them, and only by their acknowledgment can we deal with those critical controversies adequately. Genre and mode are limina into a reading (or viewing) of a piece of literature, and we are subject to misreading if we ignore them.

4

Comedy: Reflection of Life or Unreal Angle of Vision?

The topic *comedy* has been subjected over the years to a dialectic approach to literature: the effect upon the reader and the formalistic nature of comedy, which separates it from tragedy. One approach does not exclude the other. Comedy has been read moralistically as a means to instruct by holding a mirror up for us to view ourselves (the reflection of life), or it has been defined in formulaic terms of structure, devices, and wit. The reflection of life supposedly "leaves nature as it is." Deconstruction rejects even the possibility of "reflection of life" when it rejects the mimetic as viable. When the mirror distorts the reflection of life, emphasizing one of its parts only, like the various mirrors lining an amusement park fun house (an unreal angle of vision), a satiric property may enter, leading to ridicule and expected rejection of the exaggerated type, whether character or plot element. Or distortion may lead, not to the satiric, but to the aggrandizement of the good and pleasing, with a corresponding collapse, or at least dwarfing, of the ugly and distasteful. The angle of vision may be created or enhanced by structures, devices, and wit. Deconstruction concedes angle of vision, though rejecting both the author and the substance, in considering the only access to reality to be anamorphic.

Much modern literature has employed the unreal angle of vision to comment on the absurdity of life, not to satirize. Thus suggested is either the comedic property of a work like John Hawkes's *Second Skin* or the inherent tragic propensities that this kind of view may offer in a novel like Nathanael West's *Day of the Locust.* In the latter case the aggrandizement is of the ugly and distasteful. Clearly the reflection of life or its unreal angle of vision, to allow classification of a literary work as comedic of mode, must involve authorial intention and expected reader response, and, as comedy generically, some appropriate form.

Differences between the reflection of life and the unreal angle of vision can most specifically be seen in the contradiction or paradox of life that underlies the literary work as the coordinates of its action and characters. Søren Kierkegaard concluded that the comical involves "painless contradiction," for it manifests a way out of the contradiction, and that what separates the only comic from the satiric comic is, in the latter case, a teleology in the direction of a cure.[1] The reflection of life presents such contradiction from outside the consciousness by presenting those elements of life in which humor resides (it never exists in the abstract, Kierkegaard reminds us); the unreal angle of vision forces such contradiction upon the consciousness by a refocusing of elements of life that appear to offer little humor within them. In James Joyce's *Ulysses*, for instance, the picture of "Stately, plump Buck Mulligan" at the top of the stairs in his "yellow dressinggown, ungirdled . . . sustained gently behind him by the mild morning air" and "bearing a bowl of lather on which a mirror and a razor lay crossed," intoning, "Introibo ad altare Dei,"[2] subtends the contradictions in religion and human living, in religion and medicine (for Buck is a medical student and some of the problems for Stephen Dedalus are the incompatibilities of knowledge and religion), in religion and art, and in the basic conflict for the novel of religious emphasis on the afterlife and Joyce's philosophic emphasis on the acceptance of the now. At the same time the satiric view of the church and its ritual is created by an unreal angle of vision, the teleological cure being the rejecting of the church and its morality by Stephen through a universal and mythic morality. The cure is most strongly advanced, as the novel proceeds, in the Jewishness of Leopold Bloom, with his clearly regenerative associations. The novel is formed from symbolical paradoxes that fill every page: the paradoxes may reflect or distort the actual of reality to be seen within us and around us, symbolically, if not congruently, as when Bloom defecates soon after having prepared a kidney for ingestion, or metaphorically as when Stephen urinates "In long lassoes from the Cock lake . . . covering greengoldenly lagoons of sand, rising, flowing," his "ashplant" seeming to be almost floated away, or mythically as when Bloom and Molly[3] sleep head-to-foot imaging generative continuity. The angle of vision has collapsed what might be most commonly considered ugly and distasteful by acceptance of it as nonvicious because it is natural. The unreal angle of vision has become congruent with the reflection of life. And perhaps most significant ultimately is that this seemingly very personal and biographical novel has avoided the personal and subjective by its distancing. The metanovel that the "Wandering Rocks" chapter delineates is a clear example of such avoidance and such distancing.

Basically a reader response has been expected when comedy is seen as a reflection of life that will lead ultimately to some reform—of oneself, of those one may influence, of one's approach to life and its cast of characters.

Historically either there is an imitation of unacceptable types of people with respect to manners or there is ridicule of that which is considered vicious. Comedy may thus become a "vehicle of corrective satire." In contrast there has been postulated a character or characters who represent that which is acceptable and who are opposed to vice. Comedy thus becomes an "exemplary display of social grace and witty refinement."[4] Aristophanic comedy and Jonsonian comedy partake generally of the first with an exemplary character here or there, and Plautine comedy and romantic comedy (particularly that set in or against a green world)[5] partake generally of the second with a ridiculous character here or there. The structure may involve (1) movement through the potentially tragic to a happy solution, (2) interference of a dramatic movement in terms of Henri Bergson's geometric concepts,[6] and (3) variant story patterns subtended by varied but persistent characters or character types. Devices derive from plot lines and are often standard, and wit, while it may drive home the instruction positively or negatively, is often a device to portray a character or to comment on an action. The reformative view of comedy emphasizes reader response, but one manipulated by the author; the structural and witty view emphasizes the author's writing. Comedy implies the completion of its geometries and nullification of its structural interferences and inconsistencies. Thus in its movement through and minimizing of the tragic it offers inherent hopeful and positive views of life. Clearly the structure of comedy says that the artifact defines its whole world and is not to be viewed in any relationship with any other world. There may be parallel worlds, there may be many artifacts that offer the same structuralistic underpinnings so that, in a sense, each one is every one, but the individual comedic artifact is self-contained. The contrast of *A Portrait of the Artist as a Young Man* and *Ulysses* in this regard is instructive: the world of *Ulysses* is self-contained and only structuralistic concepts will be repeating as we close the book, like a theme and variations; but the world of *A Portrait* only appears to be self-contained, with the future supposedly being a fulfillment of the work read. Rather, as we rethink, *A Portrait* implies the indecisiveness that life's future always holds, for Stephen, born out of the womb that is the novel, faces, as he leaves mother and mother Ireland, a transitory world equivalent to that of the newborn child. *A Portrait* in itself cannot be labeled a comedy; it is instead a proem to the comic or the tragic in life, depending upon Stephen's (that is, any person's) view of reality and his interfacing with it.

Hugh Blair in his survey of literary types toward the end of the eighteenth century emphasized the first of the two basic reader-response concepts: it is the comic poet's business "to give us pictures taken from among ourselves; to satirize reigning and present vices; to exhibit to the age a faithful copy of itself, with its humours, its follies, and its extravagancies."[7] The scene, subject, and time should be the author's own world, he adds, and in terms of what I call the "unreal angle of vision" Blair notes that at times comedic elements are too exaggerated. But this reflection of life bifurcates into two areas as well: Is the emphasis on action or character, on plot or discourse? "Do the characters exist to carry out the action, or is the action contrived to display the characters?"[8] Blair labels these two approaches "Comedy of Intrigue" and "Comedy of Character," and though he remarks that "it is what men say, and how they behave, that draws our attention, rather than what they perform, or what they suffer," he concludes that "In order to give this sort of Composition its proper advantage, these two kinds should be properly mixed together."[9]

Aristotle in his definition of tragedy specifically states that it lies in the dramatic action, not in the narrative, emphasizing therefore the persons performing the action. Implied is empathy of the personal, involvement of the self in the emotional world of the actors, and this leads to the concept of catharsis.[10] While I would suggest that Aristotle, working out of drama only, is wrong for nondramatic literature to which one might assign the genre *tragedy* in that there may be a "Tragedy of Intrigue"—perhaps Céline's *Journey to the End of the Night* or Kenneth Patchen's *Journal of Albion Moonlight*—I would agree that the tragic does involve the self more intricately than does the comedic and that in an admixture of "Tragedy of Character" and "Tragedy of Intrigue" the greater emphasis lies on the "character." By contrastive reasoning, in an admixture of "Comedy of Character" and "Comedy of Intrigue," which Blair notes should be properly mixed together, the greater emphasis lies on the "Comedy of Intrigue." In *Day of the Locust* we have tragic emphasis on Tod Hackett, Faye Greener, and Abe Kusich, for example, who proceed through a series of episodes, and in *Second Skin* the emphasis is on the life force within Skipper, which persists through the tragic world of Fernandez and Cassandra. In the one instance the reader is surely more concerned with Tod (note the onomastic value of the name as *Death*) and the futural end of life pointed to by the title, drawn from Exodus 10.12–20 and Revelation 9.1–11, and shown in the great conflagration of 2 Peter 3.10, "The Burning of Los Angeles." In the other instance, the reader is more concerned with the persistence of life's continuancy that Skipper's nickname implies as pilot of the ship that is man's body moving through the sea of life, the title of the novel pointing to cyclical continuance rather than end. The past is gone; the future is begun. That it is the serpent that shucks off its skin to reemerge with a second skin is, of course, significant: the serpent is both a positive symbol, as in the serpents entwining the caduceus of Aesculapius, and a negative one, as in the false kenosis of Satan when he seduced Eve and

Adam. The spoil discarded, the individual can be the self in its positivity and in its negativity, in its self-deception and in its self-cure. If
there is moralistic instruction here, it is to accept life as it is, and this in
itself is positive and minimizes life's consuming tragedies. Certainly the
novel has been skewed in ways that make its action—and the emphasis is
on the stages of action—unreal and anamorphic.

In order to consider comedy as genre rather than as a category (drama,
poem, prose) I have chosen examples from fictional prose. Unfortunately
most discussions of comedy and tragedy have been relegated to dramatic
presentation only,[11] since the Aristotelian dichotomy of literature gave us
only the mimetic and the descriptive (or poetry). Indeed Aristotle said
little about comedy, focusing the mimetic on tragedy, and thus elaborating
the mimesis of character, but always meaning dramatic presentation.
Genre in no way implies authorial attitude toward the content, as I have
argued. Its importance, again, is what it tells us about the author's intentions for the work since the author chose the genre: it implies what the
author wanted to communicate by its use or variation (according to what
can be inferred as his or her understanding of the genre), and it thus may
be evaluated for craft alongside other examples of the same genre. The
implications the author believes are being imbued within the work depend
on the internal evidence of the work itself, and certainly intentional
fallacy could occur. But the internal evidence of the work itself leads us to
an intentionality of the text, a more viable concept, one demonstrable by
the text itself without recourse to considering the author. Genre is a sign
that makes explicit certain literary conventions, places a work within a
literary context, and thus partakes of a semiotic system. It provides a limen
into a novel in one area of genre meaning, and another limen into the
same novel in such an area as "tragedy" or "comedy," once we divorce
those generic signs from only the play area of genre meaning. As such,
genre should be important for structuralist concerns as a component in
literary discourse and its operation. It does involve the writer writing; it
does involve authorial intention, determinable interiorly; it helps define
an intentionality of the text. That the term genre has been abused and
misunderstood should not remove it from literary-critical concerns.[12]

Comedy refers to the work as artifact, its form and its structure and its
characteristics; comic refers to the effect on the reader and should reflect
the author's attitude toward his material. I am urging, first, that the genre
comedy be divorced from the mode comic or comedic,[13] and, second, that
comedy be more specifically delineated as dramatic comedy, prose comedy,
or poetic comedy, just as we have begun (though loosely and not always
with definition) to talk of verse satire and prose satire. Satire should pose
an overall generic definition that will divide into verse satire and prose

satire on more issues than simply one's being in verse and one's being in prose. Accordingly the work that, by holding up a mirror for society to view itself whether reflectively or distortedly, exhibits the superiority of the group or the inferiority of a segment of the group, and that achieves a perspective distance for the reader, is a comedy. Such a work of necessity involves thought, an emphasis on events (although a character type may be emphasized, as in Molière's *Le Misanthrope*) and a deemphasis on cause and effect. The intentionality of its form and structure (a term used by Husserl and the phenomenological school) is fullness and completion, and yet continuance through repetitive cycle or duplication in parallel worlds. Its form and structure do not allow interiorization or reform; those elements may enter through content or mode, and the relation with satire here is one of degree in modal terms. The social aspect of the work avoids the personal and subjective and presents to the audience the means to infer the learning that motivates such works as Bernard Shaw's *Heartbreak House* and *The Simpleton of the Unexpected Isles*. Shaw's comedy is drawn generically from concepts in George Meredith's "On the Idea of Comedy and of the Uses of the Comic Spirit,"[14] which emphasized intellect, not emotion. Shaw is concerned with the act of thinking rather than specific ideas; he does not indoctrinate but rather raises issues to be considered, perhaps approaching conclusions thereon.[15]

This approach to comedy as genre denies reformative aims in the usual sense: it offers instead the elements and contexts to be thought on with expectation only that the future of the reader will be tempered by such thought in one's own being, in the world of those whom one may influence, and in the approach to the world or worlds in which one will find oneself. It is apparent, then, that emphasis is not on character or the individual, nor on causal concerns, events thus neither being determined by character nor shaping character. The answer to the question posed before—Do the characters exist to carry out the action, or is the action contrived to display the characters?—is the first, and when the literary work slips over into the second we have a different genre or subgenre, perhaps tragicomedy, with its frequent accompanying sentimentalism, whether it is Colley Cibber's *Careless Husband* or Erich Segal's *Love Story*. While both these works reflect life in one guise or another, neither takes on an unreal angle of vision except in its ending of rewarding virtue and punishing vice. (I do not credit the simplistic definition that tragicomedy is a mere mixture of tragedy and comedy or of superiors and inferiors; this may be a characteristic of tragicomedy if we allow that mixture to be symbolic. But we would thus be saying that the superiors take on the qualities of the inferiors, or that the inferiors take on the qualities of the superiors, and such thinking about qualities is based on outdated and invalid societal prejudices, based in their turn on economic and political crutches for society's psychological escape.)[16] In comedy vice is rebuked or nullified, and virtue as the positivity that society provides persists. The moralistic reading of comedy is acceptable only when it coincides with the customs and conduct of society as they persist through time and space, not when it involves judgment of a righteous nature. The visage in the mirror in which we view ourselves should coincide with ourselves (thus leaving nature as it is), but the visage can be cognizant, highlighted, perspective, and evaluated meaningfully only by an angle of vision that, though ultimately distorting, will allow us to see the warts, the asymmetry, the ever-present selfness of that visage.

Moving to the boundaries of the satiric is such a fine prose comedy as Randall Jarrell's novel *Pictures from an Institution.* Its society would seem to be the circumscribed world of Bennington College (as well as Sarah Lawrence College and Vanderbilt University), but, no, it is that part of society called the academic, but, no, again, it is society itself walking in various spheres peopled with poseurs and the avaricious. The form seems almost episodic, each chapter another view of the whole, each portrait part of the total canvas. These are pictures from an institution, an asylum for those adjudged mad, the asylum that is the world itself. These are pictures to be compared with those of Mussorgsky at an exhibition of Viktor Hartmann's paintings as we promenade the gallery: chickens in their shells, or catacombs, or querulous Jews, or the Great Gate at Kiev. The form is similar to that of verse satire, as previously described. Jarrell has exhibited "to the age a faithful copy of itself, with its humors, its follies, and its extravagancies."

Moving to the boundaries of the tragic is Jean Giono's *Chant du Monde,* in which, in his words, he has "not had to invent anything at all, not even the people. They all exist." It moves into but through the tragic, yet it is always concerned with the triumph of people and the land. The view is always a bit skewed, the impact is always the persistence of life and the cast of characters who repeat their performances generation after generation. It begins:

> La nuit. Le fleuve roulait à coups d'épaules à travers la forêt, Antonio s'avança jusqu'à la pointe de l'île. D'un côté l'eau profonde, souple comme du poil de chat; de l'autre côté les hennissements du gué. Antonio toucha le chêne. Il écoute dans sa main les tremblements de l'arbe. C'était un vieux chêne plus gros qu'un homme de la montagne, mais il était à la belle pointe de l'île des geais, juste dans la venue du courant et, déjà, la moitié de ses racines sortaient de l'eau.[17]

The inclusiveness of the imagery and its contrasts and fusions in terms of the constituencies of life—cyclic, vegetal, and animal, isolated and companioned, water and earth and air—offers the whole of the world seen through the experiences of one who moves through it. Surely this is the song of the world, and the shivering of the aged oak implies the internal and external forces that may defeat part of that world sometimes, but the world will go on still, much as before. We start in night; the novel ends with a dawn. The ending (with excisions to conserve space) reads:

> Le courant portait dru. Il n'y avait plus à craindre les souches et les hauts fonds. On était sur le gras de l'eau. Il ne restait plus qu'à donner de temps en temps de petits coups de gouverne. Au fond de la nuit, on entendait souffler les gorges.
>
> Au jour levant, on touchera l'île des Geais. . . .
>
> Il pensait que maintenant. Clara et lui, tout le temps ensemble. . . .
>
> Antonio pensait qu'il allait être libre et la garder près de lui dans l'île. Tout doucement. Pas à pas. . . .
>
> Il pensait qu'il allait prendre Clara dans ses bras et qu'il allait se coucher avec elle sur la terre.[18]

The imagery is similar to that of the novel's beginning, when not the same; the concepts of continuation and generation are seen as well in "Step by step" ("Pas à pas"), in the newness of feeling and touching life by the inexperienced, in the potential generation of lying down on the earth, out of which generation comes. Perhaps we should also note the spatial structure of the novel, which has three parts, divided into nine, seven, and three chapters respectively. Three as symbol of godhead relates with seven, the number of creation, and suggests fullness and completion as ten, while Part One has moved toward such perfection as the number nine implies in symbolic meaning.

I purposely cite *Le Chant du Monde* to separate *comedy* from "funny" and "ridicule," and to impress that the angle of vision, askew, may aggrandize the good and pleasing while collapsing or at least dwarfing the ugly and distasteful. For the ugly and distasteful are a part of life and must be a part of the reflection of life, if comedy indeed does engage the reflection of life. But the comic vision sees beyond the ugly and distasteful and underscores indelibly the movement past and beyond. The tragic vision is consumed by what it sees, overwhelmed by the black, blank wall it erects. Recognition of Giono's novel as a comedy has led not only to a different reading of it but also to a realization that any tragic reading of it lacks cogency.

The imagery of the last paragraph of Günter Grass's *Hundejahre*, the ending of Part Three, will recapitulate the points I have made here. Significantly, the third part is entitled "Materniaden," the histories or epics of Matern, the main character of the novel. Here we have allegedly a hundred stories plus three additional ones. The descent into the mine and reascent to the world complete the epical novel, and its last paragraph emphasizes the mythic underpinnings of comedy that have been outlined— emphasis on more than individuals by themselves, the shucking-off of the accoutrements of the past, the emergence out of the world of the dark where artificial light is needed, and the new beginning that each must undertake, freed of the past as each one becomes an individual self again, unable to duplicate exactly "the whistle" ("die Pfeife") of another:

> Und Dieser und Jener—wer mag sie noch Brauxel und Matern nennen?—ich und er, wir schreiten mit abgelöschtem Geleucht zur Steigerkaue, wo ens der Kauenwärter die Schutzhelme und die Karbidlampen abnimmt. Mich und ihn führt er in Kabinen, die Materns und Brauxels Kleider aufbewahrten. Aus Untertageklamotten steigen er und ich. Für mich und ihn wurden die Badewannen gefüllt. Drüben höre ich Eddi plätschern. Jetzt steige auch ich ins Bad. Das Wasser laugt uns ab. Eddi pfeift etwas Unbestimmtes. Ich versuche ähnliches zu pfeifen. Doch das ist schwer. Beide sind wir nackt. Jeder badet für sich.[19]

The interplay between the tragic and the comic in Henry Roth's wonderful but neglected novel *Call It Sleep* also summarizes the point of this chapter, and indicates the importance of considering these generic and modal concepts in reading a piece of literature, here the novel with its multiple modes and ambiguities of placement. For early reviews of this 1934 work looked upon it as a "proletarian" novel that was not quite radical but that nonetheless stressed the tragic world of the Jewish immigrant in New York City, the squalor and poverty, the prejudiced and inescapable economic stratifications for those who did not fit the dominant society into which they had been thrust. The emphasis was on the tragic, yet because it was not a doctrinaire novel with a message of revolt but rather a novel offering a view of life through the eyes of a six- to nine-year-old boy it was dismissed by the more politically extreme commentators. It is not essentially a novel of social protest though one can certainly read its discrepancy between the dignity of humankind and the actualities of life for its characters as a protest. Basically, as with so many other pieces of literature we are looking at in this study, it was not being read early on as the work it is but as a work that the critic thought it should be. Later, the novel was discussed by a few astute readers like Alfred Kazin and Leslie Fiedler as one dealing with the growth, particularly the psychological growth, of a boy, a growth echoed by many, a different kind of bildungsroman from *David Copperfield.* But the novel has fallen again into neglect.

Throughout *Call It Sleep* a reader can encounter the tragic in the forces of society shaping David Schearl's world, in the bitterness of his father and the sadism of his teacher, in the ugly introduction to sex with the older crippled girl, but such emphasis on the character as character only, rather than like David Copperfield as one of many who undergo various paralleled experiences, misses the nullification of these things in the hopes of transcendence in this "Golden Land." The view of society and of human growth that is mirrored in the novel involves the tragic and even "tragedies" (the father, Albert, for instance), but there is movement through this world when it is understood as the reflection of an angle of vision that ultimately distorts. David is shocked, as the novel ends, by the current of the streetcar track when, on a double dare, he inserts a zinc milk ladle:

> A blast, a siren of light
> within him, rending, quaking, fusing his
> brain and blood to a fountain of flame,
> vast rockets in a searing spray! Power!
> The hawk of radiance raking him with
> talons of fire, battering his skull with
> a beak of fire, braying his body with
> pinions of intolerable light.[20]

The descent into darkness, so commonplace in ancient epics as a metaphor for understanding or rather self-understanding and then transcendence, follows:

> Down! Down into darkness,
> darkness that tunneled the heart of
> darkness, darkness fathomless. Each
> step he took, he shrank, grew smaller
> with the unseen panels. . . . At
> each step shed the husks of being,
> and himself tapering always downward
> in the funnel of the night.

Later, perhaps recovered and home in his own bed, perhaps dead, David is seen putting all these tragic worlds and potentialities behind him: they and this ultimate transcending experience "He might as well call . . . sleep."

It was only toward sleep that ears had power to cull again and reassemble the shrill cry, the hoarse voice, the scream of fear, the bells, the thick-breathing, the roar of crowds and all sounds that lay fermenting in the vats of silence and the past. . . . One might as well call it sleep. He shut his eyes.

The intentionality of this text is not reform, social protest, or communistic need, nor is it the recognition of the Alberts of life and the plight of the Jewish immigrant: it is, rather, the reflection and distortion of the mirror of a society to which one, David, has been subjected before there can be the shucking-off of the accoutrements of the past and the emergence out of the world of the dark before he hears the *"(Mister! Whistle! Whistle! Whistle! / Whistle, Mister! Yellow birds!)."* Critical estimates of this novel have misread its intentionality as social/political reform and found it somewhat wanting or have stressed its substance as only psychological growth of the individual in a Jewish world: it encompasses these, yes, but it presents the results of that coal of Isaiah (6.6–7), so frequently cited in the novel, that has touched the lips of the fictive voice and offers up the hallowed fire of life and its joy of living. Recognition of the preeminence of the comedic within the whole of the work directs the reader to that overarching concern.

While chapters 3 and 4 have dealt with other creative forms than poetry, the generic and modal definitions and employment of tragedy/comedy, the tragic/the comic are meaningful for poetic forms. The prototype of the tragic is the basis for George Herbert's "The Sacrifice"—the Incarnation and the Crucifixion; the sense of the comic pervades Herbert's "Man" and its intertext, Vaughan's "Man," though the latter criticizes the hope of the former. What Vaughan's "Man" points out is that Herbert's poem is insufficiently a reflection of life as life realistically is, though his poem too ends with open-endedness:

> Man is the shuttle, to whose winding quest
> And passage through these looms
> God ordered motion, but ordain'd no rest.

David Schearl's passage reflects that winding quest.

5

Genre and Seventeenth-Century Poetry

The significance of genre for the poet may be summarized thus: The poet writes consciously within this genre or that. The poet writes consciously within a genre to prove to her- or himself and to others that she or he can accomplish a poem in a specific genre. The poet writes consciously within a genre to communicate to readers the ideas or connotations that are attached to a specific genre because she or he relates such ideas or connotations to the meaning. And the poet writes consciously within a genre in order to transcend that genre, thereby achieving another level of evaluative comparison with other writers working within that genre, and also thereby achieving further meaning for the poem through variations from the standard. In this way genre becomes a liminal entry into a poem, bringing the reader from outside the poem into it as a space to be encountered.

One other point needs to be made before looking at examples, which will be drawn from that very genre-conscious period, the British seventeenth century. What I have just said so positively contradicts an all-too-frequent belief about writing, particularly about poetic writing, that is seldom acknowledged and always deleterious: the belief that most of the time a poet puts into words a strongly felt emotion or idea or experience, either directly and almost spontaneously or after reflection in tranquillity, without planning or strategies or what the Elizabethans called the foreconceit.[1] Critics may admit that a poet has a plan for a work, but they do not always really acknowledge that plan, nor deep-down subscribe to belief in such planning. They will not really admit that the poet is working from much more than a kind of rough outline. This kind of erroneous belief has led to many indefensible critical stances: T. S. Eliot's theory that John Donne's songs and sonnets represent undissociated sensibility because he thought they were basically raw biographical data is one case. Donne is too seldom given credit for vision or imagination.[2] Or one can think of the antagonism toward those critics who perceive geometric and arithmetic structures behind literature, for example, in Spenser's "Epithalamion" or Milton's "Nativity Ode." Or consider the aversion to psychological analysis which suggests that, say, Milton consciously implied phallicism when Comus waves his rod at the Lady. The fault ultimately lies in this all-too-frequent and erroneous belief that a poet does not sit down and plan out a work, does not, that is, know what she or he is doing or why. So many people assume that the poet gets some kind of inspiration and sits down and puts pen to paper, sometimes to succeed without much time lapse and without much revision, and sometimes not to succeed except with revision over a good period of time.[3] Is this not as well the point behind the cliché that Henry Vaughan wrote fine first lines, but then his poems fall apart? An instance sometimes cited is "I saw eternity the other night." After a great first line, the critique goes, the poem disintegrates. Such a statement about Vaughan ultimately derives from the lack of acknowledgment of the poetic act, and so the would-be critic does not examine the poem to see what Vaughan is doing and how he is doing it. The poem examined is the poem the critic thinks should have been written. I am sure that only one concerned with structure can know how fine a poem "The World" is, let alone a maligned "secular" poem like "To Amoret Weeping."[4]

I think it is clear that my views of genre oppose such a belief about the writing of literature as I have been impaling. I believe the poet—at least most poets, and the good ones, surely—knows what he or she is doing, where the poem is going, what the reader is expected to experience, and if the poet does not, the poem will fail or be a mere effusion of emotion, like a Joyce Kilmer's "Trees." And one of the means of planning that the poet uses is genre. None of the factors of genre definition can exist without forethought. Maybe the author decides to eschew a genre, but that implies in itself some kind of nonstructure and a different kind of characteristic and authorial point of view. An author may alter the received generic form or characteristics, though most will probably stay within the rough contours of the definition. If the change is great from the standard type or if the generic earmarks disappear, we may have instead a new kind of subgenre; and if the authorial point of view is unclear or vacillating, we probably have an inept poem.

In this chapter a few different poetic genres (and kinds of genres) are examined for their importance in reading and more fully understanding the examples used. More "kinds" could, of course, be cited, and many more examples of each kind looked at, but the conclusion should be adequately demonstrated by the poems discussed: genre is important to a reading of a poem and may, indeed, direct the reader to a cogent reading, thereby, at times, obviating false readings.

The sonnet will provide illustrative discussion and point up the way new readings may arise—particularly since it is a well-known form whose generic implications are usually overlooked. The sonnet has a form and structure: fourteen lines in iambic pentameter with a definite rhyme scheme and definite sections. Early sonnets (meaning "little songs") and a few later sonneteers vary the number of lines, the meter, the rhyme, or the lack of rhyme, and the sections, or the lack of sections. But the Petrarchan or Italian sonnet and the Elizabethan or Spenserian or Shakespearean sonnets had these characteristics of form and structure. "Little songs" are not really to be classified under the current genre *sonnet;* and sonnets that do not exhibit the form and structure described should be evaluated for their variations from the description—for example, George Meredith's sequence "Modern Love" (each sonnet has sixteen lines). The Petrarchan sonnet, which I wish to talk about here, was divided into two sections, an octave and a sestet. The octave provided the background out of which the thought or conclusion of the sestet came. The important element in terms of thought was the sestet. That thought might be somewhat commonplace and the octave might present the more imaginative substance and expression. Separating the octave and the sestet was the *volta* or turn; that is, there was a sharp break between the two sections. Now surely a person who sits down to write and chooses a sonnet as the form and structure into which she or he is going to put the thought or emotion has made a planned decision before writing. If the poet is going to work in the Petrarchan sonnet form, the material must be planned so that the background is set forth in the octave and the conclusion is set forth in the sestet. (If the poet is using a different sonnet form with a different structure, the planning is going to be different. And always there may be the poet who is not aware of all the characteristics.) If the sestet represents a "philosophic" thought that the author has come to and wishes to communicate to the reader, the obvious material for the octave is that experience or set of actions that has provoked the philosophic thought. But such material provides only a background, not the major statement. This is one of the most important characteristics of the Petrarchan sonnet, and at the same time it defines the evidence for the authorial point of view toward the genre and the content presented through it. Evaluatively, it is often the octave that is important as an imaginative, striking statement of a "new" background for the rather commonplace idea or emotion (e.g., in Shakespeare's "When in disgrace with fortune and men's eyes").

We can see this Petrarchan form in Milton's seventh sonnet, "How soon hath Time the suttle theef of youth," where the background out of which the thought comes is his lack of accomplishment, his youthful appearance, and his seeming lack of maturity. The philosophic thought is explicitly stated in the sestet—whatever is depends upon time and the will of Heaven as long as he is worthy. There is a sharp break at line 8, and we know that Milton was not really concerned with his seeming lack of internal and external maturity, not only from what he says in the poem but even from the demands of the genre employed to express his consoling and yet resolute thought. In other words, by knowing what the characteristics and authorial point of view of a genre are, we can better understand what the author implies by using a specific genre and thus come to a better understanding of what the author wishes to communicate. Supposedly the thought of the sestet could also have derived from a different background (perhaps Milton's lack of preferment for a clerical fellowship such as that won by Edward King, who is mourned in "Lycidas"), but in that case the content of the octave would have been different though the sestet remain exactly the same. We have no trouble with Sonnet 7, for it is all quite explicit, critical stress having been showered on the sestet, but critics have sometimes missed the point of Milton's eighteenth sonnet, which cites the Piedmont massacre, because they have not paid attention to the genre.

> Avenge O Lord thy slaughter'd Saints, whose bones
>   Lie scatter'd on the *Alpine* mountains cold,
>   Ev'n them who kept thy truth so pure of old
>   When all our Fathers worship't Stocks and Stones,
> Forget not: in thy book record their groans
>   Who were thy Sheep and in their antient fold
>   Slain by the bloody *Piemontese* that roll'd
>   Mother with Infant down the Rocks. Their moans
> The Vales redoubl'd to the Hills, and they
>   To Heav'n. Their martyr'd blood and ashes sow
>   O're all th' *Italian* fields where still doth sway
> The triple Tyrant: that from these may grow
>   A hunderd-fold, who having learnt thy way
>   Early may fly the *Babylonian* wo.

The question of the position of the volta or turn can be belayed for a minute. The first part of the poem, the ostensible octave, relates the events of Piemontese Easter, on which day armed forces in the name of the Duke of Savoy attacked the Protestant Waldensians (the Vaudois); the second part of the poem, the ostensible sestet, makes the plea that God sow the blood and ashes of these martyrs over all of Italy so that more of the Protestant persuasion will be generated who will flee from Roman Catholicism, its earthly head, the Pope, and the destruction that will result with its fall. The emphasis is not upon Milton's indignation for the massacred Vaudois—not that he was not horrified by that massacre, but he is not stressing that set of events. If he had wanted to stress it, he surely would have written a very different poem, and that very different poem would probably not have been a sonnet. The poem is concerned with regeneration for those who discover the error of (for the Protestant) false religion and denounce it; Milton's reference to the fall and desolation of Babylon, recalling Jeremiah 51 and Revelation 18, underscores that. But so do the facts that, first, the hundredth word of the sonnet is *hunderdfold*, implying that Milton's sonnet will itself generate those who learn the evil of the Papacy from it, and second, that there are eleven words after *hunderdfold*, implying regeneration and salvation. (We have in these meaningful numerological considerations another liminal entry into the reading of the poem.) The reason for this emphasis on fleeing from Babylon and the ensuing regeneration and salvation has not been fully observed: the poem was written in May 1655, and it was believed, metaphorically at least, that the millennium preluding the Final Judgment would take place in 1657. Milton's poem, whether he actually joined the Millenarians in this or simply used a convenient metaphoric situation, has a relevance for his times that has gone unrecognized—I think primarily because the sonnet has been misread as one exercised over the Piedmont massacre only. Milton's point is that more should recognize the pope as Antichrist and flee from him before it is too late—and in 1655 it was already late.

Milton has stayed well within the generic form, structure, characteristics, and authorial position of the Petrarchan sonnet in this particular poem, but he has employed a great many run-on lines, even to the point of breaking any feeling of two quatrains as constituent parts of the octave— thus being closer to the theoretic Petrarchan mold than was standard—and he has displaced the volta. Does it occur in line 8 after "Rocks" or in line 10 after "Heav'n"? The treatment of this sonnet, and some others, led Hilaire Belloc to talk of the Miltonic sonnet, a supposedly unbroken series of fourteen lines. But none of Milton's sonnets will hold up to that description. "Their moans / The Vales redoubl'd to the Hills, and they / To Heav'n" is transitional, I believe on purpose. (Note its symmetry: two syllables, ten syllables, two syllables.) While it is part of the "octave" in that it supplies background from the event ("Their moans"), it is intended to suggest something not evidential in any material way: heaven hears humankind's moans ("To Heav'n" becoming part of the "sestet"), and it then follows for the true believer that Heaven will not allow the misery to continue. The quadruple moans imply that God has heard and will act. This leads to the prayer to the Lord to sow the martyrs' blood and ashes over all of Italy so that all may learn to flee Antichrist before it is too late. The sowing is also not evidential in any material way, but it may lead to a new material set of events when those who grow a hundredfold flee.[5] In the sonnet we move from material things to faith and to material things of the future. The displacement of the volta more closely unites octave and sestet although they remain separate, and the vagueness of its placement enhances the syllogism involved: these martyrs have died; Heaven has heard their moans; Heaven will not let them die in vain. The structure of the sonnet demands comparison with others that do not employ these meaningful variations from what had become standard. To use a genre but not be rigidly controlled by it, rather to adapt it to one's meaning, may demand high evaluation of generic execution. Recognition of the significance of genre changes our reading of this poem, helps lead to realization of its strategies and structures, and evaluates it more highly in terms of composition than it otherwise could be.

Had Thomas Newton known all this about sonnets, he never would have called Sonnet 19 "On His Blindness," since Milton's condition is mere vehicle. Milton is not talking about blindness in the sonnet; he is talking of the "deeds of substance" (to borrow a key phrase from *The Tenure of Kings and Magistrates*) that those who stand awaiting God's command achieve. Let us hope we have heard the last of that false title, as well as Elijah Fenton's "On His Having Arrived at the Age of Twenty-Three" for Sonnet 7. They definitely are not Milton's.

I turn now to a different genre and, indeed, a different kind of genre: the impossibility poem. Probably such poems will not be misread, for the device on which they depend is clear; but the earmarks of the subgenre direct one's reading as surely as the denotations of its text. We ignore the writer writing if we do not acknowledge the subgenre which has controlled that writing. Here the form or structure is reduced to a series of impossibilities, presented in any one of several meters or patterns, to be followed by a rather quick statement of what the author purports that he really wants to happen but that seems as much an impossibility as the items he has just enumerated. The main characteristic of the impossibility poem is the negative statement followed by a negative conclusion that only miraculously can be positive. The authorial attitude toward the work clearly involves the attempt at wittiness and variety; we should not extrapolate the poet's beliefs from such a poem, although it is certainly possible that the author does believe in the impossibility of the impossibilities cited and in the miracle relegated to impossibility.

Robert Herrick's "To Find God" is a good example of the impossibility poem: the impossibilities are things that a human cannot achieve but that the faithful believe that God can cause to occur. For those who do not believe in God's miraculous powers, the conclusion ("then shew me Him / That rides the glorious cherubim")[6] will not be feasible; for those who have faith, the conclusion is possible through the powers of God. Herrick will see God upon ascent to Heaven, he believes. I do not doubt that he had faith in God, and this poem from "Noble Numbers" can be read as an example of his faith. Under attack is illogic, for most see the impossibilities as impossibilities, yet they believe in God. If God is God, then he could make possible a person's weighing of fire, measuring of wind, Herrick implies. But the poem's *literary* significance lies in the recognition of the poetic genre that has been wittily manipulated to exemplify faith.

Comparison with Herrick's "Impossibilities to His Friend" makes the same point about literary significance:

> My faithful friend, if you can see
> The fruit to grow upon the tree:
> If you can see the color come
> Into the blushing pear or plum:
> If you can see the water grow
> To cakes of ice, or flakes of snow:
> If you can see that drop of rain
> Lost in the wild sea once again:
> If you can see how dreams do creep
> Into the brain by easy sleep:
> Then there is hope that you may see
> Her love me once, who now hates me.

Here the expressed impossibilities are all easy realities, and the conclusion should logically be as easy a reality—the loved one's hate will turn to love. The so-called faithful friend has apparently denied that the loved one will come to love the poet; but this could be a natural development, says the poet, just as by analogy a tree grows fruit after a bleak winter; just as the water that is fluid becomes tangible as ice or snow; just as nonactive periods can be filled with activity. By imagination and experience we can project the fruit, the ice, the dream; why not then her love? Here the friend sees the impossibilities as realities, yet denies a paralleled impossibility as alterable. The attack is really upon logic through false analogy since the poet makes things parallel that are not, and that is a common tactic for debaters in order to draw analogous conclusions. But the significance of the poem is literary: the poet's manipulation of the genre—not the thought that the loved one will change, and not the attack on logic.

Again let us take up a different kind of genre. A hymn is a song of praise of God or gods or heroes and is often sung by a chorus. Its form is not prescribed, and it appears in stanzaic and nonstanzaic patterns. Thus what structures are employed in a hymn may be peculiar to the individual poem. The characteristics of the hymn and the authorial point of view are more distinctive: not only must there be praise, but the hymn represents praise by a group though it may be sung by one person; not only is it poetic, but it must soar as vocal music; not only does the author look toward the person to be praised as a superior, but the poet implies that person can achieve something desirable for her or for him and for the group. At times what is desirable has already been achieved, and the hymn becomes one of thanks.

Ben Jonson's "Hymn" from *Cynthia's Revels* consists of three stanzas of six lines of truncated iambic tetrameters;[7] it praises the moon, that is, Cynthia or Diana, and her realm. Specifically it praises Queen Elizabeth, who was called Cynthia. The meter of the poem is perfect throughout (by which I mean each line is exactly syllabled and accented). For what is Cynthia being praised? At first we may think only for the existence of Night, which contrasts with day and gives respite from day's activeness. The poem appears in the play toward the end, and it has thus been read only as praise of Elizabeth and as a way to start to end the masque and get people home to sleep. But remembering that the hymn implies that the person addressed can achieve something desirable for the speaker and the group represented, we wonder whether that would not be something more than just simply rest, "space to breathe," as the poem expresses it. The first line praises Cynthia as huntress and as goddess of chastity. By putting up her bow of pearl and her crystal-shining quiver she will give the flying hart (HART) space to breathe, even if only for a short while. In the play it preludes the end of the activities on the stage; thus Cynthia as huntress. Knowing the genre, we ask, Is the poet concerned only with an animal? Well, no, for "hart" is metaphor and pun. Cynthia as chastity is being asked to help the pursued lovers (HEART) get a little rest from pursuit—or, rather, from the sexual action that follows completion of the pursuit each night. The speaker of the poem is Hesperus, the evening star, who is an aspect of Venus, the goddess of love.

Putting apart the bow and quiver equates with the moon's shining forth, for now it becomes a steady light. The shining of the moon will dispel the darkness that ensues when the sun has descended, for in the darkness the pursuit and its aftermath will proceed. Darkness always seems to imply acts of love for love poets of this period, and light interferes (we remember Donne's "Sunne Rising"), even when it is moonlight, apparently. With the moon shining, the flying hart (male) can avoid the hunter (or rather huntress) and rest from pursuit.

I think recognition of the genre makes us read the poem more deeply, although in this case we might have been astute enough without such recognition to see it as a witty plea for men to get some relief from sexual intercourse—though no one has previously suggested this. Once said, we can reread the poem with some new emphases and puns: "now the sun [a male symbol and symbol of passion] is laid to sleep" contrasts with the flying hart. "Earth [a female symbol], let not thy envious shade / Dare itself to interpose" recalls the evil that an eclipse portends. "Space to just breathe [not pant], how short soever." And we remember again that it is the male personification of Venus who is singing these lines.

In contrast is Abraham Cowley's "Hymn to Light," which is an attempt to define and depict what light is in mythic and scientific terms. He defines by exclusion and by inclusion; and he depicts by analogy and by effects. The ultimate praise of the poem is for God, who has created light, and for his creation, without which a person could little enjoy the desirable things mentioned in the poem. The genre is quite evident with a single reading, and recognition of it does not really extend our understanding. On the other hand, Donne's "Hymne to Christ, at the Authors last going into Germany," which has many biographical contexts, presents problems. Our understanding of the characteristics of the genre *hymn* makes us realize that the poem has been misclassified, mistitled; it is more correctly a prayer. The "I" of the poem is an individual and his supplication does not call up praise. The "I" does take on some representation, however. The torn ship is not just the ship the poet will sail in to the Continent, but a person's body—a common metaphor. The island the poet sacrifices to Christ is not just England, but the Isle of Man, the body again and its concomitant bodily demands. The paradoxes of the poem underline the applicability to more than just Donne the person: "To see God only, I goe out of sight"; "And to scape stormy dayes, I chuse an Everlasting night." For Christ died so that humankind could live, and Death becomes the Gate to Life (as Milton's Adam phrased it). What the poem is about is the regeneration of spirit or self by the death of former spirit or former self, and the septenary (seven-foot line) that caps each of the four stanzas specifically points to mystic creation—the meaning of the number seven in numerology. There are four stanzas since four is the number of Man. If we read the poem only biographically, we will miss its real import, and its imagery, and its structure. It is a prayer to Christ from all beings, not just from Donne. It is not, therefore, a hymn, and that label misdirects a reader, who would be better served by the descriptive title of the Dobell manuscript, "At his departure with my L: of Doncaster," or by the generic title "Prayer."

Another genre, the painter poem, became very popular in the Restoration as a vehicle for political satire (such as Marvell's "Last Instructions to the Painter"). The poet instructs a painter how to paint a canvas: this goes here, that there; something lies in juxtaposition to something else; one object is colored red, another black, another white, with the common connotations of each color pulled into play. The form of the painter poem is a series of couplets, each couplet or each set of two couplets presenting another aspect or element of the total picture to be painted. When the poem is completed, so is the picture. It becomes something more than the sum of its parts. The technique derives from "Ut Pictura Poesis," which is the principle behind many seventeenth-century poems, not just the painter poem. Jonson in "Timber; or the Discoveries" explained the principle in this way: "Poetry and pictures are arts of a like nature, and both are busy about imitation. It was excellently said of Plutarch, poetry was a speaking picture, and picture a mute poesy" ("Poesis et pictura," 703).

Thomas Carew's "To the Painter" first berates the painter for thinking he can "catch that face" in his canvas. The poet's description of that face involves comparison ("those eyes that outshine the day's"), denial of implications in the painter's colors ("Instead of that same rosy dye, / You should have drawn out modesty . . . Or can you color just the same, / When virtue blushes or what shame?"), objection to the plasticity of any painting ("'Tis taken ill by some that you / Should be so insolently vain, / As to contrive all that rich gain / Into one tablet"), and argument that affective being is more significant ("His eyes the pencils are which limn / Her truly . . . His heart the tablet which alone / Is for that portrait the truest stone"). Is Carew essentially concerned with presenting his loved one? Is he really concerned with denying achievement in painting—or in poetry? Or is he not concerned with writing a poem in this genre and working up something that will not be merely standard but that will compare and contrast with others of the same genre written from a more standard point of view? Is this not an essential factor in the lyric as genre? a genre that has never been defined to everyone's satisfaction, it seems.

Alongside Carew's poem we might choose Herrick's "To the Painter, To Draw Him a Picture," which takes the standard approach and defines the subject by his instructions to the painter. The author's aim seems simply to illustrate "Ut Pictura Poesis":

> Come, skillful Lupo, now, and take
> Thy bice, thy umber, pink, and lake;
> And let it be thy pencil's strife,
> To paint a bridgeman to the life:
> Draw him as like too, as you can,
> An old, poor, lying, clattering man:
> His cheeks be pimpled, red and blue;
> His nose and lips of mulberry hue.
> Then for an easy fancy, place
> A burling iron for his face:
> Next, make his cheeks with breath to swell,

> And for to speak, if possible:
> But do not so; for fear, lest he
> Should by his breathing, poison thee.

Let me turn finally to the epigram, a seemingly easy genre to describe and exemplify, though less easy than it first appears. It is a short poem, often witty, presenting a pointed idea tersely. The epigram can be classified as showing *laus* (praise of some kind) or *vituperatio* (censure of some nature). An epigram by Martial, translated variously over the centuries, illustrates this definition; I use a version by John Weever (1576–1632):

> Sabidi, I love thee not, nor why I wot,
> But this I wot, Sabidi: I love thee not.[8]

In English an epigram is frequently a couplet, or in two to nine couplets. But at times a more complicated form will emerge, for example, Richard Crashaw's "On the Saviour's Wounds":

> Whatever story of their cruelty,
> Or nails, or thorn, or spear have writ in thee,
>   Are in another sense
>   Still legible;
>   Sweet is the difference:
>   Once I did spell
>   Every red letter
>   A wound of thine,
>   Now (what is better)
>   Balsam for mine.[9]

This epigram fits the description above, even though its structure, characteristics, and authorial point of view seem to be different from the usual epigram. Crashaw's poem is really three couplets with internal rhyme in the last two and separation into two lines for each line of these last two couplets. I am not sure that this has been observed before, and if not, it probably has not been because genre is seldom looked at from a definition of form. While employing a "standard" structure, then, Crashaw so alters it that it *seems* to be a totally different stanzaic structure. (Good illustrations of this kind of obscuring of form are William Butler Yeats's "Leda and the Swan" and e. e. cummings's "next to of course god," the specific genre of which has not always been clear it seems; both poems are sonnets.) There are variations in structures of epigrams: some exist that are longer, some use tercets, some use alternate rhymes, some use meters other than pentameter. The main characteristics of the epigram—wit and terseness—are present in Crashaw's poem, but the wit exists in the irony of Christ's suffering's becoming a restorative agent and the terseness demands a kind of paraphrase. These are not the earmarks of the usual epigram, for example, Sir John Harington's "Comparison of the Sonnet and the Epigram," where the wit lies in the puns on the opposites "sugar" and "salt" and the point is clearly made that sonnets may arouse man's lecherousness, whereas epigrams are more truthful in their trenchancy. Crashaw has altered the wittiness in his poem away from puns to paradoxes and has thus created an expansive meaning.

Harington's point of view toward the genre he is using is encased in the content of the poem: the epigram should be short, to the point, attention catching, and memorable. He wishes to have the reader take away his epitome of the two genres without long explanation or discussion and remember it. Crashaw's poem evidences this kind of point of view toward the genre externally; but in reality Crashaw is not presenting a pointed idea tersely. His poem demands an extensive background of religion and symbolism for full understanding. As generic example Harington's poem probably should rate high and Crashaw's much lower; as poetic expression the poems should receive a reversal of evaluation.

For generic theory in seventeenth-century poetry the *Epigrammes* of Ben Jonson have proved critical stumbling blocks. And it is too thorny a problem to go into very much here. But examination of all the epigrams shows that the majority fit the description of the epigram already given without any additional remarks. Alterations of meter seem purposeful in the few cases where they occur, and many of the longer epigrams (twenty or more lines) appear to be extended epigrams, by which I mean they show all elements of the definition except that they have more couplets attached to them, giving more details or epigrammatic examples of the point being made, than is usual. The parts are terse, though the entire poem may be rather long. Our examination will also show that the epigram as genre does not exclude the other genres whose forms are not rigid. That is, a sonnet would not be an epigram, an ode would not be an epigram, a sestina would not be an epigram; but an impossibility poem could be considered an epigram at times, a painter poem could be an epigram. Our examination will also show that the epigram as genre does not exclude other genres whose characteristics are not dissimilar. That is, a satiric verse (not a verse satire) could be an epigram, an encomium or epitaph or verse epistle could be an epigram; but a love elegy could not be because of its narrative quality; a stanzaic funereal poem could not be an epigram because its characteristics are different; a monody or threnody could not be an epigram because of the nature of its authorial involvement. In Jonson's

Epigrammes we do indeed find the satiric verse, the encomium, the epitaph, the acrostic, the verse epistle, a kind of envoi, a canzone, and a mock epic. It is this last item that has caused the most critical trouble; it is the last epigram in Jonson's collection, No. 133, called "On the Famous Voyage." The others have been easily recognized as epigrammatic and almost all of them are short. In any case, Jonson shows that the term epigram should stress the wittiness and the presentation of a pointed idea tersely, not the total length of the poem, and that we should understand that some genres may overlap, just as we may see Milton's sonnets Nos. 20 (to Edward Lawrence) and 21 (to Cyriack Skinner) as sonnets and as verse epistles, or Waller's "Go, lovely Rose!" as a song (its title), as an envoi, and as a *carpe diem* poem. I think we may rationalize the inclusion of "On the Famous Voyage" in the collection of *Epigrammes* on the basis of my previous remarks: it is epigrammatic in style despite its length and narrative quality. And maybe Jonson is experimenting to see how that subject which is narrative can be made nonnarrative through epigrammatic couplets and how technique that is nonnarrative can be made narrative through connections of those couplets.[10]

What I am urging in these remarks is a recognition, first, that genre in poetry existed for the seventeenth-century poet (and others); second, that the poet consciously wrote within a genre and this then demands that we know what the elements of that genre are; third, that the poet's choice of genre begs the questions of Why? What is gained by this rather than that genre?; fourth, that deeper understanding of meaning and achievement will be gained by examining the poet's use of genre; fifth, that genre emphasizes technique rather than content, although both may be important; sixth, that such emphasis reorients our thinking about the poet's relationship with the poem; seventh, that genre emphasizes literary significance and thereby may reduce the significance of biography and of philosophic content; and eighth, that evaluation may depend more on the execution of the genre or on the transcendence of that genre than on the poem's content. Genre is manifestly a liminal means to reading literature.

Having said that, let me add that for me the higher evaluation lies in the variation in the execution of the genre, in the breaking down of supposedly rigid rules of genre, and in the transcendence of the genre. It was rigid theories of genre and the wont to classify that Shakespeare was lampooning at the very start of the seventeenth century by having Polonius talk of "The best actors in the world, either for tragedy, comedy, history, pastoral, pastoral-comical, historical-pastoral, tragical-historical, tragical-comical-historical-pastoral, scene individable, or poem unlimited" (*Hamlet*, II, ii, 415–18). But in the middle of the century, in 1650, Thomas Hobbes laid down what had been developing into a very closed system that was to determine the course of literature and literary criticism for almost 150 years. In his preface to Sir William Davenant's *Gondibert,* he talks of "three sorts of poesy, heroic, scommatic, and pastoral. . . . For the heroic poem narrative (such as yours) is called an epic poem; the heroic poem dramatic, is tragedy. The scommatic narrative, is satire; dramatic is comedy. The pastoral narrative, is called simply pastoral (anciently bucolic), the same dramatic, pastoral comedy." Near the close of the century William Wollaston, in 1691, in *The Design of Part of the Book of Ecclesiastes,* remarked in the introduction to his poem,

> The principal kinds of Poems are, either those that tend to *the advancement of Vertue:* as, *the Epic Poem,* which sets before us the achievements of those, that have been famous and Heroic, as patterns for others in their circumstances: *Tragedy,* which teaches us not to over-value or rely upon temporal advantages, by the falls of those who have had the most of them; to be tender-hearted, by using to pity their misfortunes; to be couragious, by evoking at their patience; and to be humble, by observing what the greates of men may come to: *Ode,* that excites our devotion, by singing the attributes of the Deity; or a laudable emulation, by celebrating the praises of some Worthy; *Eclogue,* that continues a pious remembrance of the deceased Friends of our Country, of Learning, or our selves: Or those, on the contrary, that tend *to depress and discredit Vice:* as *Comedy,* which presents to view the faults of common Conversations: and *Satyr,* which by its arguments exposes, not so much men, as their unreasonableness and enormities. (7–8)

The seventeenth century had moved from the play of writing poetry, and with it the possibility of alteration of generic limitations, to emphasis on exactness of generic characteristics and moral significance, with an attendant decline in certain subgenres of the "private" type (the sonnet, the verse epistle, other lyrical forms) and a stress on certain subgenres of the "public" type (the ode, the verse satire, the encomium). The ludic spirit had generally been lost and the aim of imitation of models had ascended. These strictures continuing for some have led to the disregard of genre that a number of current critical circles espouse, but as a sign of communication between author and reader and as a sign of authorial intention and evaluation genre is still important for criticism. Genre is one liminal means to reading, a reading that may lead to revision of understanding, of appreciation, and of evaluation.

6

The Lyric

The most common definition of the lyric, a vague one that really does not limit, is that it is a short musical poem; added is often some concept of a personal element and a unified impression of a circumscribed topic. Poems that have been called lyrics over the ages have shown such attributes, although in more recent times a musical context is usually missing, and the individual and personal emotive element emphasized. Certainly those who have pointed out a shift in the meaning of lyric since the Renaissance are correct in chalking it up to the increase of the visual over the auditory, a result of printing and the decline of the oral tradition. But a major problem in definition, it seems, has been the confounding of genre and mode for the same term. Separation is made traditionally for three broad poetic genres: the lyric (melic), the dramatic, and the epic (narrative).[1] While such division of poetry contrasts form and length, it should be clear that genre has not been the basis of division. In this division all one has said is that poetry that partakes of narrative is epical—it is certainly not necessarily epic; that that which partakes of at least an implied character visuality in a setting and character speech is dramatic, but a dramatic poem is not a drama in verse; and that all the rest is lyric, being given over neither to narration nor to drama. By this then the mode "lyric" is being used for poetry that has as its subject matter not story but thought or emotion and as its form not the scenic but the reflective (not the reader viewing but the reader thinking). We have not defined a genre, nor have we adequately defined the mode. We have simply used a term to cover poetry that is not two other kinds of poetry. The fact is we have misused the word lyric because we have inherited from the Greeks only three genres and modes, one being lyric. And as other genres and modes emerged they were either lumped under that same rubric or left in an undefined abyss.[2] The term "lyric" as genre has been the most abused generic term because it has been a catchall classification and because relatively little attention has been paid to definition, in distinction to attitudes about it.

The reader must disengage certain past concepts. First, the reader must disallow only three literary genres—the poetic, the dramatic, and the narrative—since these indicate only the ostensible physical form of the work and do not define genre. (Fusions of these literary forms are also possible. I think of Milton's *Samson Agonistes*, a "Dramatick Poem," or William Faulkner's novel *Requiem for a Nun* with its partial format of character speeches as if it were a stage drama.) Second, the reader must disallow only three literary genres under poetry—the epic, the dramatic, and the lyric—for these basically classify only the form and length of the poem, and are indeed ultimately meaningless for those poems (say, the verse satire) that fall under none of those classifications. A work like Spenser's "Shepheardes Calender" has epical proportions, it is set up as characters speaking (together or in soliloquy), and it certainly includes numerous lyrical forms, but it is not, as genre, an epic, a poetic drama or a dramatic poem, or a lyric. (It is a sequence; see chapters 7 and 8 for discussion of two kinds of sequence, both of which Spenser's poem partakes of.) As suggested before, this inattention to genre and this threefold classification have been a main stumbling block in discussing lyric, for everything not epical or dramatic seems to be cast as lyric with no critical definition. Third, the reader must recognize that there are subdivisions, or subgenres, under the classification *poetry* that deal with something different from what is understood by the collocation epic, dramatic, lyric.[3] Though we classify each as a lyric, verse epistle is a special kind; encomium is an obviously special kind; sonnet seems to cause no definitional problems; and impossibility poem may cause definitional problems. If these are lyrics, then we need a definition of the genre lyric that subsumes each type, differentiates it from nonlyric poetry (including verse satire, epigram, etc.), and allows us to talk of a poem that is an undifferentiated lyric (that is, a subgenre of the genre lyric that is not a member of lyric subgenres like verse epistle, encomium, etc.). What is required of each lyric subgenre for generic definition is what I have been outlining as structure/form, characteristics, and intention.[4] And the genre lyric itself must sustain the same kind of definition. It should be considered on the same genre or subgenre level as epitaph and epigram, which are not lyrics, except that lyric as genre may also subdivide into further literary subgenres like ode and hymn.[5]

In the eighteenth century Joseph Trapp succinctly stated an important factor in lyric: "Hence, then, we learn the chief Property of Lyric Poetry, *viz.* that it abounds with a Sort of Liberty which consists in Digressions and Excursions."[6] The century also emphasized the property of "enthusiasm,"[7] the innumerable harmonious meters in which lyric might be written, and the elegance of language. While noting that lyric's "peculiar character is, that it is intended to be sung, or accompanied with music," Hugh Blair postulated that its distinguishing feature is "chiefly the Spirit, the manner of its execution, that marks and characterises it."[8] He also remarked the increased lack of regularity and the increase of digressions and disorder in lyric; its enthusiasm, boldness, and passion; and the extravagance that overlies it as its musical relationship has decreased. A major point of discussion has been imitation, whether *mimesis* or *imitatio* is involved and whether the poem is distinguished between them or not. Thomas Twining concluded that "The Lyric Poet is not always, and essentially, an *imitator*, any more than the Epic. While he is merely expressing his own *sentiments*, in his own *person*, we consider him not as imitating;—we inquire not whether they are the assumed sentiments of the Poetic character, or the real sentiments of the writer himself; we do not even think of any such distinction. He is understood to *imitate*, in the most *general* view, no otherwise than by *fiction*, by *personation*, by *description*, or by *sound;* in the view of Aristotle, only by the *two first* of these."[9] Northrop Frye sees the lyric as an internal mimesis of sound and imagery, standing in opposition to external mimesis, or outward representation of sound and imagery, which is drama.[10]

For Andrew Welsh, writing today but basically sidestepping the issue of definition, "Lyric is finally less a particular genre of poetry than a distinctive way of organizing language."[11] Yet his conclusion puts a finger on what I consider the most significant means to defining the genre *lyric:* "It is the voice of the poet as an individual maker, the voice of someone standing above the archaic functions of language and concerned primarily with his art. . . . We may hear in the roots of [Wyatt's] rhythms the sorcerer's voice using language to charm, the communal voice chanting or singing for the society, and the personal voice of a man speaking to men. But we also hear the voice of a maker speaking to his own art—to the craft and sullen art which the age of Wyatt had not yet named lyric poetry."[12] This is basically a point made by George T. Wright: "a love sonnet does not present man in love, but man singing of love; an elegy is not a presentation of man's feeling about death, but of man singing about death. The poet appears not as a man undergoing experiences but as a man singing about his experiences."[13]

The medieval lyric that preceded Sir Thomas Wyatt is really a song, according to Stephen Manning.[14] A song has always been classified as a kind of lyric, which represents the melic voice in the triad with epic and dramatic. While the speaker presents "his thought, feeling or emotion as an intense experience which he at this moment undergoes, . . . he places his audience between himself and his experience and merely reports it in terms which his audience associates with that experience."[15] The emphasis is thus on the substance of the poem rather than the techniques, whereas the Renaissance lyric reverses the emphasis, developing the technique and moving out of the more regular metric form with stress on rhyme into the metrical irregularities and increased enjambment of a dramatic lyric. But the substance of that poem is past: it is an experience undergone, it is reported, it is presented in terms that will allow the audience to realize that experience, and in this way the song and the lyric are one. The song is a lyric, but it lacks the "deeper and original thought, subtle psychology, strange imagery, or social or philosophical implications" often assigned to the general category lyric.[16] "In the song, the speaker is not sharply characterized; he tends to be anonymous, or Everyman. In the dramatic lyric, the speaker is sharply characterized because, among other things, the experience of which he speaks is so intense that he unconsciously (or consciously, for that matter) betrays a considerable part of his personality in presenting the experience. Moreover, the speaker in the song removes himself from his experience to sing of it rather than to dramatize it."[17] The "I" of the lyric, thus, is a focal element in the definition of lyric. For Nietzsche that "I" presents a different projection of oneself from that *in propria persona;*[18] for Ing (16), "the emotion is made sharper and deeper by its immediate association with a personality"; and for Frye, the lyric is an utterance that is overheard.

The foregoing distinctions between other lyrics and song can be seen by comparing Edmund Waller's "To Phyllis" ("Phyllis! Why should we delay") and "Song" ("Say, lovely dream! where couldst thou find"). The point of congruency of both as the genre *lyric,* however, is noteworthy: the speaker is reporting experience undergone in terms allowing the audience to realize that experience. As we move into "techniques" (which may differentiate the speaker from Everyman) the speaker may *appear* to be intensely involved in an experience and a describable personality may emerge, but the speaker is still not the poet *in propria persona;* the emotion only *appears* to be more immediate; the utterance is planted for the reader to overhear; and the lyric has been produced with the audience placed between the poet and the poet's experience.

Waller's "Song" is in regular quatrains, rhyming *a b a b;* the emphasis is on the experience, which, while it emphasizes the present tense, implies action of the past (the "dream") and of the future ("Perhaps . . . surprised she may fall"); we feel that we are looking at the experience through the speaker's eyes; the speaker and the experience are not particularized. The contrivance of imagery and allusion is generalized: "shades," "angel-like disguise," "heavenly face," "Pale, wan, and meagre," "graves," "death resembling," even "Cruel Sacharissa," "the brook / Of Lethe." The singer asks his dream to appear to his loved one, who thwarts his love, as one escaped from the grave to express his woe in her dream, equating thus his woe with death. Even naming his loved one, who appears in other poems of Waller, does not particularize the loved one for the reader. The image pattern allows an emphasis on its substance rather than on its technique, yet it is clearly built on a poetic language brought externally to bear on that which is supposedly internal. It betrays the poem as the work of a "maker," "standing above the archaic functions of language and concerned primarily with his art." The undifferentiated lyric "To Phyllis" is in rhymed couplets with some amount of enjambment; the emphasis is on the present with a future experience proposed; the past is dismissed. There is an urgency in the thought built on the brevity of time (the *carpe diem* theme) and the metrical treatment that pushes us forward. We feel a poetic voice that is concerned with someone he calls Phyllis, who has as yet not succumbed to his blandishments and who seems to need being reminded that time flies by swiftly. It will become obvious that he is not "sincere," but that he is simply using a flattering argument to get a reluctant woman to bed. The imagery has a more involved point, is more intricate than in "Song": time is fleeting, so is life, and physically so are the sexual "pleasures" he solicits; beauty flies as does the shadow cast by the sun, the demarcator of time (here is a submerged *carpe rosam* theme), and with it youth and the sexual implications that *youth* suggests. Love becomes a bird, and since birds climb to heaven, so does love; but this movement involves change, and so must love change—only "change" now means "a change in love partners." The specious equations of language remind that heavenly beings are eternal (do not change their state) and therefore so will the couple be eternal after the "change in love," which is like the gods' changing actions toward humans by love and hate. The second stanza makes clear that both (or at least the poetic voice thinks both) have had romantic attachments and desires in the past; these are all forgotten and lost in the cosmic world, just as their sexual union now will be. The seductive voice is saying, our sexual union is of the present; it is no more than all those we have had with others in the past; no one knows or cares about them, nor about ours now. "Prove," of course—"For the joys we now may prove, / Take advice of present love"—also meant "test": he is arguing that until we make love we will not know whether our lovemaking will bring joys or not. He implies that if their lovemaking brings joys, they will continue their union; but we are fairly certain he is only looking for a one-night stand.

We can observe from this contrast of Waller's poems some general attributes of lyric that arise to encompass both "dramatic lyric" and "song": the time of the lyric is not necessarily the past or involved in reflection and may at least appear to be synchronic; the experience is important as occurrence rather than as purposive example of something else; a speaking voice is the focus, with some degree of supposed congruency between that speaking voice and the reader. The song, because of its more direct descent from musical performance, has a regularity of form, frequently in shorter lines and stanzas (often, in fact, the quatrain); there may be a sense of end-stoppage for lines and stanzas because of the form. The lyric (a term used here to mean all lyric forms) may have a regularity of form but does not require it; its lines, even when the unit is the couplet, often tend not to end-stop through enjambment and a sense of continuance (or drawing out and through a thought or image).

The time of the song is synchronic but its emphasis is on the present; the lyric so emphasizes the present that the experience leading to its articulation may be submerged. Both imply a future time as a result of the present and its treatment, but, most important, both are created out of an experiential past that, while seemingly submerged, is recollected. The time of the lyric (including song) therefore is present, but it arises from an experiential past reflected upon. That experiential past contains the basic importance for the speaking voice which that voice contemplates as a continuing present; the implied future is only a poetic of possibility as outgrowth, but not really expected outgrowth, of the present. Rather, the realistic future will be a continuance of the present and in no way involves a purposive example of action to be taken.[19] While metaphor may establish a range of subjects and contexts, lyric does not create an allegoric or philosophical attitude to be applied to any specific other subject or context. The reader takes on the poetic voice's understanding as meaningful for the poetic voice, for others, and for her- or himself.

Moving out of medieval song/lyric, Jerome Mazzaro[20] stresses the emphasis in Renaissance lyric on the conceit, the proper *res/verba* relationship: "Since the final value of each work would lie outside the author's style and the relationship of word to word, the writer's paramount consideration became the fidelity of his words or signs to a reality which he sought to capture and interpret" (7–8). When divorced from music, the lyric became a vehicle for consciousness; with aesthetic distance, its aim came to be "to imitate, invent, and present things which would render men virtuous and happy" (20). Mazzaro's intention in his study seems to be to indicate that creative literature cannot be separated from philosophy and theology, a thought I can in no way subscribe to. For him, the moral dimension sets up the boundaries for defining the lyric and the lyric poet. W. R. Johnson seems to advance a similar concept in seeing great lyric as involving "community," an authentic *vates*, and "eternal moments." The change from the nineteenth- and earlier twentieth-century lyric monologue has in more recent poets given way to lyric discourse, which involves public voices and public themes.[21]

While the English Renaissance stresses in its poetic theory a fusion of *utile* and *dulce*, most importantly stated by Sir Philip Sidney in *Defence of Poesy* (composed 1580–82), a work written as argument within a specific moral context as counter to such attacks on morality in drama as Stephen Gosson's *School of Abuse* (1579), it is the visionary line of poetry, generally working through larger forms like epic, that is being evoked. While the genre lyric might be used to visionary purposes, like Spenser's "Fowre Hymns," it in itself does not normally partake of the line of vision.[22] Like Manning, Mazzaro talks of the increase in drama and the use of a persona in the Renaissance lyric.

In chapter 5, it will be remembered, I remarked that Thomas Carew in "To the Painter" was concerned, not with depicting his loved one or denying achievement in painting, but with writing a poem in the subgenre *painter poem* and working up something that would not be merely standard but that would compare and contrast with others of the same genre. And I asked, "Is this not an essential factor in the lyric?" I repeat the question and thus point up something that may aid in definition. What I suggest is that the concept of lyric that sees it as a personal, emotional idea or attitude, that is, a subjective poem, a "private" poem in a meaning not implied by Earl Miner's private-public-social triad, is inaccurate. It is the product of a maker concerned primarily with poetic art, to use Welsh's language. A well-used handbook of literature calls a lyric, "A brief subjective POEM strongly marked by IMAGINATION, melody, and emotion, and creating for the reader a single, unified impression," and adds, "The conception of the *lyric* as the individual and personal emotion of the poet still holds and is, perhaps, the chief basis for discriminating between the *lyric* and other poetic forms."[23] What I suggest, instead, is that the key to the *genre* lyric is the intention of the poet to write a poem—to write a certain kind of poem, or use a certain kind of technique, or employ a specific device, and the like—but basically to write a poem, not to advance a philosophy, not to get the reader to do something of importance as a result of reading the poem, not to point out a virtue or a vice or poke fun in order to influence the reader and the reader's thinking, not to argue a position. A lyric, indeed, is not many other things that it has fallen heir to because people have not paid attention to a theory of genres. All of these intentions involve the author's attitude toward the subject matter and indeed put the emphasis on the subject matter (the content). A concomitant aim of the lyric is reader response, whether emotional or intellectual, but not reader action, whether physical or mental. The poem that exhibits, at least primarily, the function of advancing a philosophy or a position, or a virtue or a vice, and so forth, is not a lyric. The author who writes an epic has an attitude akin to the didactic, whether it is a national epic like *The Iliad,* a moral epic like *Paradise Lost,* or a sociological epic like *Paterson.* The author who writes a verse satire has an attitude of exposing vice and virtue through *vituperatio* or *laus,* and while it need not be reformative, it can involve purposive authorial influence. The author who writes an epigram aims at presenting a single thought in a pithy, memorable way; such thoughts may evoke character types or human characteristics or the ways of the world, but all with an intentionality of influence or authorial position (the author in the poem, as it were, being more important than the reader in the poem, since the author has delimited the reader's reaction and thought). The author who writes an epitaph—and comparison with the funereal elegy and particularly the monody or threnody makes the generic differences most clear—is concerned with pointing out the dead one's virtue or vice, significance or influence in life, the heritage left for others. It may be humorous, certainly, satiric, epigrammatic; it may seriously advance a philosophy of "there but for the grace of God go I" or of the significance of any person's life or its insignificance as of a grain of sand. All of these intentions and the subgenres that sustain them involve the author's attitude toward the subject matter primarily, not toward his or her art, and such poems are thus not, I contend, lyrics.[24]

For the lyric genre encompasses many different elements in form/structure and characteristics. It is constituted, first, by poems taking various forms that are short enough to be encompassed as individual poetic units (wholes); subgenres under the broad genre may take on specific forms in terms of line or stanza, meter or rhythm (e.g., the sonnet), or may employ comparable but undesignated forms (e.g., the song), or may be built on individual forms, both those that are comparable to the preceding (e.g., the stanzaic form) and those that are not comparable (e.g., a form employing the verse paragraph as metric unit or the line as metric unit). It is differentiated from such as the verse satire by its overall development as a poetic unit rather than as a series of concatenated poetic units; it is differentiated from such as the epigram, elegy, and pastoral by certain characteristics that they exhibit (e.g., pithiness, "narrative," setting and characters, interrelationships of sections). Second, it is constituted by a seeming lack of direct development since it moves by "Digressions and Excursions," to use Trapp's words. Such indirect movement is actually involute through images, image patterns, language, and emotional and/or logical connections, though such connections be submerged. The organization of language presents a seemingly unorganized development of emotion, idea, attitude, occurrence (or experience), which thus appears to be internal for the lyric voice. Subgenres under lyric may digress and organize around an attitude (as in the ode), an idea (as in the Petrarchan sonnet with its background octave and a sestet logically extractable from that octave), a relationship between voice and reader (as in the verse letter, whether given to the epideictic or the paraenectic), but the movement within the lyric is similar in these subgenres and very different from that in the epic, the dramatic poem, or, say, the elegy. The lyric emphasizes the present though it may recollect and reflect upon an experience past and suggest some futural result. The hymn or the encomium is a good example, opposed to the nonlyric threnody or epitaph.

The most notable element in definition of the genre lyric, however, involves the third requirement in my definition of a genre: the authorial intention toward the act of writing the poem. The lyric presents an authorial presence but its function is fully reader response; it presents a mimesis of experience for the reader to comprehend or sense; it presents a calculated mimesis devised by the maker, whose concern is poetic art. The lyric as I define it unites the *Erlebnislyrik* and *Gefühlpoesie*, being neither one only and being a contrived poem to reflect that experience or that feeling. As the Renaissance developed, the shift into making influenced all the categories of literature, but the difference of the lyric from other kinds lay in the development by techniques and devices of varied structure/form, characteristics, and authorial intention toward the poem. A focus came to exist on variety that nonetheless remained within the parameters of structure/form and characteristics. The decline of certain lyric subgenres in the eighteenth century and the near-dominance of nonlyrical forms (except for the ode, the sort that often exhibited the modally almost nonlyric nature of Joseph Warton's "Ode to Fancy") is in accord not only with the shift from mimesis to imitation, but evidences the moribund quality of much of the lyric and nonlyric work—resultant from the lack of individualism in making—that the *Lyrical Ballads* of Wordsworth and Coleridge set out to replace. The lyric emphasizes the speaker, the circumstance of the speaking, and the "statement" that is the tangible poem; the lyric does not emphasize the content, which constitutes, rather, the occasion (to use Hamburger's language, 266). The "I" becomes a personality that emerges, but it is not the author *in propria persona*. The "I" presents an experience (tangible or intangible *and past*) that the author may have or may not have in reality undergone through a mimesis that appears to arise from within the "I" as the author reflects upon it or as he or she offers it as an occasion that will evoke reflection.[25] The "I" allows for inclusion of the reader as experiencer and reflector of the occasion: the occasion may offer a narrative subtext or present a scenic placement, but neither is the focus for the statement, which calls forth the reader response (as if it were the response of the "I") in thought or emotion.

W. R. Johnson's emphasis on lyrical rhetoric is in agreement. Countering "romantic notions of lyric poetry as unpremeditated warblings," Johnson argues for an understanding of "I–You" constructs within the lyric, since it is "discourse" rather than "expression" (by which he means the poetic voice musing alone), except that such "rhetorical modes" are "means," not "ends," whereby "the speaker becomes wholly lost in, wholly indistinguishable from, his discourse and the technical repertoire that structures and ornaments it" (31).

A lyric is thus a briefer poem in which the author intends to produce a successful literary creation by specific chosen techniques, devices, form, language, strategy, and the like in an ultimately competitive spirit for evaluation by the readers. It implies a fictive voice that may appear to be an authorial one, and that may owe its substance to an authorial voice; it is a fictive voice speaking to an auditor, implied or also fictive, who always also is the reader. The voice does *not* turn his or her back on the audience, although the fiction may purport to sustain that view; the voice is never Eliot's meditative voice. The *primary* aim is not catharsis, despite the implication of many prior statements about lyric;[26] rather it defines the poet's concept of the poet's role as poet. The poet's relationship to the subject is an "esthetic closeness but with an ideological distance *as far as the writing of the poem is concerned.*"[27] The presentation of the emotion or idea is not primary; the creation of the literary artifact to sustain that emotion or idea is.[28] What we have been "defining" is the third element in the requirement for a definition of a genre: the author's intention toward the piece of writing.[29]

Lyric as mode (perhaps we should use "lyrical" for differentiation) indicates that the poem is intended to elicit a reader response that is a mimesis of the purported experience or feeling of the voice. In song the lyrical mode is only enhanced by the musical proportions; it is not equivalent to it. A poem that is not a lyric by genre but that is lyrical in mode, for example, is Whitman's "When Lilacs Last in the Dooryard Bloom'd"; comparison with the lyric "O Captain, My Captain," in lyrical mode, makes the point obvious. The problem with the latter poem is that it tries too hard at its "poetic/lyrical" devices, undoubtedly because the relationship of author to poem was so strong that it dictated "standard" structure/ form and characteristics rather than allowing them to be devised to sustain the mimetic emotion. The obverse of lyric genre/unlyrical mode may be seen in the nonlyrical mode of Ransom's sonnet "Piazza Piece," discussed in chapter 1.

7

The Lyric and Ben Jonson

About twenty-five years ago the teacher of seventeenth-century poetry could remark that there was little criticism published strictly on Ben Jonson's nondramatic poetry. The studies of George Johnston and Wesley Trimpi were available, but only more recently has interest in his poetry elicited extensive comment.[1] Unlike Donne's work, there seemed to be little that needed explication: the poetry was clear and understandable upon a first reading (or, if something like "Execration upon Vulcan," with informative footnotes); the style did not set up ambiguities and wrenching of meanings and syntax; the philosophic (and religious) element was not seething as in Donne or not prominent as in Milton. Apparently there was little to say about the nondramatic poetry, just as there has been—invalidly—little to say about the poetry of Thomas Carew, Sir John Suckling, Richard Lovelace, and Edmund Waller.[2] One of the problems has been, I have long thought, that so many of Jonson's poems are lyrics. That, of course, begs the questions, What is a lyric? and Why should a lyric be less susceptible to critical statement than another genre? The answers help explain the lack of attention in the past because of inadequate critical understanding of the lyric, and help explain the rise in critical statements because of the growing critical importance of what are the earmarks of lyric. My view of Jonson's work is quite contrary to Swinburne's comment on the lack of "the quality which lyrical verse ought to have and which [Jonson's] lyrical verse almost invariably misses; the note of apparently spontaneous, inevitable, irrepressible and impeccable music."[3] My concern in this chapter, therefore, is to examine some of Jonson's poetry as lyric, employing the descriptions and conclusions of chapter 6, both to reevaluate that poetry and to indicate the significance of those conclusions. The limina that definition of lyric as genre offers become means into a reading of Jonson's lyrics whereby we see authorial presence and reach "new" understandings of them.

"The Forrest" was published in 1616 as contrast to *Epigrammes.* It is a miscellany, translating Statius's *Sylvae*, trees or woods. The metaphor suggests that each poem, like a tree, has its roots in the stuff of the ground but ascends to the supernal; it also implies the concepts seen in Ezra Pound's employment of the image in "A Pact":

> I make a pact with you, Walt Whitman—
> I have detested you long enough.
> I come to you as a grown child
> Who has had a pig-headed father;
> I am old enough now to make friends.
> It was you that broke the new wood,
> Now is a time for carving.
> We have one sap and one root—
> Let there be commerce between us.[4]

Jonson's revision of Statius's plural images to the composite "Forrest" tells us to view the individual trees, but also to step back and see the unity that they provide. His individual trees have been carved, but they quite literally have one sap and one root. There are fifteen poems in "The Forrest," contrasting with the 133 epigrams. Varied forms are found among the fifteen, involving a few lyric subgenres: 1, tetrameter couplets; 2, pentameter couplets (a topographical or country-house poem); 3, rhyming pentameter and tetrameter lines (an encomium); 4, tetrameter quatrains (*a b a b*) without breaks (a satiric dramatic monologue); 5, headless tetrameter couplets (a song); 6, headless tetrameter couplets (a song); 7, tetrameters (rhyming *a b a b c c / d e d e c c*); 8, headless tetrameter couplets; 9, tetrameter and trimeter lines in alternate rhyme (a song); 10, pentameter three-line stanzas in one rhyme; 11, pentameter and trimeter couplets (an epode); 12, pentameter couplets (a verse epistle); 13, pentameter couplets (a verse epistle); 14, ten-line unbroken stanzas, rhyming *a b c c b a d d e e* (an ode); and 15, pentameter couplets. The lengths vary as well: 12, 102, 106, 68, 18, 22, 12, 48, 16, 30, 116, [100],[5] 124, 60, and 26 lines. It is evident that Jonson has purposely set up his collection to contrast and compare verse forms and lengths. The subjects are likewise varied or similar and so placed as to contrast (such as No. 1, "Why I Write Not of Love," and No. 15, "To Heaven") or to compare (such as No. 4, "To the World: A Farewell for a Gentle-woman, Vertuous and Noble," and No. 5, "Song: To Celia"; or No. 10, untitled, but ending, "And now an *Epode* to deepe eares I sing," and No. 11, "Epode"). The maker has been concerned, we see, with literary matters: meters, genres, forms, comparison, and contrasts. The poems constitute a sequence, not one developing a narrative line like most sonnet sequences, but one interrelating the poems in form and content with a development of change for the fictive poet. There is a thematic plotting emphasizing the art of poetry and, as we shall see, with a strong apostrophe to patronage. Jonson's collection is among the first well-organized "little poetry volumes"[6]—the most thorough one—the forerunner of our present-day publishing achievements.

Jonathan Z. Kamholtz has discussed "The Forrest" as sequence: it "contains a poetic and dramatic 'plot' which Jonson develops within and between groups of poems." Kamholtz groups the poems 1–4, 5–9, 10–11, and 12–15 (with some indecision about the last two groupings) and sees the sequence as making "broad claims about the powers of poetry": the only artifact is within the self and the only true audience is God.[7] Lawrence Venuti, taking his title from the first poem in the sequence, argues that "Jonson did not write many poems about love because he valued a close relationship between language and reality for didactic purposes." "Jonson was dedicated to establishing a close relationship between res and verba, in which the writer's matter is selected primarily for his observations of reality."[8] While Venuti would seem to be interested in those aspects of the lyric that emphasize craft, the thrust of his essay stresses subject matter. The thematic sequence and the employment of certain topics or forms are particularly well set forth by Alastair Fowler. These poems, connected by themes of retirement and religious aspiration, provide "a ladder of love, ascending to God," fifteen symbolizing such ascent and being a pyramidic number. The concept of silvae (compare J. C. Scaliger in Poetices libri system [Lyons, 1561]) allows for the "forest" entanglement that the treatment of the lower forms of love up to No. 11 provides and then for ascent to the higher forms.[9]

The collection has, thus, been viewed as sequence, one developing themes and belief. Sequence as narrative is discussed in chapter 8. Individual poems in "The Forrest" have been examined, largely through explications, but here I look at them as examples of the lyric as I have defined it, ignoring for the most part the subject matters but yielding a further dimension to the claim for the power of poetry.

The main concern of the lyric writer is the art of writing itself. There would seem to be certain topics that are appropriate to lyric, as Scaliger says of silvae, just as there are for other genres. But it is not topoi that concern the lyric poet, I would argue, except, for one like Jonson, to see how far the author can stretch the "normal" employment without breaking the boundaries. (We have already cited Ransom's "Piazza Piece" for the lyric and Jonson's own "On the Famous Voyage" for the epigram.) Indeed one way of testing boundaries is purposefully to employ a not-usual topos in an unusual genre. No. 8, "To Sicknesse," is a clear example. It has been called "an unpleasant satiric epigram" (Fowler, 175) because it does not fall neatly into a preconceived mold and because it is not being read in context.

The sequential position of No. 8 alone should have deflected such assessments: it appears after a poem to Celia to bestow limitless kisses (No. 6), which is followed by one styling women but men's shadows (No. 7), and before another to Celia, the popular "Drinke to me, onely, with thine eyes" (No. 9). If we understand Celia, as in *Volpone* (where No. 5 appears and lines 19–22 of No. 6), to be supposedly virtuous (as her name implies) and thus more of a challenge to be seduced, we should recognize the ironies of these poems. No. 5, employing the theme that Carew's "Secrecy Protested" is all about, wants Celia to "prove" "the sports of love" in the "light" against the challenge of "household spyes": it is "no sinne" "to steale" such lovemaking; only being "taken" (found out) or "seene" are "crimes accounted." By No. 6 she has succumbed, and in No. 7 the poet recites an aside (to the reading audience) that cynically and with sexism says woman will simply be opposite in the game of love ("So court a mistris, shee denyes you; / Let her alone, she will court you"), but she is as eager as man and simply uses this coyness as a ploy. When we get to No. 9, we have the male's sincere avowal of love: he has been trapped in his own seduction. It illustrates on one level the last line of poem No. 11, "Epode": *"Man may securely sinne, but safely never."* (That is, sinning may bring more than the person expected though it also have its intentions fulfilled.) However, there is No. 8 intervening, and this illustrates the pun in that last line of No. 11: the sinful lovemaking not only may backfire by the male's falling in love, but such careless, promiscuous lovemaking may not be "safe" (in terms of the spread of disease). In "To Sicknesse"[10] the poet first asks, "Why, *Disease,* dost thou molest / Ladies?" Men, he goes on, by their nightly surfeiting of desire, constantly are, or may be, assaulted by disease. Women should not be such victims (should not be infected by their sexual partners), or if they must be, let them be only the "wast Livers, round about the towne" (prostitutes), not "them the best" (upper-class women). The poet wants to relegate disease to those who "maintayne the truest trade," or at least to those avaricious wives who may be "mann'd / With ten Emp'ricks, in their chamber" (with a clear salacious joke), thereby "dis-tilling" (with sexual agricultural pun) "their husbands land / In decoctions" (with obviously obscene pun, joining the "Emp'ricks"). He asks Disease thus "to molest / None but them, and leave the rest," among whom he implies Celia is. For as No. 9 avows, he has fallen in love with her. Is she free from such disease as make men "Bald, or blinde"? The poet considers that she may not be. Maybe those thousand kisses requested in No. 6 are not so uncommonly given as we first thought; maybe we should remark the possibility of sexual puns in the "kisse ... in the cup," the apparent soul kissing, the "rosie wreath" (with vaginal pun) that "growes, and smells" of her. It all sounds innocent at first reading, but was not the poet's mind going the same route that he has directed some readers to?

Poems Nos. 5, 6, 7, and 9 are all songs, and so labeled. They should therefore accord with the definitions previously offered for lyric and the specific subgenre of lyric, song. First, they are short units in varying forms. Nos. 5 and 6 are both in headless tetrameter couplets, linking them as contrasts between the situations before and after succumbing. No. 7 falls into two unseparated six-line stanzas of tetrameter, rhyming *a b a b c c / d e d e c c*, with lines 1 and 3 (*a* rhymes) and 7 and 9 (*d* rhymes) employing feminine endings and thus playing on feminine and masculine stereotypes of weakness and strength just as the poem itself does. No. 9 combines tetrameter with trimeter in *a b c b* rhyme patterns, falling into quatrains (strong end-stoppage occurs in ll. 4, 8, 12, and 16), although it appears as one continuous unit. The song, as has been remarked, most often consists of quatrains in couplet, alternate rhyme, or *a b c b* rhymes. No. 7 alters this slightly by adding a couplet (the same couplet) to each discrete quatrain (ll. 4 and 8 are end-stopped). Each poem moves by seeming "digressions" and "excursions" in what may appear like linear conversational relationships, as in No. 6, or in distinct images as in No. 7, which distinctiveness, however, is nullified by the repetition of the same conclusive couplet. No. 9 centers on an attitude, posing a relationship between the poetic voice and the fictive auditor. A romanticist would like to believe that the auditor is reacting favorably toward the poetic voice and following his excursions into a concept of immortality and the metaphors of cup and wreath. But we should not be surprised if the Celia of No. 6 found an appropriate and obscene comment to make, one suggesting his misunderstanding of her compliance with his advances and her annoyance at his persistence for exclusivity. Like Waller's "Song" discussed in chapter 6, Jonson's songs emphasize the present tense but use action of the past and imply action of the future. The imagery and allusion may at first not appear to be generalized (for instance, "All the grasse that *Rumney* yeelds," No. 6), but it is replaceable without loss; more usual is the look of love in one's eyes, the exaggeration that anything like the rosy wreath touched by true love will never die (in No. 9)—certainly generalized imagery used meaningfully. These are poems betraying themselves as work of a "maker," "standing above the archaic function of language and concerned primarily with his art." They are the reportage of an experience supposedly undergone, the speaker appearing to be intensely involved and overheard in his thoughts with discernible change in him and in his speech acts: from seductive ploy to erotic heights, to "philosophic" observation, to validity of newfound emotion. The poetic voice is made to appear to be *in propria persona,* but surely No. 7 indicates an audience other than Celia between the lyric and the lyricist and makes clear the fictiveness of what precedes and *what follows.*

The topic of "To Sicknesse" hardly seems the kind of thing one lyricizes over—that is, if one imagines that a lyric must encompass personal emotion and elegance of language, that it cannot address such an uncouth auditor as (sexual) disease, except perhaps with satiric intent. But if we do not delimit ourselves so and if for genre we stress the craft, we will not be unhappy to consider this poem as a lyric. Like its surrounding songs, this (undifferentiated) lyric stresses the present, but contrastively the present thinking is a result of the submerged past, and only vaguely glances at a hoped-for (but obviously unlikely) future. Here it is the reflection that is paramount, not the reported experience. Here reflection arises out of the submerged experiential past through a speaker, a personality, certainly not Jonson *in propria persona,* who can call forth identification for the male reader and distanced comprehension for the female reader. This speaker is "overheard," but he has not turned his back on his reading audience. That reading audience is prominently before the writer writing. Jonson has treated a subject that in context is appropriate, though its topos has stretched the boundary of the "pretty room" for those expecting "sugared sonnets." (Of course, Donne and Shakespeare also stretched boundaries from time to time.) I cannot attach "satiric" mode to the poem; it is not "unpleasant" because the venereal diseases implied and their transmission are treated so wittily; and there is nothing of the epigrammatic, not even of the broad epigrammatism of Jonson's companion collection.

From this eighth poem of "The Forrest" (its central poem) we see clearly the way in which misreading arises when genre and context are not heeded. My readings of Nos. 5–9 are frequently different from those of others, perhaps most in the treatment of the speech act and its attention to *res* and *verba.* The lyric for the critical past has been an avenue into an emotion or thought, unhidden and on the surface, of which there was little to say beyond appreciative generalities. But to me the lyric is a springboard into experiencing the poet's craft, and when that craft supports levels of meaning, there is much to comment on.

The opening and ending poems of "The Forrest" afford instructive contrasts here, the "lower" forms of love "ascending" to divine love, according to Fowler. Their contrast capsulizes the change for the fictive poet that the development within the sequence has wrought. Yet there is also comparison, but that is possible to see only if we refuse to be led by prejudice to believe that anything concerned with God is best, higher, unreproachable. No. 1, "Why I write not of love," is a short poem in six tetrameter couplets; Fowler labels it a palinode, which means that the poet is retracting something said before. In the poem the speaker says he has tried to write of Cupid and thus bind him in his verse, but Cupid would not be so fettered, fled, and could not thereafter be made to enter the poet's lines. Thus his verse is cold and he grows old. The palinode in English is not strictly a genre, although it originally had strophic form in Greek. What occurs by the rejection of love as a theme is that the poet in poems two and three writes praises of place, the *beata ille* theme. In contrast is "To Heaven" in thirteen heroic couplets. Even the marriage number six in the first poem is altered to the prime number thirteen, as the earthly god of love is exchanged for the divine god of heaven. Fowler calls No. 15 a hymn. Preceding it are two verse epistles to titled ladies and a birthday ode to a member of the Sidney family, whose home, Penshurst, was apostrophized in No. 2.

The rejection of mundane love as theme (No. 1) leads to place as theme and praise of "owner" (Nos. 2–3); the nonsexual compliments of women (Nos. 12–13) and praise of an earthly being (No. 14) lead to praise of divine place, not simply God, but where the "owner" is even more coterminous with place than the "owners" in the previous encomia. The Sidneys and specifically Sir Robert Sidney are lauded in No. 2, the household at Penshurst then being headed by Sir Robert; in No. 3, Sir Robert Wroth being Sir Robert's son-in-law; in No. 12, the Countess of Rutland being Sir Robert's niece; and in No. 14, Sir William Sidney being Sir Robert's son. The acceptance of divine love in No. 15 brings together the mundane of the earlier poems (Nos. 1–3), the rejection of earthly love (Nos. 5–9), and the nondivine of the earlier poems and its acceptance (Nos. 12–14). (Poems 4 and 10–11, which we will look at shortly, create two transitions and work on rejection and acceptance themes.) In "To Heaven" Jonson reprises the sins and disease of poems in the middle of the sequence (ll. 3–4), noting in ll. 17–18 their transcendence, and talks of the potential falsity of human intentions: "Is it interpreted in me disease, / That, laden with my sinnes, I seeke for ease?"; "I know my state, both full of shame, and scorne, / Conceiv'd in sinne, and unto labour borne." But divinely "rap'd," he can contain within him God ("Dwell, dwell here still"), despite his "state." The play on sexual imagery in this divine context is clear and particularly points the reader toward the poet's craft and toward a revision of the usual definition of lyric. The play on the three persons of God indivisible in ll. 9–12 continues in the human history of the fear, the horrible fall, and the judgment of ll. 19–20 ("As thou art all, so be thou all to mee, / First, midst, and last, converted one, and three; / My faith, my hope, my love: and in this state, / My judge, my witnesse, and my advocate"; "Standing with feare, and must with horror fall, / And destin'd unto judgement, after all"). The plea that his apostrophe to heaven is sincere and out of love of God rather than out of discontent and weariness with the world poses the dilemma of humankind's attitude toward death, but it also works to argue that the pleasures sought and unachieved in earlier poems (representative of people's adherence to principles of pleasure) are now truly transcended and that the substance of poems 12–14 is indeed "sincere."

No. 12, as noted before, made reference to Rutland's impotence through a wish that the Countess might yet bear a son. The suppressed ending, thus, plays ironically upon the transcendence of the pleasure principle, for "It is the *Muse*, alone, can raise to heaven" (l. 41). To Lady Aubigny, Jonson talks "Of [her] blest wombe, made fruitfull from above, / To pay [her] lord the pledges of chast love" (No. 13, ll. 95–96). No. 14 praises a birthday of one still rather young and unmarried, but its subtext suggests the expectation of approaching death and thus his nonmarriage and lack of progeny when Judgment Day comes.

"To Heaven," thus viewed, is something other than just a statement of a religious theme and of belief. The negative criticism of it—what is read as not very heartfelt sincerity—has not understood what it is doing *as a lyric*. As a hymn, that is, as a dislocated poem, noncontextualized, it may present "his best religious work in an area which he never learned to handle very well."[11] But as a lyric under the definition advanced in this book (while still being subgenerically a hymn), it would not be expected to render high emotion, overflowing with heartfelt sincerity and eschewing such therefore questionable language as "reynes," "rap'd," "Conceiv'd," "Upon my flesh to'inflict another wound" (although this, of course, contrasts with the wounds Jesus sustained in his redemption of humankind).[12] Rather it would be expected to do what it does, though it be "sincere": pull together themes in the sequence, work as a capping of the movement seen from poem 11 onward, illustrate the craft of the poet, and move through seeming digressions as it surveys the self of the past with hope for a future although its time emphasis is clearly a present. Indeed that craft and that present suggest a final tribute to the Sidney family by juxtaposition of the mundane and the divine through the means of encomium and by juxtaposition of the Sidneys and their circle with the sacred matter of the final poem.

The date of the sequence, or of some of the poems in it at least, is after 1609, when Katherine Clifton married Lord Esmé, Seignieur d'Aubigny (see No. 13), and after 1611, when William Sidney was knighted, and before 1612, when he died (see No. 14). Prince Henry, who died in 1612, may or may not have been alive when No. 2 was written; Sir Robert Wroth died in 1614 (see No. 3); *Volpone* was produced in 1606; and Elizabeth Sidney became the Countess of Rutland in 1599 and died in 1612. In No. 14 the birthday celebrated was William Sidney's twenty-first ("This day sayes, then, the number of glad yeeres / Are justly summ'd, that make you man"); that is, in 1611. No. 10 had previously appeared in Robert Chester's *Love's Martyr* in 1601. As a collection put together in

1611 it roughly coincides with Jonson's return to Anglicanism, often dated around 1610.

The foregoing points us to a principle of organization for the sequence and a reason for it: praise of the Sidneys (perhaps in an attempt toward greater patronage—and indeed the 1616 *Works* was dedicated to William Herbert, Earl of Pembroke,[13] a nephew of Sir Robert Sidney). Much has been written about "To Penshurst," and Don E. Wayne's study, *Penshurst: The Semiotics of Place and the Poetics of History* (Madison: University of Wisconsin Press, 1984), should be consulted. As individual lyric it manifests the validity of Wayne's statement, "Remarkably, Jonson shows a certain awareness of the extent to which in his time intellect and craft were coming to be thought of as a private property, and the product of the intellect as a commodity" (157). The whole collection, as collection, iterates this awareness, and, recognizing it, we are better able to see such individual poems as Nos. 4 and 10–11 in two ways: as decontextualized poem and as poem with a subtext placing it in a larger context. While the craft of the poem by itself may present No. 4 as a valediction, No. 10 as an invocation, and No. 11 as an epode (I use Fowler's classifications), the poem within its collection exhibits further craft, implying an attitude of the author toward his work that is different from what appears to be the usual reading of these poems. Further, Nos. 5–9 take on readings that suggest interrelationships among themselves, demanding revised readings of Nos. 8 and 9 at least, as I have argued, and that place them in a schema organized to advance the bid for patronage. Jonson is not like so many other poets—the coterie versifier, the supposedly private, "overheard" poet wallowing in his thwarted love, the courtier poet dabbling in emotions and satire, nor even the allegorist or *vates* idealizing the road back to the Golden Age. He is *poet*—craftsperson, artisan, the generic type, who is the Muses' priest (No. 13, ll. 100–1) and who can rear "a rich, and golden *pyramede*" to raise one to heaven and make fame abide (No. 12, ll. 83–84, 41, 48). As lyrics we see Nos. 5–9 evidencing certain forms and characteristics but, in their larger context, as examples of the poems moving around in the world of other poets. Such examples, though Jonson can write them as well as others, he rejects as representative of his total worth. The attitude of the poet toward these poems (when placed in context) is that they demonstrate his poetic ability in this amatory vein, including its wordplay, and give the lie to the thought that they represent true experience and "sincerity" (as so often, say, Donne's "The good-morrow" or "The Autumnall" is misread to do). These central poems constitute seeming digressions and excursions, separately and as a group, but their emphasis on a mimesis of experience and their individual and interrelated craft defines that distanced maker concerned primarily with his *art*.

"To the World. A Farewell for a Gentle-woman, Vertuous and Noble" (No. 4) is a valediction consonant with and advancing the rejection theme of the whole sequence. The subgenre valediction indicates content; the subgenre "dramatic monologue" indicates its method. Spoken by a woman,[14] the poem has the female in the game of love renounce such amatory pursuits; thereby is she proved "vertuous and noble." But, of course, we know from No. 8 that even the supposedly virtuous and noble women may be subject to disease, and not only through its transmission from their husbands. The world demands for virtuousness "narrow straits," whereby one may find its "subtle ways." However, the allusion to Matthew 7:13–14[15] is undercut by that word "subtle," for we remember that "the serpent was more subtile than any beast of the field which the Lord God had made" (Genesis 3:1). The gentlewoman knows she must refuse the world's baited gifts, which, when she was younger, "stird'st up jealousies and feares." Now that she has reached the "houre upon [her] morne of age," she has reconciled herself to bear "age, misfortune, sicknesse, griefe," and stay at home rather than remain in attendance in the corrupt "soile" of the court. Is the gentlewoman saying farewell to the world or has not it already said farewell to her? Are the strengths of her bosom a hint that she has finally succumbed to having children and thus staying home? The "gentlewoman" (we must now put it in quotation marks) also grows old when love is fled and becomes an ironic contrast to the people of the worlds of poems Nos. 2 and 3. At the same time, this poem allows transition for the lyrical voice, grown old too, to pursue Celia one more time, to beg kisses, to recognize that "women are but mens shaddowes," that disease strikes all, and that perhaps he has fallen in love. I qualify *perhaps,* where previously the word has not entered our discussion of poem nine, because re-viewed it may become the ultimate seduction ploy rather than avowal. Does it contribute to the movement from the "lower" forms of love to the "higher" by illustrating deep human love of another human? Or does it illustrate the falsity of stated intention so common to humankind, whereby a human even seems to convince the self of its truth?

As decontextualized lyrics these poems may set up different interpretations from those when they are contextualized. As decontextualized lyric, No. 4, like these others, offers a maker "overhearing" one who meditates on the past and the future but who is concerned with the present, one who presents an attitude that allows mimesis of experience. The reader takes on that attitude when the poem is read as a dramatic lyric wherein "the speaker is sharply characterized" and "the emotion is made sharper and deeper by its immediate association with a personality." But once distanced by the reader through its contextualization, the poem comes to present a speaker who "tends to be anonymous, or Everyman" and a writer writing who has devised "digressions and excursions" to create a voice singing *about* experience. The seeming internal mimesis of the decontextualized poem (suggesting Frye's concept of the lyric) has become the external mimesis of the contextualized poem,[16] and the "You" thus understands the poem as "discourse" with "I" rather than I's "expression," as the means to rhetorical mode rather than its ends.

This is undoubtedly made more cogent for my reader by the fact that the speaking voice is a gentlewoman rather than Ben. But understanding of the point being advanced proclaims that in poem 10 the "I" is and is not Jonson.[17] An internal mimesis is presented but is not a recording of the experience; rather it is a telling about the experience. The poet begins, "And must I sing?" following immediately upon the song "To Celia." In context, No. 9 must be reconsidered as example of such demand rather than as heartfelt statement of the poetic voice's truly being in love (which is the sentimental reading/hearing of "Drinke to me, onely, with thine eyes"). The poetic voice may believe he is truly in love and may thus be presenting an internal mimesis, but the fuller context indicates that the writer writing knows differently. In poem 10 the poetic voice recounts various subjects that others' muses have proffered, ranging over potentially epic and vatic subjects to the Dionysian, the didactic, erotic hetero- and homosexual themes, the overtly fanciful and poetic, or commissioned work. Some of these have been pursued in the previous poems, but now are rejected in favor of his "owne true fire," and he writes an epode to be understood only by those with "deepe eares."

The epode starts by justifying the writer's excursion into certain aspects of poems 5–9:

> Not to know vice at all, and keepe true state,
> Is vertue, and not *Fate:*
> Next, to that vertue, is to know vice well,
> And her blacke spight expell.

The morality that this defines in ll. 7–16 rejects "The thing, they here call Love, . . . blinde Desire" and accepts "true Love . . . / That is an essence, farre more gentle, fine, / Pure, perfect, nay divine." The play of this poem, which divides the sequence into three-quarters and the final four poems we have already looked at, establishes the unity of the sequence. The various lovers, as well as those who are chaste of necessity or who abstain, and especially those who declare "there's no such thing, / As this chaste love we sing," are set against a man who is like a faithful turtledove[18] and a woman who graces him as perfect Phoenix. The chaste love that "so divine a creature" begets in this "person," of "noble, and right generous mind / . . . That knows the waight of guilt," counsels *"Man may securely sinne, but safely never."* While we have seen in other poems those who securely sin (that is, carelessly or overconfidently), we are presented here with a person who knows that one cannot sin safely (that is, without some retribution or reprisal or ill). We are now ready for the positive subjects and views of poems 12–14 and the apostrophe to divine love in No. 15. But within the full context of the sequence the epode suggests that Sir Robert and his wife, Barbara Gamage, are intended.

An epode is the last strophe of a lyric ode (a song in honor of gods or heroes) and etymologically indicates a "singing afterwards"; that is, in this case, Jonson's lyric reprise of what has preceded and his "completion" of the thought to which the previous poems have led. Following will thus be demonstrations of the thought in the womanhood of Elizabeth, Countess of Rutland, who was childless, and of Katherine, Lady Aubigny, whose "blest wombe [was] made fruitfull from above" (l. 95), and the hopes for Sir William Sidney, whose virtue shows "whose sonne, / Whose nephew, whose grand-child you are" (ll. 41–42). The praise implied by the ode that the full sequence equates is directed toward the Sidneys, specifically toward Sir Robert Sidney, and its contents range over the world of generation and place. Some of that generation involves "securely" sinning, for that is a way of the world, but others "will refrain / from thoughts of such a straine." The wakeful reason that rules our affections (see l. 13) can lead to "god-like unitie" and preserve "community" (ll. 53–54). These we see in poems 12–14, and, in the final poem, the poem and the poet unite to praise God, distancing what has gone before.

The individual poems and the sequence as a composite odic form fulfill the definition of lyric set forth in chapter 6. The rereading of some of the individual poems, as well as of the sequence, arises from our consideration of those lyric dimensions: the author's craft; the ultimate distance of the writer from the writing, and especially from the fictive voices (which range not only over seemingly different people but over differing degrees of direct authorial involvement); the present concerns despite a past and an implied future; and an internal mimesis that is not capable of remaining internal. In these generic lyric dimensions we have limina into a rereading of literature and evidence of the author's continuing presence.

8

Henry Vaughan's "Amoret" Poems: A Jonsonian Sequence

I turn now to consideration of a different kind of genre, the poetic sequence, which we have examined in chapter 7, and a kind of literary device, structure, by which I mean something more organizational and geometric and arithmetic than what "form" implies. Structure results from organization within space, and such organization may depend on mathematical proportion, duplicative building blocks (imagery, language, ideas), and relationships of parts. These aspects of structure provide limina into an understanding and fuller reading of the individual poems and of the sequence they subtend. While the sonnet sequence seems to be well known, most critics of poetry seem to avoid the sequence,[1] and those critics dealing with Renaissance literature are particularly immune even after having attended to Sidney's "Astrophil and Stella" in the realm of the "secular" and Herbert's *The Temple* in the realm of the devotional.

Despite the efforts of E. L. Marilla to raise the evaluation of Henry Vaughan's secular poems, they seem to have attracted few readers and even less scholarly attention.[2] Primarily Marilla argued that the "secular verse is characterized by craftsmanship that is distinctly similar to and but little less skillful than that of the religious poetry."[3] Yet, while the religious poems are praised, the secular poems are condemned. James D. Simmonds has been one of the few to champion Marilla's position in print. In his *Masques of God*[4] he calls the secular poems a "cool, deliberative statement and reasoned argument rather than passionate ardors and hyperbolical enthusiasm." He finds a variety of form, meter, imagery, and language, and at times "an awkwardness in development of thought and in the handling of the complex stanzaic patterns" that "too often produces a heavy, turgid effect." Perhaps. But there is more going on in at least *Poems, 1646,* than has been acknowledged, and to my way of thinking what is going on calls for praise of Vaughan's craft.

I propose that Vaughan's 1646 *Poems,* which number thirteen, constitute a sequence and that, aside from the very different sonnet sequences of the Elizabethans, the force behind it is Jonson as seen in "A Celebration of

Charis in Ten Lyrick Peeces."[5] There are no love-poem sequences, let it be noted, in Donne's canon, nor Cherbury's (despite the series of Lady Diana Cecil poems), Herrick's, Carew's, Waller's, Suckling's, Lovelace's, or Marvell's. Habington's "Castara," owing sustenance to Jonson, is an elaborate series of sequences, and Cowley's "The Mistress," owing style to Donne, qualifies as a series of related poems. Jonson's sequence, put together from poems written at various times, supplies Vaughan's literary fountainhead. It depicts the progress of an affair with lacunae between the individual poetic narratives (though they are easily filled in) and with Petrarchan complications, turned as a result of evaluating the affair from the woman's point of view. The ten poems have titles helpful in following the progress of the affair and in interpreting them. There are varying verse forms in Nos. 4 and 7, giving a sequence of three in iambic tetrameter couplets, one in stanzas, two in iambic tetrameter, one in stanzas, and three in iambic tetrameter. The sequence mocks Petrarchan narrative and imagery, and it revels in some supposedly autobiographical lines (like "Of your Trouble, *Ben,* to ease me, / I will tell what Man would please me") and sexual double entendre.[6] Vaughan's sequence is more ambitious, more crafted, and more "sincere." It rebuffs the Donnean form of love plea, rejection, and sour grapes (differently, of course, from the way this appears in Carew and Suckling) as the lover alters through the influence of the woman and her point of view. It is more firmly autobiographical and it reverses Jonson's ambiguities by employing them toward the beginning of the sequence, not primarily at the end. Jonson starts with the sympathy-evoking lines:

> Let it not your wonder move,
> Lesse your laughter; that I love.
> Though I now write fiftie yeares,
> I have had, and have my Peeres,

and ends with ridicule by a woman of the game of love:

> What you please, you parts may call,
> 'Tis one good part I'ld lie withall.

Vaughan begins bathetically and in Donnean language:

> When we are dead, and now, no more
> Our harmles mirth, our wit, and score
> Distracts the Towne; when all is spent
> That the base niggard world hath lent
> Thy purse, or mine . . .
> Wee'le beg the world would be so kinde,
> To give's one grave, as wee'de one minde.

and ends exaltedly at Priory Grove, with a topographic poem in plain style:

> So there againe, thou'lt see us move
> In our first Innocence, and Love:
> And in thy shades, as now, so then,
> Wee'le kisse, and smile, and walke agen.

Marilla discerned a continuity of theme in the 1646 *Poems* from rejection of the author's initial overtures through a succession of changes in Amoret's attitude and finally to marriage and a peaceful reminiscence of the courtship. The poems, nonetheless, have not been read as a sequence and have therefore been found lacking as individually successful poems. What few comments have been printed see no context for a poem beyond what is on its surface and this has led to negative evaluation.[7] A verse epistle introduces the sequence, followed by a poem entitled "Les Amours," and the first poem in which Amoret is named. Next are two "non-Amoret" poems, then three more Amoret poems, and then two more poems; and finally two Amoret poems and "Upon the Priorie Grove." The pattern of "non-Amoret" and Amoret poems is 2, *1*; 2, *3*, 2; and 2, 1.[8] Simmonds's analysis of Vaughan's poems, including those under discussion here, stresses Vaughan's employment of balance and symmetry. We see structural balance and symmetry in this sequence in the placement of those poems specifically referring to Amoret. As sequence, all the poems impinge on Amoret; as sequence, they demand awareness of the lacunae in the love affair being depicted through the continuity of theme and the continuity of imagery. Each poem requires an analysis in terms of itself and its relationship to the sequence. So little has been published on any one of the poems that detailed explication is necessary. The sequence tells the story of the reversal of a disrupted love affair, which indeed may have existed at first more in the poet's hopes than in reality. The individual poems become steps away from despair and rationalization to arguments that wear the loved one down—his guilt, his loss, his love, his contemplated life without her—until she repents as if the guilty one, leading ultimately to marriage and serenity.

The first poem is the verse epistle "To my Ingenuous Friend, *R. W.,*" which divides into halves. Lines 1–28 indicate the poet's and his noble friend's harmless mirth in carousing and running up debts, and postulates a time when they have put such crass matters behind them through death. At such time, the poet says, they will beg burial in one grave since they have been of one mind. Thus equally will they proceed to the Elysian

Fields, where their spirits will meet others like themselves. Such burial in poetry of the period, however, was usually sought for the lover and his beloved, as in Donne's "The Relique," a form of the bed-grave image. The implication is that the poet has found only man of his mind and, by unexpressed analogy, woman to be only bodily. This Donnean attitude as expressed in "Loves Alchymie" is further reenforced by Donnean phrases: the clause "When we are dead," which begins the poem, and "When I am dead," which opens Donne's "The Dampe"; the reversal of the idea of "Wee'le beg the world would be so kind," which contrasts those of the mundane world in "The Canonization," who invoke the lovers in their heaven to "Beg from above / A patterne of your love!" The first half of the verse epistle relates the "ancient love" of R. W. and the poet, a love based on compatibility of mind; it plays upon a comparison between the friendship of men and the sexual love of man and woman. The souls of the poet and R. W. will meet and proceed to the Elysian Fields when "Freed from the tyranny of clay." The first half moves through death to a rebirth, and from the concerns of the world (the outer view) to spiritual or mental union (the inner view).

The second half, lines 29–56, balances the first by indicating whom the poet and R. W. will meet who are "More of thy Genius, and my mind." First, such spiritual or mental union leads to forgetfulness of the outer world of perjured love and bodily things. Lines 43–50 are specifically concerned with male-female bodily love, a love that is "unhappy" because murdered (as in Donne's "Apparition") "by some perjur'd face." Lethe will allow the poet's spirit no longer to be vexed in death by the "inconstant, cruell sex." Second, the latter half moves from their souls' rebirth, when they meet Ben Jonson and Thomas Randolph and when they dismiss the past alongside the stream that can subdue all sorrow, to potential birth into a new life. Lines 51–56 discuss the pregnancy of their souls, "bigge with delight / Of their new state." Only now will last thoughts appear; now will their souls have come to rest with "all sense and cares" drunk away. The intoxicating liquors of the world with which the poem began have been replaced at the conclusion by the waters of Lethe. The two halves of the poem are directly correspondent in reverse. And whereas the pints drunk in The Moon or The Star (rooms of the Globe Tavern) apparently lead to assignations upstairs, where the "calm whisperers" await payment, the draughts of Lethe negate care since they do away with "all sense"—that is, bodily appetite and gratification of the senses. Where the worldly of the first part proceed to the skies (The Moon, The Star, the upstairs chambers), the spiritual of the second part are already in the Elysian Fields. Reversals of imagery are everywhere in the two halves of the poem. The basic reversal, however, is the use of materials of "love" poems (like Donne's) to express a state where love in a sexual sense is missing. The heaven after death envisioned by the poet becomes one of stasis (the present only); it contrasts with the view of the mutable earthly heaven of sexual love, which is built on concepts of the past and the future.

The verse epistle concludes with a couplet, "So they that did of these discusse, / Shall find their fables true in us." Again it is Donne in the background, where the poet of "The Relique" would have the age taught "What miracles wee harmless lovers wrought." The summary couplet indicates the kind of solace that the thwarted lover has allowed himself: rationalization. The fables that have discussed the spirits of the dead allege their nonbodily concerns and oneness. And R. W. and the poet will illustrate this "truth" well. The union of two such minds in this peculiar form of coition will beget "delight of their new state." Throughout the poem we should have been remembering the double meaning of "die" (as orgasm) for contrast with this kind of love-death. The fables concern the meeting of minds without bodily implications; yet the poet dwells on this subject because he has apparently fallen in love with one who has proved (he says) inconstant and who has lied about her love or her lack of love for him. The fables he alludes to have therefore also discussed man's constancy and woman's fickleness (a staple of Renaissance love lyrics), and again their "truth" is "proved" in the poem. But this is only the way the poet sees the situation. Surely man's "harmelesse mirth" might instead suggest man's fickleness to a woman. Possibly the schism in their love affair has arisen from a difference in the couple's conception of this "harmelesse mirth," a not uncommon source of marital difficulties.

The opening poem has set up a narrative out of which the sequence will grow. It has employed some crypsis—unfortunately, for critical understanding. The poet has fallen in love, has found his loved one to be perfidious to him, and has been accused of unseriousness and of too much attention to male escapades. He has reacted by rejecting his beloved, by wallowing in a sentimental rationalization that true love is the meeting of minds as the ancients proclaimed, and by consoling himself with his poetry. At this point in the sequence we see the poet, deceived by self-pity, disparaging that which has not been attained. The poem represents, as Simmonds notes (204), the thwarted suitor's retreat into masculine convivialities, but it also serves a double function: it posits the supposed dialectic of love—the body or sexual love and the mind or spiritual love—and introduces a sequence that, being concerned with dialectic, will culminate in the poet's, not the mistress's, encompassing of both. It is the poet who changes. His opposition of the world of men to his personal world, as in the first poem, will be shown to be in error, and only then, mind-set changed, can he enjoy "His usuall Retyrement" at Priory Grove.

In the Elysian Fields, R. W. and the poet meet Ben Jonson and then Thomas Randolph.[9] The lines immediately follow "More of thy Genius, and my mind." Is the poet suggesting that R. W. writes more in the manner of Jonson than he, and he more like Randolph? What is cited for Jonson are "sacred Layes" and poems on so many topics that the spirits throng "To catch the subject of his Song." Neither seems apropos of Vaughan in the present sequence, although the nature of many poems is Jonsonian—for example, the last with its relationship to topographic poetry. We do not know who R. W. was, although it has been suggested that he was the person killed at Rowton Heath in 1645, for whom Vaughan wrote an elegy. But the equation with Randolph, who was a Son of Ben, just as R. W. shows genius and the poet only mind, is carried out in the sequence. Vaughan cites Randolph's "Lovers" (his comedy, "The Jealous Lovers"). *"Amyntas"* (his pastoral of that name), and "Nightingale" (his poem "On the Death of a Nightingale"). Vaughan's sequence continues with an excursion into matter for jealous lovers, "Les Amours"; to a poem appropriate to Amyntas, "Song," which begins "Amyntas *goe, thou art undone"*; and to "An Elegy" such as the nightingale is said to sing for itself (the nightingale appears in "Upon the Priorie Grove"). That is, poems 2, 5, 9, and 13—a rather definite pattern of placement—present the poet of the sequence as one of Randolph's mind. As Simmonds has suggested, the unfavorable comparison of Vaughan with Donne has been misplaced because Vaughan should rather be compared with Jonson. Indeed, as I read the sequence, it becomes a rejection of the Donnean pattern by employment of motifs, language, and metaphor found in Donne's poems to epitomize the false view of love. The poet of the sequence must become more like Jonson, though he can attain only to kinship. This first poem, a kind of fountainhead for the sequence, employs imagery of supposed death, which contrasts with life concepts, and imagery of the monetary world, which contrasts with a world free of care and discontent. Its devices of balance, symmetry, and reversals will appear in the other individual poems as well.

"Les Amours" follows the narrative of the first poem by envisioning that time when the thwarted lover is dead. He begins "Tyrant farewell," thus saying farewell to his beloved, but also to his body and bodily needs as comparison with the first poem shows. Since the rest of the poem manifests that he is not really saying farewell to either, we are prepared to read the poem as a rhetorical ploy—a commonplace for the Petrarchan poet. The ultimate point is that the poet must learn to reject such a ploy and achieve sincerity by simplicity and directness. But at this point he is still Donnean as in "The Dampe," "The Prohibition," and "The Legacie." The attitude of a kind of martyrdom hinted at in the first poem is reprised in the "sacrifice to Heaven" of his heart. While his ardor has turned his body (heart) to ashes (or cold dust), a tear from her eyes, which have been scornful of him but that have made him her victim, will allow his heart's flames to partake of new life. Her eye can be "quickning," and from his grave will arise "Crimson flowers" to curtain his head. The male-female imagery of fire and water, in this proposed emblematic intercourse, will beget a different kind of delight from the pregnancy of the first poem, and since the flowers are crimson they represent resurrection and immortality for the dead lover but acknowledgment of sin and remorse for the woman. The poet in the bed-grave and his loved one's creation of flowers by her tears shed over him are symbolic of union but reverse the sexual roles expected in a seduction poem. The nonloving situation between them is different from what we were led to believe in the first poem. In the first poem— appropriate to such rejection of female love as the poet hypothesized—we have been led to believe that he has been faithful, at least in his fashion, to her and she has been inconstant and has perjured herself. But the second poem makes it clear that he has only been thwarted in loving her and that she has not shown love for him as he would wish it. Her former inconstancy has become only rejection of love for him, and thus her "perjur'd face" comes to suggest that she has said or implied only that she does not love him. The unnamed woman referred to in these first two poems is the Amoret of the rest of the sequence.

The poem divides into six, twenty, six, and two lines. In the first six lines the poet sacrifices his heart as he prepares to die. The poem moves to a point beyond the first poem. While "To my Ingenuous Friend, R. W." has talked about "When we are dead," this second poem has postulated a later time, "Yet e're I goe." The first poem shows a rather immediate reaction to the poet's love affair as one on which he supposedly can turn his back and adopt a surrogate relationship; in "Les Amours" he contemplates his loved one's reaction to his death with the hope expressed underneath this vision that she still can care for him and that in death at least they can be united. The central section of the poem (twenty lines) proposes such union in male-female imagery of fire and water with resultant flowers springing "o'er all the tombe." The next six lines, balancing the first six, describe the emblems that this union-after-death will achieve: two hearts, one hers, which has withstood his love, and one his, which has succumbed to her allure. His heart will retain a drop of dew on it though it is "washt in bloud" (thus pure in theological terms) and though it should give off heat. The drop of dew reprises the Petrarchan tears he has shed, while it also suggests what a tear from her quickening eye will yield. The two six-line sections balance each other in imagery as well as structure, and the central section proposes the result, through the bed-grave image, of what their union might be. A final couplet summarizes the poem: "Thus Heaven can make it knowne, and true, / That you kill'd me, 'cause I lov'd you." The common metaphor of "die" and "death" as sexual union determines the main image of the poem, and the final couplet, like that of the first poem, evidences that the fable of love-death is "true." This truth is made known by Heaven's emblems on each crimson flower. Possibly he refers to the flower called "love-lies-bleeding"; it is the *Amaranthus caudatus,* one type of the flower symbolizing immortality. Or possibly he refers to the flower called "bleeding hearts." The bed-grave image in "Les Amours" is thus related to the context of the sequence that the first poem has set up. The poet has picked up the vision of his mortal death—death being his hoped-for end in sexual terms—and presented it now symbolically, so that it is mortal death and a kind of sexual death at the same time. It develops and advances the sequence. His strategy is obviously to get her to feel sorry that she has treated him as she has, and accordingly the central lines of the poem are "But blesse my ashes with a teare: / This influxe from that quickning eye." Man consumed by his passion becomes but ashes; he needs woman's love—the influxing tear of her eye (with its clear double entendre)—to compound those ashes (or dust) into the living "clay" that is man. This is not a contrivance, but a meaningful metaphoric statement—commonplace though its imagery may be. The crimson flowers that their love will produce contrast with the delight of the new state in the first poem and with the flowery banks of the Lethe.

While the first poem divides into two and the second into three sections (plus epitomizing couplet), with the first and third being symmetric, the next poem, "To Amoret. The Sigh," is stanzaic, seemingly an ordinary form. The sigh for the Petrarchan lover is standard and repeated. There are four stanzas of five lines each; the rhyme schemes of the first and fourth are identical, and those of the second and third vary. The lines range between seven and eight syllables. Though there is a suggestion of regularity, the meter and rhyme scheme really move toward a kind of sighing, which is enhanced by the fitful phrasing: "Take this Message, and depart, / Tell Amoret, that smiles, and sings / At what thy airie voyage brings, / That thou cam'st lately from my heart." In the previous poem he had mentioned tears and sighs, and went on to develop the imagery of tears. In this poem sighs are the subject. In the former poems death has been postulated; in this poem death is still to take place soon, but the time relationship is earlier than the death of the previous poem. He is not yet even in a symbolic grave. The first three poems move from a kind of real death to a symbolic death to a contemplated death. We therefore should expect that the sequence will continue to move toward a concept of life, and it does, the last poem ending with an idea of renewal.

There is a break between poems three and four as implied in the pattern of Amoret/non-Amoret poems given in note 8, above. The fourth poem, "To his Friend Being in Love," introduces a section of the sequence that modulates from reaction against conventional attitudes toward love to a change within the poet. The poem divides into twelve and six lines: the first section gives the words of his friend to him; the second records his compliance with that advice. But his friend here is his other self, his reason, and his "real" self is his heart. The tone of the first section is arrogant, impatient, unkind; but its advice is worthwhile: ask her whether she loves you and do not keep your love bottled up inside. But in the crucible of the heart the words (or the metaphoric tears) become kind and warm and loving. The heart needs only half the space the mind does to express itself. The time of the poem seems to be that of the previous one. The poet has advanced well toward rejecting the arrogant male attitude, which underlies the sequence up to this point. This fourth poem is compounded of the imagery of the previous ones: death, sighs, his but not her love, her coldness, his warmth, the eye, tears, tyranny, his sacrificed heart, and her white bosom and tears falling on it. Fire, water, air, and earth and their supposed properties also appear in all four poems.

The next poem (No. 5) is a "Song," addressed to Amyntas, that is, the poet; and since its "origin" is not the poet himself, it is printed in italics. It is in unbroken quatrains and, as a song, consists of only iambic tetrameters without variation. It contrasts with his own heartfelt lines in the previous poem. There the lines are iambic pentameters, but phrasing and enjambment disallow an artificial feeling; the last six lines sound as if they are the true words spoken by the poet's heart. The speaker of "Song" is again the poet's other self, but now more gentle, though it still berates the tyrant who has slain many servants in order to achieve glory in their pain. Though death is mentioned, the poet is not envisioning his being dead. Tying this poem to poem four, the reason now counsels recognition that his loved one does not love him any more than others she has known, and it would be best therefore just to forget about it and her. Casting this advice as a song subtly suggests its own artifice and its lack of individuation.

In contrast is poem six, "To *Amoret*. Walking in a Starry Evening." Here there are four stanzas of six lines each in a varied pattern of two or three rhymes, and a frequently altered meter of 8, 6, 4 and 8, 4, 6 syllables per line. The effect is one of walking and stopping without pattern. It suggests thought, a necessary transition from the colder reason of the previous two poems into the Fancy that accompanies the poet in poem seven. The thesis of the poem is that the poet and Amoret were destined for each other; thus the advice of the immediately preceding poem is rejected. There is no reference to his death, and time has caught up to the present, when his love has been born. However, it really deals with a time before the present: it speaks of their destined love and it uses imagery of the sun and the stars and their creation in the heavens. This second poem citing Amoret compares and contrasts with the first poem citing Amoret; it has four stanzas of six rather than five lines, and it varies rhyme schemes and metric patterns, but now the effect is a kind of external indecision rather than internal fitfulness. "Walking in a Starry Evening" effects an important change: the poet takes on hope (though not explicitly stated) that there is sympathy between the lovers and that theirs are "two conspiring minds"; that is, minds that are mutually inspiriting.

With the seventh poem, "To *Amoret* gone from him," we have reached the middle of the sequence. The poem is in twelve tetrameter couplets. The imagery of walking and the night reappears, and the poet again talks to another self, now Fancy. As hinted in the previous poem, Amoret is equated with the sun. Its descent symbolizes Amoret's leaving him; with its descent comes night, symbolizing unhappiness. The poem becomes the vehicle for him to take the previous advice of reason and tell her of his love, but it must be done fancifully. The poet should not be arrogant, as we have seen him before, nor should he act the martyr. The fanciful image will grow to simpler expression as the remaining poems are developed. The sequence we are reading is his fanciful recitation of his love.

"A Song to *Amoret,*" in quatrains, supposes a time when he will be dead and Amoret has a new lover ("some fresher youth"). He would not be able to give "So rich a heart" or "true resolved minde," for the poet "not for an houre did love, / Or for a day desire," but with his soul "had from above, / This endles holy fire." Past the middle of the sequence, the poet now confesses his love and does not try to excuse it or accuse her of thwarting it. He has turned from arrogance and admits that she could find other men with more fortune and beauty, greater men, than he. Those things that others may have in greater store than he are held in high esteem by the world, but they are ephemeral and material; yet his love, endless and spiritual, balances all those other worldly "goods." Stanza two implies that the poet has not been so faithful as the sun in its orbit, nor chaste in his passions, nor temperate in his lament:

> Were he as faithfull as the Sunne,
>   That's wedded to the Sphere;
> His bloud as chaste, and temp'rate runne,
>   As Aprils mildest teare.

It affirms our view of the poet as the unfaithful one in this relationship, who now has repented like the sentimental hero of eighteenth-century comedy, a kind of reformed rake.

There are affinities in this poem with various poems by Donne, particularly "The Apparition," but Vaughan has begun to transcend the assault on woman as inconstant and mere "body" and to accept the fault for the lovers' amorous disruption. Donne's persona is most often (though not quite always) driven to philandering by woman's unfaithfulness and insincerity. The cold Petrarchan mistress only sometimes causes Donne's lover problems; Vaughan's lover at first tries to cast his mistress in that role, but reason, knowing better, is causing him now to begin to cast her in her true role.

The next poem (No. 9) is both a love elegy and a funeral elegy for himself when he is dead from love melancholy. "An Elegy," in pentameter couplets, ends with an appended half line as if the poem were cut off before being completed. It is an effective stroke, as if the speaker is so overcome that he cannot go on. The Latin quotation from Martial says, "Oh, 'tis now enough." Reacting to the opening line of "Song," spoken by the poet's other self, the persona says in the elegy, "'Tis true, I am undone." But not yet dead, he will write an elegy for all lovers like himself, an elegy, however, that is a love elegy of praise of the mistress as well. His strategy here is to win her by letting it be known that when others scorned her he upheld her beauteous worth. It is he whom she owes for hyperbolic praise—and the similes, depicting her face, might be expected to have been continued in a blazon, had not the poet broken off.

The fusion of elegies wittily replays the meanings of "die" and enhances the import of "the Metamorphosis of Love." For through death as through love man and woman are changed into other beings: through love will come "death," through (his) death will come love (hers for him, should his strategy here win her sympathy). Even though the poet's ruse is not very subtle, at least the poem does not continue to accuse the woman. And though no blame is seen accruing to the poet in this particular poem of the sequence, at least he praises his loved one without moderation.

In a reprise of the first poem (the tavern is specifically identified as The Globe—the one in Fleet Street—whereas in the first poem only two of its rooms, The Moon and The Star, are mentioned), the poet envisions in poem ten a meaningless life of carefree drinking and its concomitants—all because his love has not been fulfilled. But unlike the first poem there is no bitterness, no "I'll show you" attitude. Rather it is a sorrowful tone that pervades the poem, one of regret but resignation. For he is not a "Rich, happy man! that canst thus watch, and sleep, / Free from all cares." One of the effects of sack is poetry (that which we are reading), but it is clear that this is not the kind of poetry he would prefer to write as an apostrophe to his love (those poems that we will be reading soon afterward, Nos. 11–13). Doomed by his thwarted love, his world would become the London he sees before him, all "riotous sinful plush." And he progresses to another dish and another, and still more until he and his companions "After full cups have dreames Poeticall."

The last eight lines are separated from those preceding and printed in italics.[10] As in "Song" it is the poet's other self that speaks—again with irony:

> Lets laugh now . . .
> And in our merry, mad mirth run
> Faster and further then the Sun;
> . . . So we men below shall move
> Equally with the gods above.

The poet has talked himself out of this kind of life, as we can realize when we remark: "*As though* the Pot, and Poet did agree, / Sack should to both Illuminator be" (my italics); the Painter's "fiery Nose" (an allusion to syphilis) and the phallic pun on "his pencill"; and the emphasis on the dreams with which the cup is pregnant, the only means of yielding for the drunkards "more soules, and nobler fire." In "A Song to *Amoret*" he had renounced popular earthly achievement; the satanic lure of being one with the gods above is ironic. The poem aims at eliciting so much sympathy from his mistress that she will in no way let him lead such a life. And as he proceeds to the final three poems, there being a definite break between "A Rhapsodis" and the next poem, we see that his strategy has worked.

The title (probably a misprint for "A Rhapsodie") indicates that the poem was intended for recitation—a colloquial and spontaneous tone is evident—and that it was conceived in some kind of heroic terms, as part of an "epic." What is epic is the sequence, in that it represents the history of a man who has overcome adversary forces to achieve heroic dedication to his love. As well, it is "narrative" presented episodically; this is one of the episodes, as "rhapsody" implies. There is little of the rapturous in this poem, another meaning of "rhapsody," except in ironic use as false rapture for the dissolute life.

"*To* Amoret, *of the difference 'twixt him, and other Lovers, and what true Love is*" has had few admirers. Marilla calls it "not the most effective poem," but Simmonds at least sees that the "slow, halting rhythm and abrupt shifts in line length" enrich the subject.[11] The poem confesses the poet's past indiscretions, which have engaged neither true passion nor loving spirit, and which have been but *ignes fatui.* The difference between him and other lovers is that they, base sublunary lovers, will continue to feed on "loose prophane desire," while he, "by pow'rfull Love, so much refin'd," cannot dismiss the loved one's powerful attraction, the elements that have given his life its course. A combination of Donne's "Valediction: forbidding Mourning" and others employing an alchemical metaphor,[12] the poem is an extended analogy: he is clearly now not hypothesizing his death (as in "An Elegy"), but he has become emboldened by his mistress's alteration of attitude toward him. "A Rhapsodis" has not only shown the mistress what the lover's unhappy life will be without her, but it has filled in a space of time during which the poet's former protestations have had their effect. "To Amoret" in turn sets up the situation out of which will come Amoret's weeping in poem twelve. For the poem is mainly gauged to assert what love is: the conspiring of spirits and stars by winged beams and mutual fire. ("Conspiring" puns etymologically on the meaning "enspiriting each other at the same time.") Love must be mutual of both visualization and directed looks of love. She, as the "cold" Petrarchan mistress, is like the polar north to which the lodestar and the enamored steel of the compass move. It is only through such guidance of her mutual love that he can steer his way through the sea of life. The poet's strategy of highflown rhetoric borrowed from affective poetry probably well known to Amoret will, of course, be successful. It should be clear that the critical comments on this poem have been opaque because they have not understood it as part of a sequence, thus again demonstrating the significance of observing such a sequence as a limen into an understanding of literature.

The is the one poem in the sequence in an odd number of lines, thirty-five, since there are seven five-line stanzas. It is built on pentameters and tetrameters, for the sets of two dimeters combine into tetrameters also. These are the two basic meters of the sequence and thus the poem pulls together the sequence even metrically. It will be followed by a poem in pentameter couplets and by one in tetrameter couplets. But the number of stanzas (since five is the number of love, a "marriage" number) and the number of lines (since seven is the number of creation) are significant. The golden mean or section of the poem occurs at line 22,[13] "Whil'st I by pow'rfull Love, so much refin'd." Not only does the line define the basic thought of the poem, it also states the theme of the sequence.

The "tone of confidential intimacy" in "To Amoret WEEPING," poem twelve, has suggested to various scholars since F. E. Hutchinson that the poem was written to Catherine Wise, who became Vaughan's first wife.[14] Whether that is true or not—and my reading of the poems does not depend on the answer—the poem indicates a further advance in the sequence, for the lovers have come to understanding and mutual love. The prior poem had almost reached this point, but not quite. The courtship seems to be about at an end; the strategy of the previous poem seems to have been successful; and we can expect marriage to ensue. At least a mutuality of love seems to dominate lines 37–58, and it is Amoret who is weeping, in remorse for the way she has treated the poet in the past.

In another reprise, now of "A Song to *Amoret*," the poet revives statements of his poor estate and of the transcendence of his—now their—love over such material and mundane concerns. Their love gives "a blessing which no gold can buye." The poem begins by recapitulating imagery and ideas of the former poems: Amoret's eyes, fortune or treasure, stars and tenements in heaven (to be contrasted with the rooms upstairs at The Globe), the sun's beams, the loved one's speech. The second verse paragraph restates the lover's ability to conquer time through his love. The third speculates on the venal life he might have led. Not having led such a life makes his estate poor but enables him, ironically, not to have sunk lower into the hell sustained by gold. The fourth verse paragraph credits the loved one with having let him avoid the mean life by her dispensing of real fortune, love. Through his love for her he has had heaven breathed into him (compare "conspiring" in the earlier poem) and has achieved courage to "dare / What ever fate, or malice can prepare."

Marilla, and probably others, felt that the poem lacks organic intensity although it is unified by its basic theme.[15] But this view is not justified, it seems to me, when we read the poem in sequence, when we see the relation of verse paragraphs to what has preceded (in imagery and idea, as well as theme) and observe the progress that the poem itself makes, and when we examine its structure. The first verse paragraph (ll. 1–8) is balanced and completed by the last six lines of the poem (ll. 53–58).[16] The treasure of her eyes should not be shed for the past, since on earth such "pious streames" are of no avail; but the treasure that the lovers have found (their "purse" and "mines," with obvious sexual connotations) emphasize a future under "a blessing which no gold can buye." (Remembering the first poem and the apparent philandering of the poet, in this context, we know what gold can buy.) The questions of the first part are made irrelevant.

The second verse paragraph, ll. 9–20, is balanced by ll. 43–52 of the last verse paragraph. In the latter the poet talks of "fate" and "providence," of wealth and wit, and of being armed with "a gallant soule and sense." The questions of the second verse paragraph are more firmly answered there than in ll. 9–20, which set the proem to ll. 43–52. The third verse paragraph, ll. 21–36, is balanced by ll. 37–42, the first lines of the last verse paragraph. The problem of birth and position is countered by an apostrophe for deliverance from what the tinsel world thinks is important. He has been delivered from a hell on earth, and this is owing to the miracle of his loved one and his love for her. The point in Amoret's weeping is that she should not weep for his death (a main theme of the sequence), since through it has come life as the better person that he now is. The "blessed pow'rs" have made him rich "by taking all away."

The turning point of the poem is at line 37, thirty-six lines in the first division, twenty-two in the second. This is the golden section of the poem. It is the artistic focal point, and the poem must clearly have been manipulated to achieve it and the inverse balances we have noted. The poem builds to this point and then returns to the beginning in terms of its content. The number of lines that sustain the poem likewise suggest numerical considerations:

verse paragraph			
1	8 lines		
2	12 lines		
3	16 lines		
4	22 lines	=	6 lines
			10 lines
			6 lines

There is a steady progression in weight (that is, in number of lines in each verse paragraph), with a greater step at the position of the golden mean, for the fourth verse paragraph balances those that precede it and is itself symmetrically balanced. At its center (ll. 48–49) are "providence" and his "gallant soule." The indention of line 58 along with the indention of line 37 frames the paragraph.

It should, thus, be apparent that the final poem of the sequence, "Upon the PRIORIE GROVE, His usuall Retyrement," will describe the further progress of this affair into marriage, into serenity and life (not the death emerging formerly), into a world of the two together rather than the world of men and whores depicted in the first poem. To contrast with that tavern of the worldly man, which was strategically revisited in the tenth "episode" ("A Rhapsodis"), the scene must be bucolic, edenic. Like the previous poem, this one divides into two at lines 22–23, its gold mean or focus. The first verse paragraph of four lines greets Beacon Priory, where the poet first fell in love with his mistress. The imagery of treasure is repeated and makes clear that this foreshadowing of Heaven, where his treasury lies, answers the injunction of Jesus that "where your treasure is, there will your heart be also" (Matt. 6.21). The past is renounced, never to return, in the second verse paragraph, and the images of sound and sun and moon and fancy merge in a consummate statement of this grove as the world he has been seeking.

Once the sequence is completed, its logical outcome is marriage. The last verse paragraph, signaled by the division of the poem as focus, immediately catches a sense of the future envisioned after marriage has occurred. Just as the grove will go on, though with signs of age, so shall the loving couple. The rhythm of their future life is caught in the last two lines as it will accrue step by step by natural episodes (like the stories of the poems of the whole sequence), though it seems finally to go on without decline:

> And in thy shades,
> as now,
> so then, /
> Wee'le kisse,
> and smile,
> and walke agen.

Each phrase is another step as they walk on, not different from Giono's "Pas à pas." The frequent references to Adam and Eve in the sequence place Priory Grove as an Eden, and the loving pair, their differences behind them and the lures of the world's gold and position rejected, as the populators of a new world. As symbol the poem transfigures the grove into an ideal natural order, as Simmonds has remarked (70), which expresses the power of love to transfigure a fallen world. But as we read the sequence we recognize that it is the poet who has "first betrayed" his "loves faire steps."

What Vaughan achieves in the sequence is an allegedly more honest appraisal of the poet and Amoret's relationship, going well beyond the usual Petrarchan love sequence where the man is faithful and loving and the woman is inconstant and cold.[17] If the sequence is truly autobiographical, it may tell us something more about Vaughan's occupational activities before 1646, when he seems to have studied law, clerked for Sir Marmaduke Lloyd, possibly engaged in medical practice, and served in the Royalist cause. He was only twenty-four in 1646, and we can surely expect him to have sown some wild seeds of carousing, whoring, and quick money and fame, in the world of men, prior to that date. But aside from autobiographical considerations the sequence has importance as a variation on a standard literary subgenre, and demands evaluation as art, not as biography or philosophy. The poet does engage in moral reflections on large general issues like the "proper" attitudes toward Fortune, Fate, and Adversity (I am citing Simmonds) and does present classic arguments in favor of a middle station in life.[18] But the significance is a literary one: the lovers are placed above the personal world and the chaos of London in comparison (or contrast) with the lovers, say, in Donne's "The Canonization," in William Habington's "Castara," and in Milton's "Comus" (see the Attendant Spirit's epilogue). It is literary comparison that should lie at the root of evaluation. Vaughan has captured much that becomes associated with the Cavaliers, as well, though his style is so far removed from Jonson's that most people have not seen the derivation. But his Donnean phrases—like "Sublunarie Lovers"—are not employed any more "metaphorically" than such echoes are by Carew or Suckling.

What is particularly Jonsonian about the sequence are (1) the social rather than the private nature of the sequence, despite the theme; (2) Vaughan's nonconceited verse, despite his borrowings from Donne; and (3) the basic plain style (for example in "A Rhapsodis" with its overlay of allusion). Remarks that Summers and Pebworth (184) make of Elegy 38 by Jonson apply equally to Vaughan's sequence: "The realism of such details serves further to particularize the dramatic context. It also places the celebrated love within a recognizable social setting, and it incorporates within that public milieu a space for the personal and the private." The jocular parodying of Donnean Petrarchanism is not unlike Jonson's achievement in "A Celebration of Charis." But it is perhaps in the style that increasingly becomes Jonsonian as we move through the sequence that Vaughan's kinship is attested. There is nothing of the high style in "Les Amours," yet even lines like

> O're all the tombe a sudden spring
> Of Crimson flowers, whose drooping heads
> Shall curtaine o're their mournfull beds:

no longer appear as we reach "To *Amoret* WEEPING":

> Nay further, I should by that lawfull stealth,
> (Damn'd Usurie) undoe the Common-wealth;
> Or Patent it in Soape, and Coales, and so
> Have the Smiths curse me, and my Laundres too.

Further, the sequence is carefully managed to achieve variety of form and prosody. Couplets are used for poems 1, 2, 4, 7, 9, 10, 12, and 13; stanzas are the basis for poems 3, 5 (although the quatrains are not separated), 6, 8, and 11. The following scheme indicates the balance and yet variety achieved in prosodic terms, a main literary intention of the poet in the sequence:

Poem	Form	Meter	Form	Number of Lines
1	couplet	tetrameter		58
2	couplet	tetrameter		34

Poem	Form	Meter	Form	Number of Lines
3			5-line stanza	20
4	couplet	pentameter		18
5			4-line stanza	24
6			6-line stanza	24
7	couplet	tetrameter		24
8			4-line stanza	24
9	couplet	pentameter		24
10	couplet	pentameter		78
11			7-line stanza	35
12	couplet	pentameter		58
13	couplet	tetrameter		36

In all, the foregoing demonstrates that there is not an awkwardness of development of thought, nor a heavy, turgid effect; that there is much here to have employed Vaughan's time and ours;[19] and that Vaughan knew very well what he wanted to say and that the individual poems and the sequence do not fall apart. To my way of thinking, what is going on calls for praise of Vaughan's craft. It is a craft so subtle that the concept of sequence, once demonstrated, first strikes one like a jolt; but then one recognizes that each poem is different from what has been one's view of it before, that Donne's poetry is used only as foil, and that the Jonsonian sequence is the key to its form and content. The concept of sequence implies an authorial control, calling up Jonson's "maker," a craftsperson as concerned with literary creation as with personal feelings and thought. It has been only through the recognition of the poetic sequence as genre and its existence for the Amoret poems (as well as the numerical bases of various poems and the sequence as a whole) that we have been able to move to this kind of evaluation for this part of the canon of an otherwise well-regarded "devotional" poet. To follow well, but not imitate, the supreme maker himself, "Great *BEN*," calls for praise indeed.

PART TWO
Poetry Reread

9

Revisionism and Some Poems of Percy Bysshe Shelley

The glories of Percy Bysshe Shelley's creativity, his great intellect and great intellectual capacity, his enthusiasm for life and action, and his fine ear for sound but even more so for tone and attitude and emotional feelings have seemed to offer to many readers poetry unlike the allusive and densely textured matter of "Lycidas" or "The Waste Land." A footnote or two may be needed for a few of the works (such as "Adonais"), and helpful for others, but for the most part one simply has to read and think and relate. Something had happened to poetry for the popular reader between the seventeenth century and the early nineteenth, and something happened again for some of the poetry of the twentieth century. This is a point basic to the thesis of Earl Wasserman's *Subtler Language* (Baltimore, Md.: Johns Hopkins Press, 1959), an important book not only for its three essays on Shelley, but for its thesis. The knowledge, educational background, and interests of the reading public had so changed between the seventeenth and nineteenth centuries that the nature of the poetry—its language, its metaphors and images, indeed its literary qualities—had sharply changed. Or seemed to have changed.

This apparent poetic change to a kind of simpler substance, I suggest, lies at the base of the negative criticism of Romantic poetry, and especially of Shelley's, which one still runs across and which is simply wrong. An Irving Babbitt looks at the poetic output of 1780–1830 and sees only emotion and little thought (or if thought, a radicalism he cannot stomach); he sees excesses due to a lack of discipline and the ascendency of "feeling." And so the trite critical stance that Shelley reaches high emotional pitches but lacks the control demanded by the well-wrought urn of poetry—not only does the urn overflow but its form is misshapen by its contents, and ultimately he is interested only in himself.

I disagree emphatically, and primarily I disagree because I think such judgments are dependent on received dicta rather than on objective perusal of the poetry. But they are dependent as well on the omission of other kinds of critical approaches besides surface appeal and immediate reaction. Literary approaches to poetry—the limina, the thresholds that will take us into the world of the poem, the devices—include genre and mode as we have been looking at those matters in part one of this book, leading to "new" or at least different readings of texts, and such signs as structures, onomastics, the self-fashioned poetic voice, the poet asking comparison with others on like themes and like creative works, image patterns and metaphoric communications, numerological concerns, allusions and imitations, contextualizations in history, authorial presence. The change that Romantic poetry is purported to exhibit has bred a superficial reading of that poetry, too frequently concentrating *only* on emotional reaction or on the thought being immediately communicated. The poem is often disembodied to a series of words and their simplistic meanings only. Or the poet may be concerned with something momentous about life—some great philosophy, some new thought, some emotion not felt so meaningfully before—and a reader may glean much from the content, emotional import, and the "message." Yet we should also observe in the poem the craft that has created the emotion or the devices that have made the thought striking and memorable. And such a *literary* approach to Shelley's poetry will not only support its craft and techniques to the rejection of the clichés that hover around it, but will also etch more deeply and significantly that thought or emotion.

The reader and the reader response is (or should be) a manipulation by the author and the author's strategies, a point I trust I have made in chapter 1. A lack of expected reader response indicates a failing of the author or of the reader or of both. Reader response is orchestrated, and some of the notes are language and form and tone and structure. Nonetheless, reader response, even though it resemble expected reader response, is important of and by itself, and may always be more or less than that which is expected. Aside from literary structure (form), structure (or structures) defines a patterning that may exist elsewhere in literature, or in life, in the past as well as in the present. Such patterning, all aspects of which may not be within an author's understanding, implies a mythic base and thus archetypal elements; herein lies the importance of the term structuralism. The employment of structures in literature predicates an aesthetic distancing of the author, and its recognition and appreciation, some aesthetic distancing for the reader. Such distancing for the reader seems missing in the so-called affective approach as it has been advanced. While a work of literature may provide—perhaps should always provide—a sense of organically continuous creation, it also provides the container that delimits the rhizomatous and points toward a construction, if not a reconstruction, of the author's thought and experience. Although such a construction cannot be congruent with the author's thought and experience (because the author cannot define the thought or experience ontologically), neither is it the locus of a reader only, since it plots the coordinates that determine that locus. While the literary work allows exteriorization, it is the product of interiorization.

Normally I am concerned that we consider the name a poet gives to his work, including generic labels.[1] When Abraham Cowley calls his poems "Pindarique odes," we should determine in what way they are odes and Pindaric, observe how they have been (deliberately?) varied, and try to infer what Cowley meant by the label. These poems come out as Pindaric odes, though with a difference, not being literal translations but rather attempts at odic feeling and form and ideas, adjusted to a new context. We can see a similar employment of terminology in Ezra Pound's Confucian odes, concluding that for Pound inward form was more important than even any vaguely employed outward form. They are odes though not Pindaric, nor Horatian, and not "English." But what do we do with "Villanelle: The Psychological Hour"? Was Pound deliberately misnaming his poem? Even if we allow Pound to be referring to a form from before the seventeenth century, at which time it seems to have taken on its exacting repetitions and rhyme scheme, it still does not smack of any pastoralism or rurality. Can we *necessarily* define poetry, is what I must ask, on the basis of a poet's concept of terms or even a poet's concept of what has been done, how it has been done, and why it has been done?[2]

Some time ago I gave a talk to an audience of practicing (and unacademic) poets in which my main argument was the planned technique of a wide-ranging group of poets, whose poems, because of a lack of attention to technique on the part of critics, were often misread and misunderstood.[3] I stressed craft and those matters that I have been calling limina. I did not rule out the "spontaneous" poem, but I did, and do, emphasize the poet's calculated approach, attention to exact language, and the like. The audience was almost totally in happy agreement, glad that an academician recognized the sweat that made inspiration into an aesthetic experience. Some commented to the effect that such an approach even reveals techniques that the poet may have forgotten as part of the process of producing the finished poem. Two demurred. One (known and published) read some of his poetry (which is quite good) with explanation of its inception and corroborated my argument, as others in the audience remarked, although he still would not accept my conclusions. And I thought, yes, even poets do not necessarily know what they do when they create; some unconsciously evidence theory without the least perception that they do. The other who demurred read some of his poetry, and it was manifest why he disagreed: the poetry was a long concatenation of disparate images in false rhythms, lacking not only overall effect and pattern, but even direction. His "spontaneous" poetry should never be written down! To this demurrer his strung-out words were poetry; to me and at least many in the audience they were strung-out words, not in any kind of familial relationship with poetry.[4]

Can we, thus I ask, always be assured that the practitioner knows what he or she means or what has been done or why certain labels have been used? I take it that Joseph Warton's "Ode to Fancy," for example, tells us that he thought of the ode only in terms of treatment, certainly not in terms of form. It is perhaps a variation of the so-called Anacreontic ode, which is not an ode at all but a short poem on such subjects as wine, love, and song.[5] "Fancy" is an obvious companion for subject, but Warton's poem is not short, and it is much too serious to be Anacreontic. Perhaps its tetrameters are a kind of approximation of the Anacreontic meter (as developed in Cowley's poems); yet their "source" is Milton's "L'Allegro" and "Il Penseroso." I conclude that Warton used the term *ode* with only one aspect of generic definition in mind, the somewhat dignified, intellectual, unified treatment of a single subject. His use (frequently observable in the eighteenth century) does not limit subject or prescribe form, and in this particular case is not really exalted. He has "misused" the term and misnamed his poem, in a sense, but it represents the way in which labels do direct the reader into the poem and may set up a disjuncture between the expected and the actual in reader response. Indeed there may be differences between the theoretical world of definition and the applied world of practitioners' use of literary terms that literary critics must acknowledge. Accordingly, literary criticism should seek (1) to determine literary definition, (2) to infer the significance of an author's employment of a literary term (such as a generic label) for meaning in a work and for evaluation of it, and (3) to recognize the inapplicability of an author's employment of a literary term at times, leading perhaps to a rejection of certain meanings and evaluation of the work—a limen that should perhaps be rejected.

In part two of this book I examine a number of devices or thresholds into a reading of a poetic text, ranging over a number of seventeenth-century poets and calling into play the signs that genre, subgenre, and mode, as we have looked at them in part one, set up for the reading. Such devices and thresholds and genres/modes are provided by the writer writing, maintaining the presence of the author in the work. In this chapter I look at a few poems by Shelley rather than a seventeenth-century author, since his poetry has so often been inadequately read as just previously noted, to see how well-wrought the urn is and to raise the question of his self-centeredness and maintenance of a private voice in the lyrics. As we have seen in chapter 6, lyrics are not or at least need not be "private" in the sense of personal concern only. We thus engage poetry reread through attention to craft, to genre and mode, to devices, techniques, and other elements in the poet's foreconceit (or pre-text). Our rereading of poetry in the ensuing chapters endeavors to advance revised evaluations and greater insight into the writing process. These chapters supply "some liminal means to literary revisionism" and aim to eradicate some of the inadequate readings one finds of these and so many other authors—Shelley, yes, but also when we look at such liminal means in the work of, say, Charlotte Smith, Walter Savage Landor, Allen Ginsberg, or Judith Wright.

The sonnet entitled "Feelings of a Republican on the Fall of Bonaparte" seems to be a kind of English sonnet (or Shakespearean or Elizabethan sonnet) since it rhymes *abba cdcd efef gg;* that is, it consists of three quatrains and a couplet if we look only at its rhyme scheme. But the three groups of four lines do not separate from each other so as to constitute quatrains, nor are the last two lines a real couplet. Observe the frequent enjambment, actually seven of the fourteen lines, 50 percent, a very high percentage:

> I hated thee, fallen tyrant! I did groan
> To think that a most unambitious slave,
> Like thou, shouldst dance and revel on the grave
> Of Liberty. Thou mightst have built thy throne
> Where it has stood even now: thou didst prefer
> A frail and bloody pomp which Time has swept
> In fragments towards oblivion. Massacre,
> For this I prayed, would on thy sleep have crept,
> Treason and Slavery, Rapine, Fear, and Lust,
> And stifled thee, their minister. I know
> Too late, since thou and France are in the dust,
> That Virtue owns a more eternal foe
> Than Force or Fraud: old Custom, legal Crime,
> And bloody Faith the foulest birth of Time.

Shelley alters the form to create coherence for the poem as if it were a lyric of one unit. It is not, of course. The volta or turn occurs in the fourth foot of line 10: "And stifled thee, their minister. I know." With its turn of thought in the reduced sestet, presenting the philosophic realization that has grown out of the circumstances recorded by the enlarged octave, the sonnet shows itself to be instead a variant of the Petrarchan form. What is important in determining the genre or subgenre of a poem is what that classification tells us about the author's intention. The subgenre Petrarchan sonnet indicates that the author's main point—a perception that he has come to, a message he wishes to communicate, an emotional tug that he has come to realize (in other words, that which is somehow different from what he previously knew or thought or felt)—lies in the sestet, as we have previously observed. Here Shelley articulates for himself and us the readers that worse than any armed power against man or any fraudulent action against him is man's attitude of faith in that which has been custom for him and made law—whether political, social, or intellectual. The octave has provided the experience lying outside himself that has driven home the perception of the sestet. Here it is the abuse of the people by Napoleon that provides backdrop, a situation that should and did call forth invective against Napoleon as tyrant. But Shelley acknowledges that he has been wrong: this was better than the political and social world that has taken over again with Napoleon's fall. I suspect that few have read the poem this way, at least with only one or two readings. It is the subgenre Petrarchan sonnet that points the way to interpretation.

The sonnet owes much to Milton's fifteenth sonnet on Thomas Fairfax, one of the leading generals of the Parliamentary army in its fight against the Royalists:

> *Fairfax,* whose name in armes through *Europe* rings,
>   Filling each mouth with envy, or with praise,
>   And all her jealous monarchs with amaze,
>   And rumors loud, that daunt remotest kings,
> Thy firm unshak'n vertue ever brings
>   Victory home, though new rebellions raise
>   Thir Hydra heads, and the fals *North* displaies
>   Her brok'n league, to imp her serpent wings,
> O yet a nobler task awaits thy hand;
>   For what can Warrs but endless warr still breed,
>   Till Truth, and Right from Violence be freed,
> And Public Faith cleard from the shamefull brand
>   Of Public Fraud. In vain doth Valour bleed
>   While Avarice, and Rapine share the land.

Unfortunately, Fairfax, rather than fight those specters of the aftermath of war that Milton cites in the sestet, retired to his country estate and the Interregnum proceeded with its failure to solve those many problems Milton foresaw. Both sonnets are Petrarchan. Shelley's, like Milton's eighteenth or nineteenth sonnet, displaces the volta, like his sixteenth sonnet ends with couplet rhyme (though neither is Elizabethan), and like his eleventh through twenty-third sonnets so heightens enjambment that the reader cannot break up the poem into neat units like quatrains and couplets. The reader must move along being led by the thought, not some mechanical device like the end of a line of sight or a period or semicolon or that kind of strong end punctuation. The lines that are not enjambed have commas only, commas separating syntactic interrupters or a series, not punctuation to separate thought. The sonnet, like some of Milton's, sounds as if it were a single fourteen-line lyric; but it is a Petrarchan sonnet with a difference.

Certainly a major avenue to evaluative criticism—not only literary criticism—is recognition of form and the author's, composer's, or artist's manipulation of that form, rather than rigid, slavish imitation of the form. Shelley has taken a sonnet form, kept within its bounds, and yet altered it in terms of rhyme scheme, volta, enjambment, and other structures. By other structures I refer to the strong medial breaks lying at various positions in the line. In line 1 the break is in the middle of the fourth foot; in line 4 after the second foot; in line 5 after the third foot; in line 7 in the middle of the fourth foot; in line 10 after the fourth foot; in line 13 after the second foot—a total of six strong medial pauses in a poem of only fourteen lines, a very high percentage, we find, if we compare Shakespeare or Spenser.

Is the urn not well-wrought? Has the urn been misshapen? Has it indeed fractured into shards? Perhaps if one construes it as an Elizabethan sonnet, perhaps if one demands imitative exactness of structure and form, perhaps if one sees the importance of the sonnet in the fall of Bonaparte rather than in the feelings of a Republican, perhaps then a reader would answer these questions in the affirmative and cast Shelley's poem into artistic chaos. But that reader would be so wrong, and so imperceptive of controlled art. The nature of this rereading poetry leads to a different reading and a different evaluation.

A very different kind of poem, "The Poet's Lover," offers a constrastive urn. At first appearance it may seem a traditional and ordered poem, built on the heroic couplet, but the last line is abruptly cut off with only seven syllables. And then we notice that the first line is only eight syllables. And then we realize that the last line is a trochee, two iambs, and a catalectic syllable, and the first line is an iamb and what sounds to our ear and reading as two anapests. And even the couplet rhyme fails: *aa bb cc dd e f g h.*

> I am as a spirit who has dwelt
> Within his heart of hearts, and I have felt
> His feelings, and have thought his thoughts, and known
> The inmost converse of his soul, the tone
> Unheard but in the silence of his blood,

> When all the pulses in their multitude
> Image the trembling calm of summer seas.
> I have unlocked the golden melodies
> Of his deep soul, as with a master-key,
> And loosened them and bathed myself therein—
> Even as an eagle in a thunder-mist
> Clothing his wings with lightning.

The lines of the poem have been so manipulated that the reader does not at first realize that the first line is defective or that the rhyme scheme is abandoned—only the abruptness of the last line has jarred our hearing. The first line seems perfectly all right because it rhymes with the next line with which it is enjambed. And the lack of rhyme in the last four lines is acceptable to our ears because the line preceding (l. 8) rhymes with its preceding line (l. 7), but that line yields a major break in the poem, separating the first half from the second. (That is, the last five lines, which break in structure with the preceding lines, each end in a different rhyme word, but the first of those five lines rhymes with the immediately preceding last line of the first part.) In the first half the lover relates herself to the poet, emphasizing his heart, feelings, thought, soul, blood; in the second half the lover—the muse, that is—relates what she has wrought for the poet, emphasizing her inspiring of him. The center of the poem is displaced: seven lines and five lines; symmetry is not possible, just as it is not quite possible between the first and last lines. The first half, dominated by the poet, is regular of rhyme scheme and almost regular of meter; the second half, dominated by the muse, is not regular of rhyme scheme and, in its last line, stentorially not regular of meter. The muse thus declares that the poet, inspired, can reject the traditional and ordered and create his own poetic.

Despite the beauty of symmetrical snowflakes, art has long been influenced by such ideas as Pythagoras's that the ideal center in a group of ten lies within 6, not between 5 and 6; and by such ideas as the golden section or mean of painting, where ratios of roughly .618 and .382 are the ideal proportion between divisions. The golden mean of the poem lies in line 8, the first line of the second part, which reads: "I have unlocked the golden melodies," the middle, third foot, being "the gold." Coincidence? Mystic improbability? I think not. Shelley is talking about that inspiring muse who unlocks the soul with a master-key so that golden melodies will flow forth. The key is purposeful structure, he implies, and he has moved from heart to feelings to thoughts to soul to pulsing blood, in the first section, which is capped by the oxymoron "trembling calm," a most exact image of the poet's inspiration. The final two lines call up the image of God, the eagle and the thunderer, too startlingly bright in all his glory for mere man to look upon (just as Moses could not)—but the poet, inspired by the Muse-God, ah, he will view his muse, her wings clothed with the lightning of his golden melodies.

Surely this poem is a well-wrought urn; surely it does not shatter or become misshapen; surely the craft of structure and image and literary device are so intertwined with thought that no one should gainsay Shelley's achievement in it.

The year 1818 was a difficult one for Shelley largely because of the falling out with Byron, and "Julian and Maddelo" provides some of the record of that year. Another important poem was "Stanzas, Written in Dejection, Near Naples," and there is a long commentary by Mary Shelley on his illness and their life at the time of its composition. Clearly it is autobiographical and must be read first on that level. But the poem is also concerned with problems that all humans face, and its literary form and language demand comparison with other works.

The poem has ten stanzas of nine lines each, rhyming *ababbcbcc,* in iambic tetrameter with a closing alexandrine. This is a variant of the Spenserian stanza, whose only difference is that the first eight lines are iambic pentameter. We perhaps remember that Byron's "Childe Harold's Pilgrimage" employs the Spenserian stanza and that the fourth and last canto was written in 1817 and published in 1818. The stanza that Shelley devised thus suggests epical longings, but the tetrameters reduce the heroic element to a merely mortal level, and the flow of thought is constantly cut off within the stanza by end stoppage. Contrast with the journey and quest theme of epic, and particularly with the Byronic version of it in true Spenserian stanzas, is paramount: the poem is sedentary and concerned with the now of time. Here is the third stanza as example:

> Alas! I have nor hope nor health,
>> Nor peace within nor calm around,
> Nor that content surpassing wealth
>> The sage in meditation found,
>> And walked with inward glory crowned—
> Nor fame, nor power, nor love, nor leisure.
>> Others I see whom these surround—
> Smiling they live, and call life pleasure;—
> To me that cup has been dealt in another measure.

Only one line allows enjambment, and that is not strong. The rhythm is constantly broken up and the phrases tend to smallness. Further the *c* rhyme is weak (feminine), as it is also in the second stanza. Forty-five of the words are monosyllables; only fourteen have more than one syllable, and eleven of these have only two syllables, such as "alas," "around," "pleasure." The poem is controlled to be reductive and confined, clearly the proper note for dejection and for sharp contrast with something like:

> I stood in Venice on the Bridge of Sighs;
> A palace and a prison on each hand;
> I saw from out the wave her structures rise
> As from the stroke of the enchanter's wand:
> A thousand years their cloudy wings expand
> Around me, and a dying Glory smiles
> O'er the far times, when many a subject land
> Look'd to the winged Lion's marble piles,
> Where Venice sate in state, throned on her hundred isles!

Byron's first stanza of the fourth canto, using more words since it employs pentameter, has fifty-seven monosyllables and sixteen words with more than one syllable, a rather rough equivalency to Shelley's; yet the verse seems expansive, not confined, shooting off to eternity of time.

Still, regardless of the biographical impetus in Shelley's writing the stanzas, the poem deals with a kind of subgenre: the dejection poem or ode. The form of the poem is like what came to be the English version of the Horatian ode—a repeated stanza of almost any length and shape—for example, Thomas Gray's "On a Distant Prospect of Eton College" or John Keats's "To a Nightingale." But in terms of the ode "Stanzas" is ironic, for it does not celebrate heroes or victorious accomplishment but defeat and despair, indeed, the failure of heroic stance and deed. The tone is the opposite of that which exalts, uplifts, or inspires. To allow a pretension to the odic enforces the lack of the heroic in the poem. Rather than the epic involving humankind or nations and rather than the ode involving praise of a hero or a nation, "Stanzas" emphasizes the "I," the one. And the "I" shows tendencies of being happy in his dejection: "Some might lament that I were cold, / As I, when this sweet day is gone," or "For I am one / Whom men love not," or "this day, which . . . / Will linger, though enjoyed, like joy in memory yet."

Is the poem only on the level of "I," however? Like the imagery of nature that lies about him on the shore near Naples, the "I" is localized and real. And like the imagery that in some form is open to us all—"The winds, the birds, the ocean floods, / The City's voice itself"—the "I" is anyone who has "Nor fame, nor power, nor love, nor leisure," or thinks he has not, though these surround others who "Smiling . . . live, and call life pleasure."

Many are they who insult the day "with this untimely moan," and even come to revel in their despair. Is the tone much different from Shakespeare's "When, in disgrace with fortune and men's eyes, / I all alone beweep my outcast state"? Or is the "I" much different in relationship to a universal "I" than it is in Coleridge's "Well, they are gone, and here I must remain, / This lime-tree bower my prison!" Should we read the Shelley poem differently in this regard from the way we read, say, LeRoi Jones's (Imamu Amiri Baraka's) "Preface to a Twenty Volume Suicide Note"?[6] We recognize the same note of personal dejection, but the poem itself says something more to a general reader who can identify with the seeming biographical voice in the poem.

I daresay a student of poetry of the Romantic period, and particularly of Shelley's poetry, will be most concerned with the biographical element in "Stanzas," and it certainly is important. The antiromantic and anti-Shelleyan will find fodder for that tired old horse of emotionalism and sentiment. But I, non-Romantic student that I am, look at the poem as poem and find two notable things: a structure and language and techniques that are consonant with the unabashed subject, and that in fact highlight and extend it, and a picture of one man so frequently duplicated in some way by reason of some kind of circumstance, psychologically drawn and psychologically valid.

What I find in Shelley stresses the imaginative and the varied (for craft is so important to evaluation of literature), and this leads to a dynamic quality that allows repeated readings with their own variety and their own recognition of further craft. These last two poems I have chosen to look at require no footnotes for the uninformed reader, as Wasserman's thesis implies, and the Napoleon sonnet calls for very little and very common historical knowledge. (One does not even have to know about Count Metternich and the aftermath of Napoleon's fall.) And so perhaps it is that social and educational change in the world of readers between the seventeenth and the nineteenth centuries has, ultimately and unfortunately, led to some of the anti-Romantic stands. But treating a poem as a poem finds the poetry of the Romantics worthy, and pleasurable, and intellectually satisfying. Viewed as craft, these poems of Shelley rise in evaluation; aware of pre-text, the reader is better able to analyze, interpret, and evaluate.

10

Neo-Latin Poetry and Henry Vaughan

Popular as seventeenth-century poetry is, and despite the attention that has been paid to many of its poets, little critical evaluation has been given the neo-Latin verse of such authors as Richard Crashaw, George Herbert, Andrew Marvell, or Henry Vaughan.[1] What studies have appeared have usually been historical or textual, and have not generally proceeded to consider the thesis that neo-Latin poetry may offer the requisites of highly evaluated poetry in English. The seventeenth century is both the waning of the Renaissance and the emergence of a new world dominated by a rising middle class whose education would become less and less formal and whose literary taste would become more and more narrowed to "meaning"—a process accelerated and entrenched by nineteenth- and twentieth-century readers and too often capitulated to by authors themselves. And so works were produced at decreasing occasions in the seventeenth century in a Latin text that was still viable as literary medium for the educated. The neo-Latin author was led into his medium, usually, by way of scholastic requirement or academic competition—as John Milton was in producing the Gunpowder Plot poems and the death tributes to such as the Bishop of Ely and Lancelot Andrewes. At times Latin was the means of reaching—it was hoped—a wide geographic audience of many tongues, and so the romances of John Barclay or Samuel Gott's *Nova Solyma*. And then there was the private aura of a neo-Latin poem in this age of language decline—Milton's "Ad Patrem" or "Epitaphium Damonis." But further, the neo-Latin poem became a kind of "trial balloon," for example, Andrew Marvell's "Hortus," which came to be a preliminary working of "The Garden"—not that Marvell in writing "Hortus" intended to compose the English poem. Rather the working out of ideas, images, allusive concepts, and prosodic experiments often proved a salutory influence on English materials because of the problems that a less common, a more intermediary language created in expressing those ideas or images or allusive concepts, and the problems that strict (or at least stricter) quantitative verse posed. Working in Latin the poet had to find words that clearly denoted his meaning but that also allowed the developed usages in both classical and medieval times to emerge.

We can compare as obvious examples Crashaw's Latin and English epigrams "In beatae Virginis verecundiam" and "On the Blessed Virgins bashfulnesse."[2] Approaching a sexual indiscretion, the Latin says that the Virgin keeps her eyes on her lap ("In gremio . . . sua lumina Virgo / Ponat?") because heaven ("coelum") is there. The English is: "on her lap she casts her humble Eye"; "'Tis Heav'n 'tis Heaven she sees." A second Latin epigram[3] on the same subject indicates that God is there on her lap ("Illic jam Deus est") and works more clearly on the paradox that one must descend before one can rise, that one must be humble before one can be exalted: "Oculus jam Virginis ergò, / Ut caelum videat, dejiciendus erit." The English epigram likewise declares, "Heavens God there lyes" and "This new Guest to her Eyes new Lawes hath given / 'Twas once *looke up,* 'tis now *looke downe* to Heaven." Each Latin epigram is two elegiac distichs; the English is four iambic pentameter couplets. (The iambic pentameter couplet was the usual English rendering of the elegiac couplet.) Repetitions or echoes or contrasts of words or forms of words occur in the first epigram: "sua lumina . . . / Ponat?" of the first distich contrasts in position and quantity with "sua lumina ponat?" in the second distich. Likewise "ubi meliùs" of the second line, being a short, long, short, short, long, with a pause after "-ùs" and before the echo of "poneret," is contrastingly reprised in the next line, "ubi, quàm coelo, meliùs," where the position and interrupting phrase give the two words quantities of short, short, short, short, long, but now the "-ùs" is the first syllable of the dactyl "-ùs sua." In the English epigram "faire starre" of line 3 contrasts with "fairer Spheare" of line 4, with the word "fixt" lying in medial position in both lines, as syllable 6 and syllable 4. Lines 5 and 6 offer contrastingly positioned and reversed phrases, "'tis Heaven she sees" and "She can see heaven." The meaning inherent in "gremium" as both lap and center is picked up in the English version, which talks of "her lap" and "a fairer Spheare." And "lumen" implies a source of light, which translates into English as "the faire starre," with mythic concepts of the stars as the guides to night wanderers to keep them safe from "ignes fatui." Finally we should note that in both the Latin and the English epigrams the language of Virgin and Son, lap and center, and light and eyes looking where no light breaks (as Dylan Thomas described it) points up the sexuality of the poems, indicating, however, that the bashfulness of the mother of Jesus, observed in her downward gaze, is paradoxically not caused by that about which most humans would seem bashful.

The entry into neo-Latin poetry is not different from the means to

understand poetry in English, as these examples show. Here our appreciation of the epigram, the connotations of words and images, the contrasts in
use and placement of language, sometimes creating paradox and irony, all
allow for an enlightened reading of these poems, only the Latin negating
communication for some. For those students of poetry knowing Latin,
however, there can be in such Latin verse whatever one finds of importance in English verse, and the means to such reading lie in like devices.

There are ten extant poems in Latin written by Henry Vaughan,[4] and
these will provide a basis for the thesis that Latin poetry should be looked
at as poetry. Eight are in elegiacs, one in hexameters, and one employs
alternating hexameter and iambic dimeter (the meter of Horace's *Epodes,*
Nos. 14 and 15). The lack of attention paid to the neo-Latin poetry
of otherwise much-discussed seventeenth-century poets can be seen in
Vaughan's "In Etesiam lachrymantem." It appears as fifth poem in a series
of seven poems on Etesia, six of which are in English, published in *Thalia
Rediviva* (1678). These are undoubtedly early poems, perhaps written
during the middle 1640s when the Amoret series was composed, although
Amoret and Etesia are not the same person, we now all agree. All that
James D. Simmonds says of this poem, for example, is, "The description of
her 'charming grief' in the Latin 'In Etesiam lachrymantem' tends to
humanize her still more and to intensify the impression that she accepts as
reluctantly as he the 'ill fortune' of their parting."[5] (Simmonds does not
mention any of the other Latin poems.) The poem is in elegiacs, which, as
noted before, is usually translated into English as iambic pentameter
couplets. Thus the sequence consists of a symmetric pattern of meters: two
poems in tetrameter couplets, one poem in pentameter couplets, one in
tetrameter couplets, the poem in elegiacs, and two in tetrameter couplets.
The Latin poem is the shortest, the lengths being 54 lines, 48, 22, 14, 8, 20,
and 22. But we recognize that in combination with "To Etesia parted from
him, and looking back" (14 lines), we have 22 lines to compare more
sharply with the preceding "To Etesia looking from her Casement at the
full Moon" (22 lines) and with the last two, "To Etesia going beyond Sea"
(20 lines) and "Etesia absent" (22 lines). Thus, in the sequence are two
longer poems of introduction to Etesia and his love for her, a poem of
transition that implies their separation through the imagery of the moon
on which Etesia is gazing, two poems indicating the lovers' parting and
Etesia's regret, and two poems placed in time after she has left. "To Etesia
parted from him, and looking back" picks up some imagery of the moon from
the preceding poem—Diana the huntress, the coldness of the moon despite
its light (its supposed fire), and its changeability; the Latin poem picks
up other aspects of that imagery—the *Sydera* (the stars) that *decorant*
(grace) the laughter *suis lachrymis* (with their tears; the earlier poem had

said, "She fed me with the tears of Starrs" and "To some in smiles . . . she broke"), and the clouds and the face and its beauteous complexion. Generally "To Etesia parted from him, and looking back" in fourteen lines (and significantly the central poem of the sequence) is directly connected with the last eight lines of "To Etesia looking from her Casement at the full Moon" (which is broken into fourteen and eight lines), and "In Etesiam lachrymantem" in eight lines is directly connected with the first fourteen lines of that poem. The three poems together (pentameter couplets, tetrameter couplets, and, as it were, pentameter couplets) create a kind of palindromic symmetry, with the implications of the first poem being realized in the next two in reversed order.

The Latin poem is basically description: Etesia's grief, her tears, her cheeks. It is quite different from "To *Amoret* WEEPING," although that poem has a similar function in its sequence to that which Simmonds assigned for this poem in the Etesia sequence. It ends with a couplet in which Chaldeans are alluded to and that contrasts the paradox of *formosa dies & sine nube* (a beautiful day without clouds) and the destroying effect (indicated by *perit*) of her parting tears, which are metaphorically rain. The paradox is implied in the earlier poem, in which the moon is surrounded by clouds but is set in golden flames. That paradox gives way to one in the Latin poem when the clouds disappear but the tears (or rain) fall and the golden flames die or are ruined. The Latin poem is tightly connected to others of its sequence by meaning and imagery, and serves in a structural pattern that creates comparisons and contrasts.

Chaldeans are evoked because of their supposed ability at soothsaying, which developed out of their alleged knowledge of astronomy. Vaughan suggests that Etesia's leaving may be part of a natural course of events such as the way in which rain, darkness, ill weather may suddenly replace bright and beautiful days (a kind of reprise of the "sad *Eclipses*" of the poem on the moon), or it may be that *fortuna fatigat* (ill fortune plagues) him, and only the Chaldeans' soothsaying will be able to answer *quae me fortuna fatigat* now and perhaps in the future. The final syllables of the first six lines all end with little stress, though of course all are quantitatively long, breathing a kind of soft and lingering quality to the lines; only lines 3 and 4 are enjambed. But the last two lines end strongly with finalizing sounds. Note too such lines as 5, with the echoes of *t, g, s, l,* and *m* (especially *-ma* in *simillima gemma*), and in line 6 of *-as* in *vivas* and *rosas*, each constituting the end of one of the two half-verses.

If one read and understood Latin, as Vaughan and others in the seventeenth century did, would not one find in this Latin poem those things that are praised in English poems of a similar Petrarchesque series? For me, the Latin has more "tone" and "mood" than its English translation, and that "tone" and "mood" are the result of the collocation of sounds and stresses and the images evoked by the words, as in *veneres,* the looks of love, if you will, or *irrigat* (sprinkle), with its implication that *tepido imbre* (a warm shower; here, the tears) will always be needed to flourish *vivas rosas* (living roses).

To take another poem: "Ad fluvium Iscam" has more to interest us than just its meter (alternate hexameter and iambic dimeter) or its relationship to the English poem "To the River *Isca,*" which begins the volume *Olor Iscanus* (1651). There are similarities of subject matter naturally in the two poems, and the reference to Orpheus in the second couplet of the English poem returns here in the final Latin distich. *Olor Iscanus* prints poems generally addressed to friends (not quite all), followed by renderings from Ovid, Ausonius, Boethius, and Casimir Sarbiewski, and a poem on Casimir in answer to Horace's ode "Beatus Ille qui procul negotiis." Then comes "Ad fluvium Iscam" and three other Latin poems, two to friends and one called "Ad Echum." Thus the Latin poem on the Usk introduces the Latin poems just as the English poem about the river had introduced English poems, the two groups being separated by English renderings of Latin works. The Latin poems of the volume exhibit elegiacs in the dedicatory poem and in the two central poems of the last group, which are preceded by "Ad fluvium Iscam" and followed by "Ad Echum" in different meters. The meters and languages were probably chosen and arranged to demonstrate Vaughan's right to the title of the Swan of Usk, and thus the reference to Orpheus as "discerpti . . . Thracis" (Orpheus torn to pieces and scattered) and as divine and old, first, obliquely reprises Vaughan's concern with the civil wars that had recently disrupted his world[6] and, second, the hopes for his work stated in the dedicatory poem,

> Si pius es, ne plura petas; Satur Ille recedat
> Qui sapit, & nos non Scripsimus Insipidis,[7]

and in the English poem,

> When I am layd to rest hard by thy streams
> And my Sun sets, where first it sprung in beams,
> I'le leave behind me such a large, kind light,
> As shall redeem thee from oblivious night, . . .
> As shall from age to age thy fair name lead
> 'Till Rivers leave to run, and men to read.

The meter of the Latin poem on the Usk may have been chosen because its English counterpart also vacillates: 34 pentameter couplets, 38 tetrameters, 4 dimeters, 6 pentameters, and 4 tetrameters. The Latin iambics are all long, long, short, and long, except for the first foot of line 8; the alternate lines are thus all strong lines dominated by enjambment except for line 8. This line has some of the most interesting images of paradox in the poem, and the slightly weakened first foot may thus be ironic. While the river that is addressed persists through all time, it will endure through its faithful (never-failing) water's "hardening" into a *fidelis latex* (in the nominative case, making it already a *fidelis latex,* an always faithful stream). The water is hardened and endures; the river is already enduring and will persist *oevumque per omne* (through all eternity); and it is by analogy possible for Vaughan to endure as a poet, though *Coelumque mortales terit* (Heaven wears down mortal men), through the publication of the volume we are reading. The hardened water recalls the miraculous gushing of the waters from the flintstone in Psalm 114, a Passover psalm, and Vaughan's emblem prefixed in drawing and Latin poem to *Silex Scintillans* (1650).

The last poem, "Ad Echum" (To Echo), iterates this version of "Not Marble Nor the Gilded Monuments" we have just looked at in its title, in lines like "Nec cedant aevo stellis" (May they not yield to the stars in age), and in the allusion to the Phoenix. Somewhat like Narcissus, beloved of Echo, man must exhibit enough self-love that he will believe he has been given the "secreta" and enough trust in himself that he will publish his work. The title page of *Olor Iscanus,* which declares that it was "Published by a Friend," is belied. The adapted epigraph from Vergil's second Georgic (486), "Flumina amo, Sylvasq; Inglorius—" reinforces that conclusion and points through psychological reversal to Vaughan's hope that no longer would he be "Inglorius."

The meter, aside from its demonstration in the volume of his ability to write in hexameters, was, I would expect, specifically chosen for its associations. This is heroic verse used for works of moment, work that has some pretension to transcend the personal and ephemeral. There is an invocation to Echo; the poem divides into half, the second part being a prayer of hope. The allusion to the *nubila flammae Panchaeae* (from the smoke of Panchaean flame [i.e., incense]), cited in Vergil's second Georgic among other places, as well as the Phoenix symbol, observes that life comes through death. That Panchaia was an island in the Red Sea accounts for its use here in Vaughan's heroic poem, for the picture he draws is an edenic one after strife and escape (he is, as it were, midstream):

> lucida sempèr
> Et satiata sacro aeterni medicamine veris . . .
> Sic spiret Muscata Comas, & Cynnama passim![8]

Perhaps we think of the Song of Songs, with its spices and cinnamon and its "fountain of gardens, a well of living waters, and streams from Lebanon" (4.15). The Usk has become a river of inspiration and a river of passage like the Red Sea to "haec Incaedua devia sylvae, / Anfractusq; loci dubios, et lustra repandam."

Read aloud, what will strike one first about "Authoris (de se) Emblema" from *Silex Scintillans*, Part I (1650), is the fitful interrupted rhythm of the lines. At most six lines of the sixteen-line poem allow enjambment, and only three and a half lines have an uninterrupted flow. More usual is line 5: "Surdus eram, mutusq; Silex: Tu, (quanta tuorum" or line 8: "Posse negas, & vim, Vi, superare paras." The contrast with the long flowing lines of "Jordanis" from *Thalia Rediviva* indicates that the latter poem aims at an equivalency to the flow of the river. Only four lines of this twenty-line poem are enjambed, but typical is the couplet:

> Ah! Solyma infoelix rivis obsessa prophanis!
> Amisit Genium porta Bethesda suum.

"Authoris (de se) Emblema" refers to the engraved title page of the 1650 edition—both title page and poem are omitted in the second, 1655 edition— that shows the thunderbolts of God held by a hand (God's) extending from a cloud and striking a rocky mass shaped like a heart. One can discern faces within that "heart," which has a bright side (the right) and a dark side (the left), signifying man's two natures and symbolic positional concepts of God and Satan. The dark side is set on fire by the thunderbolts and from this hard heart, this flint, come tears (water). The oxymoronic fire/water is commonplace for God's miraculous actions and is most prominently remembered from Dante's "Inferno," where Satan is half-encased in ice amidst the fires of Hell. But the collocation of the two as miracle underlies Psalm 114, a celebration of the Exodus, God's leading Moses and the Israelites through the Red Sea from the bondage of Pharaoh (identified with Satan). The poem makes use of the psalm. (Mythically, the Red Sea is Phlegethon, the river of fire or blood, separating the sixth circle of Hell, that of the heretics, from the seventh circle, that of the violators against one's neighbor, against oneself, and against God.) The hardening of the heart of Pharaoh (and all followers of Satan) is repeatedly cited in Exodus. The emblem, thus, says (at least as device to introduce his poetic collection that begins with the poem "Regeneration") that Vaughan considered himself one who had not properly been one of God's children, who had now been touched by the workings of God and had been saved, and who had achieved a private exodus from the bondage of the past. Clearly once this had occurred (even if fiction) Vaughan could not logically repeat it, and so neither emblem nor poem appears in the second edition.[9] (The epigraph on the title page of the second edition from Job

35.10, 11 suggests, in fact, that there were times when Vaughan felt that God had not continued to be an inspirational presence. The volume, however, is dedicated to Jesus Christ and the first poem is "Ascension-day," making the focus of *Silex Scintillans* II faith rather than an emphasis on more personal matters and change as *Silex Scintillans* I does. Even "Faith" from the first collection describes his achievement of faith; it is not a statement of faith.]

The poem on the emblem, a "private" poem with even "(de se)" of the title in parentheses and the only poem in Latin in the volume, describes the emblem in terms of his own heart: "Silex" (5), "Accedis proprior, molemq;, & Saxea rumpis / Pectora, fitq; Caro, quod fuit ante Lapis. / En lacerum! Coelosq; tuos ardentia tandem / Fragmenta, & liquidas ex Adamante genas" (9–12).[10] He has been brought to God, and his "hard" heart has been shattered by God's force. The last two lines, "Moriendo, revixi; / Et fractas jam sum ditior inter opes" ("By dying, I have been reborn; and now amidst ruined treasures I am richer than ever"), have been almost consistently interpreted biographically. Personal misfortunes are accepted, it seems, and reasons for them have been suggested as lying in Vaughan's civil-war experiences (the poems are generally dated in the late 1640s) or in the death of his brother William in July 1648. The poetic collection has been read as a "conversion." Any of this may have truth in it, but the title page, this poem, the dedication, and "Regeneration"[11] and others do not necessarily demand that reading. So much Herbert, and Donne of the Holy Sonnets, exists in the background that the concept of "conversion" should be discounted, suggesting rather that these poems represent poetic endeavors that at most offer a sincere awareness of God and of man's "depravity." While this does not obliterate a biographical context (for example, the "they" of "They are all gone into the world of light" may have been specific people for Vaughan—not just William, in any case), it does stand on the other side of the too-frequent critical position that all or almost all poetry has a biographical fountainhead. Psychologically there can be made a case for this kind of poem as opposed to that, for this subject rather than some other, but there is great difference between the two approaches. The biographical says, "This is what the poem is about"; the intentional (psychological and otherwise) on the part of the author says, "This is what the poem is"; but the unintentionally psychological on the part of the author says, "This is what we can discern about the author's psychological makeup." I do not mean for that last statement to be so restrictive as it sounds: all three ways may be avenues into interpretation and into understanding of the author. I refer in that rather unqualified statement to approaches that are rather unqualified. The first approach is what we generally have been offered for Vaughan's

Silex Scintillans, with the third approach little touched though it should really be implied as a consequence of the first. What I argue is that the first approach be generally rejected as too limited and insufficiently "literary," that the third approach, though viable, be given a wider-scaled analysis than any studies heretofore, and that the second approach—for example, Vaughan's intentionality in using the image of the flint in his emblematic Latin poem—defines his poetic strategies. The "intentionality on the part of the author" is what can be seen as the "intentionality of the poem." The collection is an organized series of poems purposefully drawn from the literature of religious experience, ending with a poem, "Begging," that has the meter of a litany and the substance of a footprayer. Vaughan's is, as the title page tells us, a variation on Herbert's *The Temple:* "Or Sacred Poems and Priuate Eiaculations" repeats Herbert's "Sacred Poems and Private Ejaculations."

The rhythms of the emblem poem are controlled to create a fitful state; it is made private, to which the Latin contributes, to enhance the fiction of "regeneration"; and it achieves emphatic effusion by its capitalization ("Vox," "Silex," "Curam," "Jamq;," "Amorem," "Vi," "Saxea," "Caro," "Lapis," "Coelosq;," "Adamante," "Petras," "Scopulosq;," "O," and "Moriendo") and by its exclamations ("quanta tuorum / Cura tibi est!," "En lacerum!," "O populi providus usq; tio!," "Quam miranda tibi manuṣ est!"). It is in elegiacs probably because of its subject matter and what it introduces.

In contrast is "Jordanis," an incidental Latin poem also in elegiacs, perhaps prompted by Herbert's two very different "Jordan" poems. I say "incidental" because it holds no relationship with the other two Latin poems following it or with the English poems preceding and following. While groups of poems in *Thalia Rediviva* do work together, there is no overall structure to the volume, no clear interplay of subject, form, effect, or thought. Possibly "Jordanis" was written around the time of the Herbertian poems of either *Silex Scintillans* group; but it does not fit into those poems' "narrative" or organization and so was held back. The poem divides into two: eight lines spoken by the river Jordan, praising itself and the sun and the stars against other rivers "combusta pyropis" (burning gold-bronze). The reason for such self-praise is given in the last twelve lines, spoken by the poet: the Jordan was "domini balnea Sancta mei!" (my Lord's holy bath). Other rivers surrounding Jerusalem have been defiled by the heathens, but "Mansit Christocolâ Jordanis unus aqua" (Jordan alone remains Christian water).

The poem does not really fit into any of Vaughan's series of poems (not even the Christ-oriented ones of *Silex Scintillans* II); the "Pious thoughts and Ejaculations" that precede it in *Thalia Rediviva* ("To his booke, Looking back," "The Shower," "Discipline," "The Ecclipse," "Affliction,"

"Retirement," "The Revival," "The Day-Spring," "The Recovery," "The Nativity" [written 1656], "The true Christmas," "The Request") seem not even vaguely related. The rather long and enjambed lines of the first section, that spoken by the river itself, should be noted and contrasted with the second section, the poet's lines, with only one run-on. The continuant sound of *m* predominates in the first section (fifteen instances), with liquid *l* not far behind (eleven instances); the sound of harsher *k* dominates in the second section (fourteen instances), with stops like *d* not far behind (ten instances).[12]

"Jordanis" is an incidental and minor poem in the Vaughan canon. It may have served a purpose connected with artistic development of other poems. It may have been intended at one time as an integral poem amidst others. Its presence in *Thalia Rediviva* perhaps represents as well as any of the poems a gathering together of inedited items. In any case it has interest as a metrical endeavor by a celebrated poet. If not so well as others, it suggests that a study of the poetry of Henry Vaughan cannot omit consideration of his Latin verse and be adequate. And this may be echoed in talking of the neo-Latin poems of Herbert, Milton, Marvell, and so many others.

11

Milton's Shorter Poems

The line of prophecy and the line of wit in poetry have continued to be used as terms designating such poets as Spenser and Milton for the first and John Donne and his so-called school for the second. We have likewise bifurcated poetry into reader-oriented approaches and author-controlled craft. Although the two sets of ideas are not confounded within today's metacritical stances, there are affinities of prophecy and affective style and of wit and craft, with the semiological approach touching both. To reduce these critical positions to two—prophecy/reader, wit/author—as *if* they were opposed and as *if* they together constituted the whole of criticism (neither of which is true), we may assign to one substance and a kind of didacticism, and to the other technique and a kind of showmanship, as their extremes. (Of course poets of the line of wit have substance, and of course poets of the line of prophecy employ many techniques and devices.) But the first critical position does emphasize what an author puts into his poem and why, and for deconstructionists what a text reads; the other, how an author produces a literary artifact that he offers for evaluation. The one involves the audience; the other has the author as focal issue.

My own view admits of the reader reading and of the writer writing, and indeed I believe neither should be isolated to the exclusion of the other. The reader reading asks us to determine not only the effect of a literary work and its "message" as we view it in completion (divorced in a sense from authorial and contextual concerns), but the literary work's place in the history of ideas, which does involve content, at least as those ideas have impinged upon the reader. The writer writing asks us to examine the structure of a literary work, the elements that make it a tangible object, the methods of incorporation of such elements into a whole, and the work's evaluation outside any place it may have in history. Authorial intention, which may involve biographical and psychological considerations, and which always exists whether one can determine it adequately or not, may appear for the reader in the affective style or in the compositorial matters that can be discerned when the writer's craft is analyzed. The writer writing produces a text, that is, which has an intentionality, and part of that intentionality involves the text's substance and part its art. The earlier poems of Milton exhibit various limina into a more thorough reading of them when we pay attention to the writer writing. One of the most notable is a break (or seeming break) with tradition.

Two early poems offer illustration of how these points of view may be balanced and suggest a means to the revaluation of Milton's shorter poems. "On the Death of a Fair Infant Dying of a Cough" has elicited discussion concerning the infant referred to, the date of composition, a textual crux, and the literary sources. Further, the *Variorum Commentary*[1] reviews criticism of a literary and interpretative nature, and I should particularly note Hugh Maclean's reading of its form and imagery and Jackson Cope's investigation of the fortunate fall underlying the treatment of the elegy.[2] The reader reading, depending of course on background, will recognize the Spenserian form, imagery, and diction, and remark in the first stanza supposedly Shakespearean overtones and similarities to Phineas Fletcher and in the last stanza inverted syntaxis. The reader will move from a metaphoric and mythic statement of death to speculations which mitigate that death, by suggesting immortality for the infant and by suggesting nonhuman being though incarnated in this world. These lines are addressed to the infant, "Thou." The infant takes on Christological proportions and is thus seen as a type who may have slaked "his wrath whom sin hath made our foe," but who "canst best perform that office where thou art." The next and last stanza immediately switches the "thou" to Milton's sister Anne, "Then thou the mother of so sweet a child," and offers a combined mythic and physical consolation. If Anne will acknowledge that she has returned God's present to him, accepting the mythic rationalization of life and death, then God will give another offspring, "That till the worlds last-end shall make thy name to live." Anne was pregnant again when Milton wrote, although Douglas Bush demurs that Milton would not have made "such a private allusion" and the birth was not dependent on any "if."

The poem has as its surface intention personal consolation, a consolation that is subtended by what seems to be authorial belief: God is all-giving, all-knowing, inscrutable but just and merciful. In God and his ways there must be faith. Milton is justifying the ways of God to men on a delimited and specific scale, but the implications of the poem, with its mythic imagery and its apparent contemporary reference—the just Maid who "cam'st again to visit us once more" in 1626–28 when Parliament was vying with Charles I and Buckingham for the people's rights— project the poem into an unlimited and wide-ranging conception. For most commentators the poem has seemed only biographical and rationalistic, but viewed anew with attention to its place in a Miltonian universe it becomes a firm teleological statement working on a personal level, a community level, and a prophetic level. Unfortunately most people have not been readers of this poem as literature, it seems, bypassing it like so many others in the Milton canon as conventional or merely biographical. I refer to the general lack of *literary* attention paid to the psalm translations, the Latin poems (with the exception of "Epitaphium Damonis"), the other shorter poems like "The Passion" or "Arcades," and even many of the sonnets. Brooks and Hardy, for instance, see the metaphors in the "Fair Infant" as being "used primarily for their decorative quality, for their function in making large and magnificent an occasion that would ordinarily seem trivial and unimportant."[3] And of course Brooks and Hardy are correct *if* the occasion is the full substance of the poem. What we should look at to judge whether there is any substance in the aforegoing "message" or intention or position in a Miltonic history of ideas is the poem as artifact produced by the writer writing.

If one assume that Milton, though young, knew what he was doing, one should not conclude that the metaphors are decoration of something trivial. Such metaphors, instead, suggest that something more is going on in the poem than only the personal level of consolation. And besides, what kind of communication would be made with Anne and her husband, Edward Phillips, when he talks of Aquilo and of Hyacinth? Milton could not have been so naïve as to think his sister and brother-in-law would have understood the poem. Addressing the infant, alone, should clue us that this is not simply an elegy on private concerns. Of course, the imminent next birth will take place successfully whether Anne accepts God's ways toward men or not, but only *if* she accepts his ways will the offspring "make thy name to live" until the Judgment, when the faithful and the nonfaithful will be judged. (Bush simply misread or refused to read without preconception.) We may find Milton's use of metaphor excessive, but we should make that evaluation on the basis of the full import of the poem and what appears to be the intentionality of the text. The writer writing such metaphors helps the reader to know what he or she is reading.

Structures are likewise pertinent. Milton employed a seven-line stanza in three rhymes, ending with an alexandrine. The alexandrine is visually enhanced in length by the indentation of the sixth line. The alexandrine, by its contrastive additional foot, allows an impression of continuance, most notably in stanzas 10 and 11, where it articulates with the sense of the lines. We note that seven is the mythic number of creation and three the symbol of godhead. There are eleven stanzas (eleven is the mystic number of regeneration and salvation), and it is in the last stanza that regenerative ideas are set forth. The allusion to Isaiah 56.5 in the last two lines is significant. They are, "This if thou do he will an off-spring give, / That till the worlds last-end shall make thy name to live"; Isaiah reads: "Even unto them I give in mine house and within my walls a place and a name better than of sons and of daughters. I will give them an everlasting name, that shall not be cut off." Chapter 56 details "The Rewards of Keeping God's Covenant" regardless of who or what one may be; verse 5 refers "even to" eunuchs (not just the childless) who "take hold of his covenant." As Bush writes, "The figurative *off-spring* is the earthly peace and strength and the heavenly life coupled in the Bible with exhortation to patience and promised to all the faithful." Only *if* Anne is "faithful" in the sense of accepting God's ways will this reward be granted. The dead infant and the soon-to-be-born infant represent a covenant perhaps not too far removed in concept from God's covenant with Abraham concerning Isaac.

The stanzas of the poem break into five (4 + 1), one, and five (4 + 1). The first five stanzas are concerned with the metaphoric and mythic statement of death, with the first four presenting natural imagery and classical allusion and the fifth being a rejection of the actuality of death. The sixth stanza is transitional, moving the meditation from one centering on mortality to concepts denying mortality. The last five stanzas speculate on mitigations of death; stanzas seven through ten are allegoric, based on Christian allusions disguised in mythic terms (a common Miltonic technique, as in "Lycidas"), and the last stanza is a consolation capped by a concept of immortality. Such balanced structure is not fortuitous.

Further, the early stanzas generally make assertions, sustained by "For since," "So," "Yet," and "Yet"; the later stanzas, although they should be the infant's reply to the charge to "say me true," are generally questions to the infant, sustained by "Wert," "Or wert," "Or wert," and "But oh why." The assertions are rejected by the import of the poem, and the questions, though unanswered, serve to anchor that import: the infant's life has seemed to have meaning by its fancied effect upon the world in which it lived. The "Nativity Ode," written almost two years later, is concerned with the effect of the Son's incarnation. Here in the "Fair Infant Elegy" we have an earlier investigation. The paradoxic quality of the poem—the mythic death/life—is displayed by these semiotic elements, as well as by the structures of the poem. Are not, then, the metaphors also concerned with death that is insubstantial when viewed as the Gate of Life, in opposition to Brooks and Hardy's dimissal of them?

Disembodied from its meanings, the poem seems to strike most people as too filled with archaic and ineffective language and diction, images that are not always appropriate (e.g., the "long-uncoupled bed, and childless eld" of winter in a poem talking of the death of a young child whose mother is again pregnant), and a tone that has been called "aureate," "commanding," "exhibitionist."[4] It is an early performance and one that Milton may have at first decided not to make available to public audience. (It was published only in the 1673 second edition of the *Poems.*) But the poem as the artifact we have seen illustrates both an attention to the writing process that will appear more successful when negativities of rhetoric, tone, and employment of metaphors have been reversed and to levels of meaning that are to complicate such poems as "Lycidas" and *Paradise Lost.*

The prophetic tag "once more" from Hebrews 12.25–27 appears in line 52, where Milton asks whether the infant might be Astraea, who "cam'st again to visit us once more." The biblical reference is to the Second Coming, after which all tears will be forever wiped from human eyes.[5] (Hebrews often refers to the Son's coming "once" before; e.g., 9.26–27.) St. Paul says, "This word, Yet once more, signifieth the removing of those things that are shaken, as of things that are made, that those things which cannot be shaken may remain." Within the context of justice on earth "once more," this suggests that during the years of the infant's life things that were shaken have been, in a way at least, removed: Parliament was presented with the Petition of Right on 2 June 1628. With "once more" as prophetic tag and the infant as a type, Milton's line symbolizes an earthly wiping of the tears of those who have experienced little or no justice in the hope for an immediately improved future. It is difficult to see the poem as intended only as a consolation for Anne. It is so developed that more than just consolation emerges as its base. Without such deeper intention, the poem is surely overwrought. The occasion, the death, is the catalyst for the meditation, and the meditation is a vehicle for certain ideas that Milton exploited later with greater art. That he should be influenced by the context of the political world around him, as I suggest, does not seem far-fetched. To recognize that Milton's shorter poems may evidence a worldly level and a prophetic level is in line with recent criticism of "Comus" that has had to acknowledge the scandalous world that whirled about its first performance, with the thrust of the most controversial Milton book of recent years, Christopher Hill's *Milton and the English Revolution,* and with the placement of "Lycidas" and *Paradise Lost* in the mainstream of prophetic literature. Perhaps an awareness that the outside world was not escapable as he wrote may inform Sonnets 19 and 21 ("When I consider how my light is spent" and "Cyriack, whose Grandsire on the Royal Bench") and lead to slightly different readings from what are usual. The prophetic voice surely sounds the English odes, as well as Sonnets 15 and 18 ("Fairfax, whose name in armes through Europe rings" and "Avenge O Lord thy slaughter'd saints"), the latter two works frequently being read in contemporary political contexts only.

Elegia prima, my second illustrative poem, has generally been studied because of what it adds to biography. It records Milton's rustication from Christ's College and his activities while at his father's home on Bread Street in London in spring 1626.[6] In the background are Ovidian poems and themes, and particularly we should note that Elegia prima is a verse epistle, as are Ovid's *Tristia* and *Epistolae ex Ponto*. Ralph W. Condee has explored the reverses between Ovid's exile and Milton's, basically built on Ovid's loss of Rome and Milton's gain of London as parallels,[7] making therefore Cambridge a place hostile to poetry and beauty, as Milton writes in ll. 13–14:

> Its bare fields are unwelcome, so unyielding are they of mild shadows;
> how improperly that place assembles the followers of Phoebus!

with ironies and puns attached to *Phoebicolis*. The sun, Phoebus, represented the dispensation of the Law; the tree, the dispensation of Grace; and thus shade, the Son's mercy.[8] Part of Milton's sense of mercilessness lay in his aggrievement over Chappell's chastisement.

The elegy is built on an eight-line introduction, followed by a sixteen-line statement of the background, a forty-eight-line résumé of his activities in London, which divides into twenty-two and twenty-six lines, an apostrophe to London covering twelve lines, and a leave-taking, eight.[9] The balance is also seen in content: introduction/leave-taking; Cambridge/London; and vicarious love/potentially actual love. This central section relates the cloistered world, imaginative and safe, and the broad way, actual and seductively dangerous. The psychological import of his relieved means of escaping Circe's infamous hall, that is, returning to the bare fields of Cambridge, is worthy of study. The structure of the poem, its balance and parallels, makes it one not just to be cast as a group of elegiac couplets attached to each other for some space of time or for a presentation of related ideas. It exemplifies what a true follower of the god of poetry may achieve under circumstances not offered in Cambridge. The free range of literary reading that Milton recounts is not just included, therefore, to show his activities but to make a subtile, ironic statement of the contrastive rigid limits of the reading program exacted by Christ's and especially by Chappell. The noncommunion with nature, the nonassociation with beautiful girls that the college confines seem to have imposed on him (if not others) are reversed in London. The strategy of the poem is to reverse the *beata ille* theme and redefine the true *locus amoenus*.

The "Fair Infant Elegy," unfortunately for its serious consideration, has not been iconoclastic of tradition in its structure, form, imagery, and diction, and has thus simply been dismissed as substantially insignificant. The reader reading has not been impressed to read very deeply. The investigation of God's ways toward men has been hidden, and the poem's only interest lies in what kind of poet Milton became and thus in its biographical relationship. But paying heed to what the writer writing was doing leads to deeper understanding, though not to particularly more positive evaluation. On the other hand, Elegia prima, while significant for a view of structuring and language use (corroborating the point of view expressed in chapter 10), finds its importance in the biographical and the psychological. While the former has been attended to in Miltonic criticism, the latter has not.

Milton's shorter poems are the full poetic canon, with the exception of *Paradise Lost, Paradise Regain'd,* and *Samson Agonistes,* although "In quintum Novembris," "On the Morning of *Christs* Nativity," "Comus," "Lycidas," "Ad Patrem," "Epitaphium Damonis," and "Ad Ioannem Rousium" are not particularly short. Perhaps some people have a tendency to replace "shorter" with "early," for we think of the three major poems as late work, written or at least completed after the composition of the last short poem, Sonnet 23 ("Methought I saw my late espoused Saint"), dated usually around 1658. "Early" is, of course, an even more vaguely relative word than "shorter." I suggest instead that we think of Milton's trip to the Continent from April 1638 to August 1639 as a watershed between the earlier and the later poetic endeavors on the basis of concepts in "Lycidas," written in November 1637, Milton's studies and activities after having returned to England, and statements in the beginning of the second book of *The Reason of Church-Government,* published in January 1642. A number of speculations rear up if we accept this inflectional point, which I have confronted elsewhere.[10] But if it had been Milton who died instead of Edward King in that fateful trip across the Irish Sea in August 1637, we would not be concerned with Milton as poet. Perhaps we can label the poems before 1634 early; those like "Comus" and "Lycidas," transitional; and those after return to England, mature.

Like Elegia prima, a number of early poems exhibit a traditional form, even though that form may be well wrought, and are either traditional or nonindividualistic in substance. Here I would place both versions of "Psalm 114," "Psalm 136," "Carmina Elegiaca," "Apologus de Rustico et Hero," Elegiae secunda and septima, the little Gunpowder Plot poems, Sonnet 1, "Song: on *May* Morning," "On Shakespear," the Hobson poems, and "Philosophus ad regem." (Elegia tertia will be discussed in note 13.) Revaluation may cast a poem like "Apologus de Rustico et Hero" into the "forgettable" category as the mere poetic exercise it is, but verses like those on Hobson, while they are not sharply distinguishable from others on the subject, engage a metaphysical treatment that is poetically pleasurable. Perhaps we should note that "On Shakespear" has—I think justifiedly— fallen in general esteem of late. When examined as poem, forgetting subject and author, it offers little beyond readers as monument (as opposed to the then already out-of-date argument about erecting a physical monu- ment) and the not-unusual genealogy of Shakespeare's being son to Mem- ory and thus brother of the Muses. We should recall its use of the heroic couplet, a metric also employed in "A Paraphrase upon Psalm 114," "At a Vacation Exercise" "Song: on *May* Morning" (partially), the Hobson poems, "Arcades" (partially), and "Psalm 1." Aside from the various verse forms in the late psalm translations and aside from the sonnet, Milton—the writer writing—does not use "standard" English metrics after the tetrameters of "Comus," that is, after what I have classified as "early" poems, "Arcades" and "Comus" being from a transitional period. The preference for a fluid- ity of line that "Lycidas" and *Paradise Lost* exhibit, as well as the later sonnets, probably accounts for Milton's abandonment of such "standard" meters, with their strong end-stoppage. "Psalm 1," written in August 1653, shows eight run-on lines out of its total sixteen, a high percentage, and helps lead us to understand that these late psalm translations were experi- ments in verse treatment. (Each of the psalms is in a different prosodic form.)

A matter of meter separates "In obitum Praesulis Eliensis" and "In obitum Procancellarii medici" from the preceding group: the employment in funereal poems of meters suggestive of other kinds of occasions makes a subtle and derisive comment on their subjects (Nicholas Felton, Bishop of Ely after Lancelot Andrewes and former master of Pembroke Hall, Cambridge, and John Gostlin, Vice Chancellor of Cambridge and Master of Caius College, Cambridge) and on the requirement of writing a poem for those occasions. The first is in alternating iambic tetrameters and dimeters, the so-called iambic strophe, employed by Horace in *Epodes* 1–10, and the second is in Alcaics, the so-called Horatian stanza employed thirty-seven times in the *Odes*. The first meter takes on the character of mixed verse developed by Archilochus for invective and satire, and in Horace's epodes (the word *epode* sometimes denotes the iambic dimeter following an iambic trimeter) it sustains harsh and indecent invective in *Epodes* 4, 5, 6, 8, and 10. Horace called the epodes *iambi*, by which he implied not only iambic meter but satiric tone, and they were published contemporaneously with the second book of *Satires*. The second meter partakes of what Stephen F. Fogle in the *Princeton Encyclopedia of Poetry and Poetics* says of Horace's odes: they are "personal rather than public, general rather than occasional, tranquil rather than intense, contemplative rather than brilliant, and intended for the reader in his library rather than for the spectator in the theatre."[11]

If indeed we recognize that the verses on the Bishop of Ely have a satiric intention,[12] we can better understand the hyperbole of "As yet my cheeks were not dry with flowing tears, / and eyes not dry, / still were they swollen with the rain of salt liquid," and the questionable punning of "you, the ornament of the race of men, / who were the prince of saints in that island / which retains the name of Eel," and the ridicule from Felton's spirit, " 'Put away your blind madness; put away your transparent melancholy and your ineffectual threats.' " The poet's professed anger at this death should be viewed—in its hyperbole, punning, and self-ridicule—alongside Ovid's invective in *Ibis* and Archilochus's satires on Lycames and Neobule, which led to their suicides. The poem is thus an intellectual joke, lampooning these required public assertions of grief to be given in tribute and pinned on the funeral bier.

The odic poem on the vice-chancellor operates on the irony that even medical doctors must succumb to death, but it is supposed to be a public utterance and smack not at all of private concerns. It is written for occasion and seems to have no general proportion other than that death is inexorable. It is the opposite of what Fogle has described its meter to subtend. It is intense, not tranquil; brilliant (in allusions and images, surely), not contemplative; and filled with pictures, not with ideas. That Horace's odes in Alcaic meter (like I.9) counsel enjoyment of the hearth and wine while winter rages without or (like IV.4) celebrate a Roman victory in the Alps or (like II.13) offer exaggerated imprecations on a tree that has fallen, just missing his head, making him realize that death comes when least expected suggests that Milton's employment of the meter for an elegiac theme is ironic, ironic to the point of saying, "All this pother over Gostlin is stuff and nonsense."[13]

While these two poems are traditional in form and subject, the indecorum of using an improper meter for the occasion and the subject places them, as products of the writer writing, into a separate niche, their evaluation depending upon the reader's recognition of that indecorum and estimate of its achievement. What all this advises is that we should not just skip over some of these poems as merely exercises, although none of the poems we have dealt with so far exhibits the poet as anything more than amateur.

Early poems that have had attention paid to them for one reason or another are "In quintum Novembris," Elegiae quarta, quinta, and sexta, Sonnets 2–6 and the "Canzone," "Naturam non senium pati," "De Idea Platonica," and Sonnet 7. Each seems to attempt something that is not standard, but the form in which they are cast is standard. I shall discuss only one of these, Elegia quinta, and note that Sonnet 7 ("How soon hath time") is the first of Milton's sonnets to break away from the ostensible "standard" subject of most Elizabethan sonnets; the remaining sonnets of his maturity will extend the subject range of the sonnet, becoming thus a prime reason for the reemergence of the sonnet in the eighteenth century with authors like Thomas Edwards, Thomas Warton, Anna Seward, Charlotte Smith, and William Lisle Bowles and leading to the great achievements in the nineteenth and twentieth centuries.

Elegia quinta does not offer something new, when compared with Ovidian example, or with Propertius or Tibullus, but there is a difference that has been little heeded. Its execution has led Harris Fletcher to call it "Milton's finest poem in Latin."[14] While I hesitate to say that, considering "Ad Ioannem Rousium" and "Ad Patrem," and with modification "Epitaphium Damonis," I also would rate it very high in achievement, but in terms of its substance as well as its craft. I think most people misread the poem by reading it on the surface only. A fine discussion of it like Don Cameron Allen's[15] stresses the manipulation of classic themes and imagery, the significance of spring as mythic concept, and thus its significance for Milton in terms of poetic inspiration, an aspect well explored by A. S. P. Woodhouse in 1943.[16] But the underlying tone—representing not only Milton's impetus for writing but the unfulfilled longings of many people—seems to go unrecognized. The underlying tone is one of contrast between the cosmic alterations of the year and their concomitant effect on most people, including especially the poet, and the lack of effectual reality for the poet of the elegy. While the poem *appears* to attest to the effect of spring on him, the effect is a surface one, one of the mind rather than of the heart. He ends:

> May the golden age restore you, Jove, to a wretched world!
> Why do you come back with your cruel weapons in the clouds?
> At least drive your swift team, Apollo, as leisurely
> as you can, and may the time of spring pass slowly;
> and may foul winter bring prolonged nights tardily,
> and may shadow attack later within our heavens.
>
> (ll. 135–40)

While we may read this as only a wish for the continuance of days, perspective suggests that the real subject of the elegy is the return of Eden, seen largely as a return of innocent sexual desire, glimpsed in the epiphany and interfacing of spring/beauty/love/poetry. The tone suggests that the poetry celebrates the hope brought forth, not the actuality. The poem itself offers what "the cleft Castalian peak" and the dreams transporting Pyrene to him in the night produce. Apollo, "his locks entwined with Daphne's laurel," descends, and rapturous imagery of male and female infusions (sun and earth) follows, which in turn leads to rather breathless

examples of the results of wandering Cupid's running through the world
(l. 97). But "that is no country for a young man" like Milton: Why else the
pleas, "ye gods . . . do not go from your arboreal home" (l. 134)? Why else
does he urge that the gods and goddesses, the shepherd and Phyllis, the
sailor, *even* the satyrs, and the sylvan deities "prefer the woods to heaven"
(l. 131)? We have here a young man (nearing twenty-one) who feels
reaction to the coming of spring but who can only dream the actualization
of that reaction in terms of others. The poem is a dream vision, and the
leisureliness of lines 25–96 contrasts with the kaleidoscope of images of
lines 97–134, which replicate one's sense of dreaming just before one
awakens, as well as sexual simulation. The poem, a cerebral thing, is the
only reaction that he seems able to actualize.

The remaining early poems have almost all evoked much criticism: "At
a Vacation Exercise," "On the Morning of *Christs* Nativity," "The Passion,"
"An Epitaph on the Marchioness of *Winchester,*" "L'Allegro," and "Il
Penseroso." Certainly three of these remain highly evaluated—deservedly—
and the reason would seem to be their new form and treatment, as well as
their substance. The major point that I have been making is that evaluation should rest on a fresh examination of a poem and that a combination
of the reader reading and the writer writing is paramount for an author
like Milton. The limina that the writer provides the reader direct such
fresh examination; we have, in these poems of Milton so far, looked at
structures, meter, numerological significances, allusion and sources,
context—the historistic but also the literary-biographic—onomastics, and
nontraditionalism. The outcome may not always be different from what is
currently available in criticism, but it may clash with some of the critical
clichés that hover around a specific poem. We will find that "At a Vacation
Exercise" is not really capable of evaluation without placing it within its
context in Prolusion 6, where it is part of a lampoon of academic orational
requirements and of his relationship with his fellow students. We will find
that the "Nativity Ode" is not about the nativity of Jesus, but about the
effect of the nativity on a person's life, particularly through the prophetic
voice of the central stanza of the Hymn, No. 14:

> For if such Holy Song
> Enwrap our fancy long,
>   Time will run back, and fetch the age of gold,
> And speckl'd vanity
> Will sicken soon and die,
>   And leprous sin will melt from earthly mould,
> And Hell it self will pass away,
> And leave her dolorous mansions to the peering day.

I imply, of course, the importance of structures to the poem. We will find that the eight stanzas of "The Passion" are but a proem, double the length of the proem of the "Nativity Ode." There the number of four stanzas stressed the incarnation of the Son as Man and the significance for humankind; here the number of eight stanzas stresses the age after the seven ages of man have transpired and Judgment has come for those who followed or who have not followed the example of the Son, whose death on the Cross is to be celebrated in the poem itself. Many look on the poem as a fragment rather than as a completed section. While this may not raise the estimate of the last line of the extant verse—we remember Louis L. Martz's comment in *The Poetry of Meditation* [17]—yet it suggests that Milton learned that mere imitation (even of himself) leads to failure.[18] This, basically, is what is wrong in the "Fair Infant Elegy": the poetic elements are not only not new, they are not employed with poetic variety. This is not to say that techniques of prosody, form, and the like may not be developed with successive improvements—think of the metrics of the Marchioness poem followed by the companion poems—but it is to point out that aside from the sonnet Milton's works generally all have a difference unto themselves, and even the sonnet is transformed in his hands. We do not find the narrowness of a Thomas Carew or a Robert Herrick; we find fewer poems, but they exhibit greater variety of poetics. I am reminded of the answer to the question in the *Athenian Mercury* in 1692, "*Whether* Milton *and* Waller *are not the best English Poets? and which the better of the two?*": "But yet we think *Milton* wrote too little in Verse, and too much Prose, to carry the Name of *Best* from all others. . . . [W]e think him not so *general* a Poet as some we have formerly had, and others still surviving. . . . [Y]et [Mr. Waller] comes not up in our Judgments to that . . . which *Milton* has, and wherein we think he was never equalled."[19] (Incidentally, "a fragment of The Passion" is considered "incomparable" by the writer of the *Athenian Mercury* answer.) We probably should ask ourselves whether we do indeed have all of Milton's poems. We might conclude that we do not have all the psalm translations written in the early period, at least, and there has been an argument for a third Hobson poem.

A main thought that I would stress for these early poems is that they should be given their due; they should not just be skipped over because they are early poems, or "only" of biographical interest, or even "only" indications of what is to come in maturity. The substance of the poems should be examined in terms of themselves, in terms of Milton's development of ideas, and in terms of their place in the history of ideas; and the elements of craft should be examined in the same terms. Revaluation of these early poems may not place many in higher regard for some specific reason than generally they are today. Yet the five poems we have looked at demonstrate concerns that the critic should pursue but will not pursue if a poem is approached traditionally, unimaginatively, insensitively, uninformedly, or with preconceptions of subject, craft, or worth.

Unexamined so far are "Arcades," dated now as May 1634,[20] "A Maske" (that is, "Comus"), dated September 1634, "On Time," "Upon the Circumcision," "At a Solemn Music," "Ad Patrem" (which incidentally ought to be translated "To *My* Father," not the ubiquitous "To *His* Father"), and the "Fifth Ode" of Horace, often dated well before 1637 and up to 1647. Whenever these poems may have been composed, with the possible exception of the Horace, all might be considered transitional, and we should add to this category "Lycidas," "Ad Salsillam," "Mansus," the Leonora Baroni epigrams, and "Epitaphium Damonis." An avenue into these poems for the reader reading is the break with tradition against which they should be evaluated. This has been a frequent approach with "Lycidas," and is a major reason why it has been called the greatest shorter poem in the English language. Critical areas to be further explored are the psychological, the religious concepts, and the fusions of form and source and of form and intention. We can cast out the epigrams as basically unimportant aside from biography; we can look on the "Fifth Ode" as an experiment in rhythms, language, and terseness of image; we can recognize that "Mansus" may be too involved in self and too little the well-wrought urn; we can adjudge "Ad Salsillum" successful in its prosodic attempts and brave in its indecorum. But we must acknowledge the new use of form or the new form of "Arcades," "A Maske," the three English odes, "Lycidas," and "Epitaphium Damonis." Success, total or partial, has not in each case necessarily been at Milton's disposal, but the works should be evaluated within the parameters of the attempt: it is achieved, I think, in "Arcades" and "At a Solemn Music" and "Lycidas," but it ultimately fails in "A Maske" and "Upon the Circumcision" and in some ways in "Epitaphium Damonis." When it fails in the latter, it is not because the elegy is so little concerned with Diodati (that is not a cogent criterion), but because Milton the poet is so close to his content that adequate perspective on universals in both form and substance becomes vague. The elegy falls apart structurally in the middle, and its ending is insufficiently prepared. Success eludes "Upon the Circumcision" because the metaphysical conceits are strained, the double vision is indecorous, and the canzone form is inappropriate. It fails in "A Maske" because the text we have has been altered from an acting text to a reading text, with attendant incompleteness or inconsistency in alteration and with a lack of control in its final version. A foreconceit (or pre-text) has not controlled the received version either in form or in substance: in form, there are problems as a masque; in substance, there are unnecessary repetitions, overextended sections, and some instances of incoherence and disunity. This is not to say that I do not admire the poem greatly: so much of its poetry is so great and it presents so much in thought. But ultimately it is not a consummate artistic achievement. The question of "A Maske," of course, raises another issue, dating, and that is too involved an issue to be taken up here. Suffice it to say, the date of "A Maske" *as we read it* has to lie in late 1637 (or early 1638, when it was published) as the pasted leaf and revised epilogue alone demand; and incidentally ll. 779–806 are not even in Milton's notebook, the Trinity MS, in which at least some of the text was worked out. The development of the text from 1634, when it was first produced as a dramatic performance, through 1637/8 has not proceeded on a full overview but has produced revisions here and there, belying a final artistic perspective.

The mature shorter poems are very few: there are sixteen sonnets, "On the Forcers of Conscience," the Greek lines on William Marshall, who drew the frontispiece for the 1645 edition of the shorter poems, the ode to Rouse, and two psalm translation groups. The ode to Rouse is a good example of a poem to be evaluated because of its craftsmanship, despite our interest in the biographical element and the comments on the rabble for a better understanding of the idealistic, republican, and psychological Milton. If we demand the maintenance of a tradition as mold, the poem will be not well thought of; if we accept the license of experimentation with form and prosody, we will rate it high, for it creates a new poetic container with concerns that are ultimately the concern of any ode: public action that advances the prestige of one's national world (such as Rouse's achievements). In other words it should be read and evaluated as one of the generic family *ode*, with awareness of its variations and evaluation of its success in such variations. The indictment of the rabble (not too different perhaps from those who cry liberty when it is license they mean, to quote Sonnet 11) is a reversed view of its odic concern. Through viewing the writer writing we become aware that we should evaluate it—and highly—on its substance.

The sonnets offer us much, from "not very important" to "magnificent." Milton's sonnets are always Petrarchan in form, although the volta may be displaced and enjambment become frequent. As form the sonnet in Milton's hand takes on a different shape, while its traditional essence is maintained. What is most ridiculous about Thomas Newton's 1751 title "On His Blindness" (the "His" should have alerted everyone to know that the title was not Milton's) is that it focuses our attention on the first two lines, as if they were the subject of the sonnet. Chapter 2 has explored the Petrarchan sonnet and the octave as background out of which the thought of the sestet emerges or against which it should be viewed. Milton's concern in the sonnet is, therefore, his inability to contribute ostensibly to God's cause in his present world; the thought that he perceives is that there must be those ready to act when called upon and who cannot, therefore, be actively engaged in other work. Milton's blindness affects his engagement in trying to dispel the ignorance of the world through his ability as an author (the imagery of "dark world and wide" and "the one Talent"), but, like Phoebus in "Lycidas," Patience stops that murmur with a thought akin to the significance of fame in Heaven. Just as Milton in "Lycidas" is concerned with his role in life (with echoes of the seventh sonnet being heard), so he is here also in October 1655, when so much was going on in the division of England into ten districts, each headed by a major general who was to enforce the various blue laws aiming at a strong theocratic world. The key to this reading is the recognition of the sonnet as Petrarchan and the recognition of the structure/content of a Petrarchan sonnet.[21]

Sonnet 23, "Methought I saw my late espoused saint," is not different. While Leo Spitzer was certainly right in viewing the sonnet as moving from a Greek (pagan) orientation (the first quatrain) to a Hebraic orientation (the second quatrain) to a Christian orientation (the sestet), most people, I think, have separated the last two lines, rendering the third group of four lines as a third quatrain, rather than as part of the sestet. The rhyme scheme (*ababab*) demands that they be part of the sestet, as well as the printed tercets (ll. 9 and 12 on the margin, 10–11 and 13–14 indented), despite the end-stoppage of l. 12. The difference that this exerts on the interpretation is to see the poem as Petrarchan in structure, but with the volta at l. 9. The primary thought, thus, is not in ll. 1–12; that is, it is not his frustration at being able only to dream of his dead wife to the point of actualization. (Dreaming just up to a point of actualization before waking is a commonplace experience we all have, but it is made poignant in Milton's case because of his blindness.)

The primary thought of ll. 10–14, and thus of the sonnet, is the questioning of religious precepts, the uncertainty of their validity in terms of the earthly tears one experiences, and the recognition that one does not really know but can only hope that salvation may be real. On the basis, first, that love can circumvent death and in turn that death can reward love (a version perhaps of Death as the Gate to Life) and, second, that covenants with God can be altered by circumstances, Milton metaphorizes his belief rather than the fact (his sight is "fancied") that goodness will be rewarded. But as he attempts to grasp this belief as an actuality, as a fact, he is dashed back to the world of uncertainty. As the seeming fact is exposed by the light of day (or the light of reason), so is it shown not to be factual, for we are ultimately ignorant in this life of the world beyond. Only through faith that one's vision has substance can one believe. We might say that it is finally "This thought [that] might lead [humankind] through the worlds vain mask / Content though blind" (Sonnet 22). And again we have the prophetic tag "yet once more" in line 7, appearing in the exact middle of the poem, and operating throughout it. Some of Milton's faith has been shaken, and some "which cannot be shaken" may remain. A wiping of the tears may be accomplished, but the tone and the statement that the vision inclines to embrace and flees when he awakens suggest that at least for a while Milton found little that was not shaken. Did the thought that the millennium would occur in the mid 1650s, or the difficulties in the government in the latter part of the decade, or the general public inaction of Milton during 1655–58 and the return, apparently, to what became *Paradise Lost,* a period capped by an addition to the new 1658 edition of the *First Defense,* provoke this mood and these thoughts? The catalyst for the poem was clearly a dream of his dead wife, but the circumstances surrounding her salvation or lack of salvation supply only the vehicle for the larger thought. They do not constitute the tenor.

Each of the mature shorter poems should be reviewed for its "new" form and poetic elements, its "new" thought, and, emphatically, its admixture of the not new, without the preconceptions that hover like vultures. We may be surprised at what we find, admiring "Ladie, that in the prime" (Sonnet 9) and never asking who she is, and ignoring much in the Lawes sonnet (Sonnet 13) as merely epideictic, finding amazement in "Ad Patrem" and artistry in the prosodic variety of Psalms 1–8. Revaluation of Milton's shorter poems as poems comes off with average marks and high marks, but in some places we might not expect.

Onomastics and Andrew Marvell's Poems

A mong the significances of names for literature is their allusive quality, and this allusiveness is why an author uses a specific name. A name may very literally mean only its denotation: when Andrew Marvell writes an encomium "To His Noble friend Mr Richard Lovelace, Upon His Poems," the title name and its occurrence in line 34 refer to the poet Lovelace and nothing more. When, however, he writes of "Bermudas," he wishes his reader to recall, first, the actual place—the Summer Isles, as they were also called; second, the metaphor for a place besieged by natural disastrous elements, which is still being described as the Bermuda triangle; third, a metaphor for a new and edenic world to the west—a type of the lost garden sought mythically by all people and actually by the colonists from the Virginia Company in London; and fourth, though the reader will discover this only by study of Marvellian image and idea through many poems, the image of the mythic island in the sun that equates the individual in the sea of life. Further, a name may add a meaning through etymology, as in "The Picture of Little *T. C.* in a Prospect of Flowers," where T. C. is literally Theophila Cornewall; metaphorically she becomes all those creatures or living things that hold promise in youth that is soon aborted—like Milton's Fair Infant or Sherwood Anderson's Egg—but also she becomes a symbol, familiar in Marvell's verse, of innocence prior to sexual awareness; and etymologically she is "This Darling of the Gods"—that is, all who are seemingly loved of God.

Excepting the satires written during the Restoration, a great many names do not appear in Andrew Marvell's poetry. Those that do refer to real people (almost all contemporary), geography (there are a few instances), biblical characters or places, and mythic and pastoral characters or places. It is this latter group that I shall focus on. One reason for the paucity of names in Marvell's poetry is that most of his poems are lyrics. A study of the poet's use of names indicates that satires and such public forms as the funeral elegy employ the majority of names, not lyrics. The reason for this would seem to be that generally lyrics employ names as devices, whereas public poems cite denotation. (The agreement of this statement with the definition of lyric in chapter 6 should be clear.) *Device,* as I here use the term, involves the metaphoric constructs suggested before, as well as strategy, and functions as a literary element of structure, image pattern, or effect—clearly a limen into reading the poem. Names, as we have said, very frequently evoke only one-on-one relationships, whatever their referent—including mythic names. But even when this is the case, the sources of those names—especially mythic names—are important to those who are interested in onomastics, for the etymology may explain the formation of the name and its assignment. The writer may use the name only for its denotation and in no way suggest that it can be a device, yet an onomastic examination may underscore the appropriateness of the name in a literary work.

Examples of this latter point can be seen in "The Gallery," which gives us "Aurora," "Clora," and "Venus." Stanza 3 expands on Aurora as goddess of the dawn:

> But, on the other side, th'art drawn
> Like to Aurora in the dawn;
> When in the East she slumbering lies
> And stretches out her milky thighs . . .

This is one of the pictures in the gallery of the poet's heart, which celebrate his mistress. The name is not used as device; there is also no suggestion here that the poet identifies with Aurora's aged lover Tithonus. The etymology of the name, however, explains the name and emphasizes the kind of desirable dawn that has been praised by making it a goddess. The name is a reduplicated form for Latin *ausosa,* cognate with the Sanskrit *ush,* to burn. It is connected with Latin *aurum,* gold, which derives from *aes,* copper or bronze; and it is cognate with Greek $\acute{Y}\omega = \mathring{\eta}\acute{\omega}$, dawn, and Etruscan *Usil,* the god of the sun. For the poet's mistress the name supplies a narrative element—her envisioned and hoped-for slumbering at daybreak with her milky thighs stretched out as she lies in bed with him—but it yields as well a symbol of sexuality for him as she lies there in her intense burning.

Another picture presents Venus in her pearly boat; that is, as born from the sea, as in Botticelli's "Primavera," where she stands on a scallop shell. The name of the goddess of love derives from Latin *veneror,* to venerate, which came to equate love and sexual desire. Like the use of Aurora, Venus is primarily denotative. The meanings of the cognates in Sanskrit, *vankh,* wish or pray, in Old Indian, *vanas,* desire, and in the Indo-European base *wen-,* to strive after with desire to be satisfied, do not emerge in Marvell's line, except as Venus connotes sexual love.

On the other hand, Clora, the name of the mistress of the poem, which occurs in a different spelling in "Mourning," is important as device. The source of the name is the Greek χλωρ, meaning greenness or verdure. She is identified with Flora, goddess of flowers. The etymology emerges in the wordplay of the final lines:

> A tender shepherdess, whose hair
> Hangs loosely playing in the air,
> Transplanting flowers from the green hill
> To crown her head, and bosom fill.

Stepping back and looking at the full poem, however, we see that Clora is an inhuman murderess: she is one associated with wooing doves that perfect their harmless loves (Aurora); still, she is an enchantress, vexing her restless lover's ghost, who has become a greedy vulture's prey. She is also one associated with the calm halcyons and perfumed air (Venus). Indeed, she is many persons, both those that please and those that torment, while she remains finally only one person, a tender shepherdess. Remembering who Clora is—the greenness and verdure of nature—we see the name as device for Marvell's evaluation of nature: benevolent and charging man with happiness, malignant and charging man with despair. Nature may be free and natural, like woman with hair loosely playing in the air, or controlled and fashioned for effect upon man, a fatally enticing effect, like woman with flowers crowning her head or tucked in her bosom. The key to our realization that Marvell is talking not only about woman as mythic object of veneration and mythic temptress, but of all nature as both good and evil, is the name Clora.[1]

Onomastic importance of the mythological and pastoral names for Marvell's lyric poetry, then, lies in their use as devices and in etymological wordplay, and for those interested in onomastics in the names themselves. The effect of these words in the lyrics is to give an air of distance between the poet and the reader, to suggest a traditional referent that may evoke metaphoric meaning, and to imply an attitude on the part of the author toward the poem he or she is writing—for as the names do act as devices, an intention is implied. Where names suggest traditional referents, such allusions may elicit connotations that have been encrusted on the name over the years. At times the significance beyond denotation is clued by etymological wordplaying.

A word list of mythic and pastoral names in Marvell's poetry (except for the Restoration satires) shows 105 instances of 55 names in 24 poems. Fourteen poems are clearly lyrics that are not public in nature; the ten public poems consists of two songs (usually designated lyrics), two encomia (also often placed under the label lyric), three elegiac poems (one of which is satiric), one satire, and "Upon Appleton House" and "The First Anniversary of the Government under O. C." The specific genre of the last two is uncertain; they are not epic or dramatic or elegiac or satiric. "Upon Appleton House" should perhaps be listed as a "country house poem" although other genres intrude, and it has been seen to have both epical and satiric modes. "The First Anniversary" may best be called panegyric. Of the 105 instances of names, 45 are in the 10 public poems, 60 in the 14 lyrics. A brief investigation of some of these names will be instructive as to the importance of onomastics to poetry and will lead to readings of the poetry not previously offered.

Illustrative of some of the things just said is the name "Ajax," which appears as a simile for "The unfortunate lover":

> Whilst he, betwixt the flames and waves,
> Like Ajax, the mad tempest braves.

The lover, born in a shipwreck in the sea of life, feels the passions of the tyrant Love and finds he must oppose the violent wind or sighs or word tempests that accompany love. Life's elements of fire, water, and air are evident in the couplet (as they have been in other places, notably stanza 3); only earth seems to be missing. The allusion to Ajax recalls the son of Oileus, King of Locri (*Aeneid* I, 41–45), who violated Cassandra in the Temple of Athena. On his way home from Troy, he was shipwrecked by Athena for his act. She destroyed his ship with the thunder of Zeus and the tempests of Poseidon. At first Poseidon saved him, until he boasted of his lack of punishment; whereupon Poseidon threw the rock on which he was standing into the sea, drowning him. The parallels seem to lie in the shipwrecks, the tempests causing them, and the superior might of the gods as each fights these elements. The lover cuffs the thunder with one hand and grapples with the stubborn rock with the other, but he too is defeated. Other parallels seem to be missing: Ajax's violation of Cassandra cannot equate the war that tyrant Love wages in the unfortunate lover's breast; the lover does not boast; and he is not being punished for his actions. Rather Marvell is driving to a statement of the masochism of love: "all he 'says [assays, evaluates by putting to a test], a lover dressed / In his own blood does relish best." The emblem of all lovers who are unfortunate is "In a field sable a lover gules"—the source of unfortunate Hester Prynne's emblem, "On a field, sable, the letter A, gules," in Nathaniel Hawthorne's *Scarlet Letter.* The lover will always be ruled by malignant stars and forced to live in storms and wars, but he relishes such spectacle of his own blood. (See chapter 13 for further discussion of this poem.)

As allusion, Ajax signifies that the lover may fight the flames, waves, and tempest that will accompany his sexual gratification, but he too will lose to the superior might of the god, living after death only as a perfume, a strain of music, or in a story. Ajax as allusion in the poem recalls part of the name as traditional referent, in order to iterate an image pattern within the poem. It is thus device.

But the etymology of the name leads us to two other matters, one involving wordplay, the other a metaphoric statement. Ajax derives from the Greek *Aĩa*, meaning earth. Thus, the couplet quoted before does contain the fourth element of life, earth, and the lover, like earth itself, will experience the other elements of life around him. He as orphan of the hurricane comes under the care of the black cormorants sailing above (stanza 4), and he has come into existence by the Caesarean section of his mother, as she through the shipwreck of life is split against the stone by a masterwave (stanza 2). If the lover, thus, is like earth, as our onomastic knowledge says he is, then we see man the lover embattled like an island—a kind of Bermuda—buffeted by the quarreling elements of fire, water, and air (stanza 3). This is a key to the interpretation of this poem, which critics have confessed in print they did not understand. No man may be an island according to Donne, but Marvell deplores man's isolation as an island in the sea of life. His thought may have been generated by his own psychological problems, but "The unfortunate lover" (which ironically would be an oxymoron if we thought of Rupert Brooke) is an Ajax—earth itself—who has tried to ravage prophetic doom (Cassandra) within the realm of wisdom (Athena). But no "lover" succeeds except in masochistic relief.

Illustrative of other matters raised before are the uses of four names in "The Garden": "Apollo" appears to allude only to the sun god, son of Zeus and Leto, who fell in love with Daphne and pursued her. Her mother Ge (that is, the earth) changed her into a laurel. In the same stanza are "Pan," god of shepherds and flocks, and "Syrinx," a nymph whom he pursued and who was turned into a reed. The stanza is:

> When we have run our passion's heat,
> Love hither makes his best retreat,
> The gods, that mortal beauty chase,
> Still in a tree did end their race.
> Apollo hunted Daphne so,
> Only that she might laurel grow.
> And Pan did after Syrinx speed,
> Not as a nymph, but for a reed.

The myths alluded to were apparently developed to explain the existence of the natural world, for *Δάφνη* is Greek for laurel tree and *σῦριγξ* means anything tubular like a pipe, that is, a reed or shepherd's pipe.

Marvell's use of the four names—all but Pan appearing only here in Marvell's poetry—would seem to be only denotative. Once love has run its course, it is translated to the realm of nature and natural beauty. But behind the myths are also the concepts of the arts, Apollo as god of poetry and music and Daphne (laurel or the bays) signifying great achievement, and Pan as god of bucolic poetry and music and Syrinx as means to such song. The extended connotations of the names recall the opening of the poem: "How vainly men themselves amaze / To win the palm, the oak, or bays." Stanza 4, reprising these lines, pushes the thought of such pursuit of love (and arts) to sidestepping bodily life to contemplate nature itself ("Annihilating all that's made / To a green thought in a green shade," he will say in stanza 6). Return to the happy garden-state will bring sweet and wholesome hours, reckoned only by a time dial made of herbs and flowers.

An adjunct myth perhaps hovers over the references to Apollo and Pan. We remember that Midas, asked to choose the more worthy music, selected that of Pan, whereupon Apollo clapped him with ass's ears. Pan in "The Garden" does not seem to be interested in Syrinx as nymph; he pursues her only for the reed she may provide. While fond love has abrogated what would have otherwise been a happy garden-state, Marvell seems to be implying that Pan's lack of appreciation of Syrinx, reflected in his pursuit "but for a reed," could lead to the kind of noise Midas praised, a noise that would dispel "Fair quiet," just hailed before, and jar with the bird's song soon after. While most of the imagery of the poem is visual or tactile, there are instances of smell and taste and sound; this citing of Apollo and Pan may be an oblique reference to sound.

There seems to be little wordplay in the etymologies. "Apollo" comes from an obsolete Greek verb, $A\pi\acute{o}\lambda\lambda\omega\nu$, meaning to drive away (it is cognate with Latin *pellere,* to strike). As the sun, he strikes and drives away from his heat that which may be scorched or consumed, such as Daphne, the laurel tree. The stanza in which the name occurs in "The Garden" does have some appropriate lines: "When we have run our passion's heat, / Love hither makes his best retreat." The Greek $\varDelta\bar{\alpha}\varphi\nu\eta$ comes out of Asia Minor from a word meaning *morning dew,* clearly significant within the Greek myth. Pan, which is cognate with $\pi\acute{\alpha}\upsilon\sigma\omega\nu$, from Old Indian *Pûsań-,* a Vedic god and guardian of cattle, literally means *nourisher.* Significance for this poem is lacking, although its uses in "Clorinda and Damon" are another matter. The word $\sigma\bar{\upsilon}\rho\iota\gamma\xi$ is related to the verb *to pipe,* from the Indo-European imitative base, **swer-, *sur-,* meaning to sound. The ending of the noun *-ιγγξ* implies a musical instrument.

We have already looked at "Clorinda and Damon" as a débat in a pastoral setting. Onomastic backgrounds corroborate our interpretation and add to the artistry and artifice of the poetry. "Clorinda" comes from the Persian meaning "renowned"; "Damon" from the Greek $\Delta\acute{\alpha}\mu\omega\nu$, in turn from Sanskrit, meaning "to rule" or "to guide." It is cognate with Greek for tame, conquer, make subject to a husband. The etymological significance is immediately mind-catching: body, pleasure, sin, and woman as temptress are renowned, talked about, sought after; and clearly it is the soul and virtue and faith that morally should rule or guide. The use of Damon by Vergil in *Eclogues* 3.17 and 8.1 following, and as the great friend of Pythias, have no pertinency. As we have seen, the resolution of the débat comes through Pan, who is both a goat god with Satanic proportions and the Great Shepherd Christ, who tends his flocks and leads them to green pastures. We see this latter aspect of Pan in the etymology "nourisher," already mentioned. The opposing concepts of Pan and many of his attributes derive from a false etymology equating the name with the Greek word for "all." Pan is a nourisher of the body as well as of the soul; both must be nourished. The resolution of this débat rests in the fusion of body and soul, just as in the fusion of the two natures of Pan.

To complete discussion of names in this poem, we should add "Flora." Marvell's line "Where Flora blazons all her pride" alludes to her being the goddess of flowers, and her name is appropriate, since it comes from the Latin *flos, floris,* a flower, which comes from *flo,* meaning to blow or to bloom, which in turn comes from the Greek $\acute{\epsilon}\kappa\text{-}\phi\lambda\alpha\iota\nu\omega$, to stream forth. The flowers that are Flora's pride are specified two lines later, and their streaming forth is seen in their blazoning, this verb suggesting the noun *blazon* or a poem graphically praising a woman's body from head downward, and then sometimes upward, to her private zone. Marvell puns accordingly:

C.   Seize the short joys then, ere they vade,
     Seest thou that unfrequented cave?
D.   That den?
C.   Love's Shrine.
D.   But virtue's grave.

The last line is printed in three separate lines, creating a hieroglyphic device, where "Love's Shrine" is surrounded by Damon's view of it as a "den" (as he stands without) and as "virtue's grave" (as he moves within).

The nine uses of Juliana in three "mower" poems offer a brief observation. "Juliana" is a descendent of Julius, Latin from Jovilios, of which Jove is a contraction. It is the same word as Jupiter, from *Diespiter,* from Old Indian *Dyauspita,* a heavenly father, from Indo-European $*d^y eu + p^e ter$, which is equivalent to $Z\epsilon\tilde{\upsilon}\ \pi\acute{\alpha}\tau\epsilon\rho$, Father Zeus in Greek. Thus Juliana is related to godhead. The interpretation of the difficult "mower" poems is suggested by etymology: the mower Damon—he is one who rules or guides and who relates to one who tames or makes subject to a husband, as previously noted—on one level is attempting to tame the godhead that woman becomes in man's eyes as man would subject woman as wife (and of course it does not work), and on another he is attempting to rule or guide, but it is Juliana who guides and controls him. The irony of the etymology of the two names is clearest in "The Mower to the Glowworms," which are his guides until Juliana is come. He rejects their natural, courteous lights, but with his mind so displaced by Juliana he will never find home (a metaphor for Heaven). The lights that have served to guide him through the world's dark masque are now ignored, and in their stead is woman as temptress, woman as emasculator through taming him, and woman as one raised to the status of godhead for him. We remember Milton's line about Adam and Eve, "Hee for God only, shee for God in him" (IV, 299) and Adam's "All higher knowledge in her presence falls / Degraded" (VIII, 551–52), and recognize the cynic view Marvell is advancing of man-woman relationships.[2]

The names of the title characters in "Ametas and Thestylis Making Hay-Ropes" pose problems onomastically, and I mention them here to indicate that names in Marvell's poems may not always be significant. "Ametas" does not appear elsewhere. Boccaccio, in a prose idyl, has a character Ameto, a young hunter, and the name could derive from Latin *ametor*, motherless (from *a* + *mater*). It could also be a misprint for the popular pastoral name *Amyntas*, which comes from the Greek $\alpha\mu\acute{v}\nu\tau\eta$s, a defender. Possibly the name is related to "amethyst," Greek $\alpha\mu\acute{\epsilon}\theta\upsilon\sigma\tau$os, from α + $\mu\epsilon\theta\acute{v}\omega$, $\mu\epsilon\theta\upsilon\sigma\iota$s, meaning "a remedy against drunkenness," or "not drunk," which in turn derives from α + $\mu\epsilon\theta\upsilon\acute{\epsilon}\iota\upsilon$ from $\mu\epsilon\theta\eta$, "wine." Or possibly it comes from α + $\mu\epsilon\tau\alpha$, meaning "not with" or "not among." None of these, however, seems pertinent to Marvell's shepherd. Thestylis, who was the bearer of garlic and wild thyme to the reapers in Virgil's *Eclogues* II, 11–12, appears in "Upon Appleton House" denotatively only:

> But bloody Thestylis, that waits
> To bring the mowing camp their cates,
> Greedy as kites, has trussed it up,
> And forthwith means on it to sup . . .
>   (401–4)

In the lyric she appears to be only a shepherdess. I have found no derivation, nor have I been able to devise any possibilities.

The second song "at the marriage of the Lord Fauconberg and the Lady

Mary Cromwell" offers a different kind of poem with three "characters," whose names appear in pastoral literature, and three further pastoral names in the text. The marriage between Thomas Belasyse, second Viscount Fauconberg, and Mary, Cromwell's third daughter, took place on 19 November 1657. The three speakers of this pastoral dialogue are Hobbinol, Phillis, and Tomalin. Hobbinol is a character in Spenser's "Shepheardes Calender" (see January, April, June, and September). The name is diminutive of "Robert" plus "goblin." "Robert" derives from German, meaning bright in fame, and "goblin," of course, is an imp or clown (Middle English *gobelin*, from Latin *gobelinus*, from Greek κοβαλός, a rogue). Hobbinol in the poem is the one who leads the praise of the married couple and turns aside the mundane concerns of Phillis—appropriately for the "Robert" portion of his name. Roguishness has disappeared and in its place is lightheartedness (appropriate enough for a clown). Marvell's Hobbinol is not different from the nature of the character in Spenser, where again he certainly is not clownish. (He is usually identified with Gabriel Harvey.)

The etymology of Phillis seems to have been known by Marvell, for it comes from the Greek φυλλίς, a green and leafy bough. Phillis wishes to

> Stay till I some flowers ha' tied
> In a garland for the bride. . . .
> Let's not then at least be seen
> Without each a sprig of green.

(Phyllis, the daughter of King Sithon of Thrace, was turned into an almond tree; and the name appears in Vergil's third eclogue, l. 78.) Tomalin is also found in Spenser's "Shepheardes Calender" in March and July. The name would seem to be diminutive of Thomas, through Latin, from the Greek θωμᾶς, a twin, which relates to the Syrian *tōmā*, twin, from the Semitic base *w-a-m*, to tally. (In Spenser it may be a brief form of Thomas of Lincoln, the real personage he depicts under this guise.) He is a less forceful person in Marvell's poem than Hobbinol, being, as in Spenser, a kind of companion (or a "twin"?) to another character (here, Hobbinol).

The three additional names are Menalcas, that is, Cromwell; Damon, that is, Fauconberg; and Marina, that is, Mary. Menalcas appears twice: "For the Northern Shepherd's son / Has Menalca's daughter won" and "Fear not; at Menalca's hall / There is bays enough for all." The name is appropriate for Cromwell as Lord Protector of England, and of course when used by one like Marvell who was employed by his government. Menalcas derives from two Greek words, Μένος [Dorian] + ἀλκή, soul or spirit + strength, courage, prowess. He is a shepherd in Vergil's third and fifth eclogues (ll. 15 and 4 respectively). "Damon" we have already looked at: as one who tames or conquers and makes subject to a husband, the name is most appropriate in a marriage song. Stressed in the song is the uniting of two politically different houses, it would seem, the Cromwellian and the Northern opposition:

> Joy to that happy pair,
> Whose hopes united banish our despair.

Fauconberg, who was from Yorkshire, was a kinsman of Lord Fairfax, who had opposed certain policies of Cromwell; he was to become privy council-lor and ambassador of Charles II. Marina, a name deriving from the Latin, meaning "of the sea," may have been used for association with the female and particularly with the innocent young girl (as in Shakespeare's "Pericles").

A final poem may serve as evidence that onomastics is significant in interpretation and that an author like Marvell is aware of the uses of such knowledge as device. "Daphnis and Chloe" has elicited various readings, primarily because its tone seems not to be pastoral but cynical. The problem lies, as it so often does with Marvell, not in the poem but in the prudishness of its readers. Looking at the names will help clear up some of the seeming difficulties. The "narrative" is that Daphnis has been wooing Chloe, who has resisted his advances and arguments; she now gives in, for Daphnis is about to take his leave of her for some spate of time. Although he was well versed in such wooing, he seemed not to have realized that "sudden parting closer glews" and thus that now he would be blessed with his supposed goal. But this is not what he really wants; he wants only the fiction of his love suit and her continuance in a "virginal" state. This is hardly an uncommon attitude on the part of many a man who seems to seek sexual gratification with "her he loved most" until she succumbs, at which time she acquires his vilification as promiscuous. Daphnis leaves and takes his pleasure with women of easy virtue; he does not blame himself for the disruption of their relationship, only Chloe, who really should not have led him on by refusing him even once.

Daphnis derives from the Greek $\Delta\alpha\phi\nu\iota s$, the bayberry. A Sicilian shepherd, he is said to have invented bucolic poetry and to have been blinded for unfaithfulness. The poem is given over to images of death, not only in the punning meaning of sexual intercourse but also to signify the death of his desire. The bayberry is popular as a scent and a floral decoration in winter, when its waxen berries appear. It is of the myrtle family, and myrtle is an opposed symbol of Venus and marriage and of death. Daphnis becomes in the poem a symbol of that man who is unfaithful to his beloved both by his amours with others like Phlogis and

Dorinda and by his lack of faith in his loved one, Chloe. He is a symbol common even today in our world of supposedly relaxed moral strictures: if she gives in to me, she will give in to anyone. The women Daphnis consorts with after he leaves Chloe are Phlogis, from Greek Φλογιτης, flame-colored gem, from Φλογεos, meaning bright as fire, who is thus understandably a courtesan in Martial's *Epigrams* xi and lx, and Dorinda, from the Greek stem *di-* (δω), to give, apparently here one who "gives her favors away." Chloe, from the Greek Χλόη, means the first green shoot of a plant, thus just beginning to bloom, a clearly appropriate name for the youthful virgin of this poem.

What commentators seem to expect in so-called love poetry, particularly that of the pastoral mode, is the romantic view of boy-girl, mutual love, and live-happily-ever-after. What commentators seem not to recognize is that seventeenth-century poets—not just Marvell—offer a range of love situations as one might find them in real life (see also chapter 13). Needless to say, I would think, but needed nevertheless for some, such poetry does not necessitate biographical or philosophical interpretation. Biography and philosophy should not be ruled out, but they have probably been overworked and oversought in lyrics such as Herrick's, Carew's, and Lovelace's, to name just three so often poorly read.

The Self as Poetry in Marvell's Work

W e are well aware of the autobiographical element in poetry. Samuel Taylor Coleridge's "Dejection: An Ode" or "This Lime-Tree Bower My Prison" represents one category of undisguised personal subject matter, but with the poetry transcending its circumscribed subject. The poetry of William Butler Yeats—say, "Easter 1916" or "A Bronze Head," which is about Maud Gonne, or "News from the Delphic Oracle"—very often represents another category, one where the personal element, though not hidden, is submerged through close attention to the meaning. It is a backdrop rather than subject. In such poetry as Shakespeare's Sonnets or John Donne's Songs and Sonets or Robert Frost's *North of Boston* collection, to cite three very different examples, it is difficult to know where the autobiographical ends and what congruencies exist with the poet's life, if any. In more recent years we have had the confessional poets, as M. L. Rosenthal has labeled them—people like W. D. Snodgrass, Anne Sexton, John Berryman—and a study by David Kalstone, called *Five Temperaments,* explores the substance of autobiography in the works of Elizabeth Bishop, Robert Lowell, James Merrill, Adrienne Rich, and John Ashbery. But at times the self is hidden by a poet, deliberately hidden for whatever reason he or she may consider important. We might think of Walt Whitman's Calamus poems, or the James Joyce of *Chamber Music,* or the way the self of much of Wallace Stevens's seemingly depersonalized poetry has begun to emerge through modern criticism.

The chapter title, "The Self as Poetry," suggests three matters: the autobiographical element in a poem; a hidden self; and an inferred self. These selves are, of course, not distinct, but I shall here not pay attention to the first. A self may be hidden, even deliberately, by a poet within the work, propelling us toward psychological analysis of him as a person, or toward eliciting data for a psychological reading of the poems. We can appreciate this immediately in the case of Whitman or Joyce, or in certain ways Samuel Johnson or Arthur Hugh Clough, as disparate examples. And

Stevens's work often exhibits this kind of self, except that we usually have the nagging suspicion that it is a "performing self," to adapt a term recalling Richard Poirier's study of mass culture.[1] A self may also be "hidden" outside the poem, as it were, in terms of the reasons for writing the poem, the tone of the poem, the ideas and attitudes of the poem. Such a self may be a performing self (somewhat fictionalized) or a self we may infer (one somewhat more true than the performing self). The self in Marvell's poetry at times is a real self (as in the poems on Lovelace or Milton) and at times a performing self. But there is also, it would seem, a deliberately hidden self and a self possible of inference from its relationship with the performing self. My choice of Andrew Marvell to examine this thesis is fraught with pitfalls, but until we test the ground section by section, we will not know where the mines are that may explode our theories or the springs that may either mire us in soggy earth or furnish us with a source of the poem's life.

That Marvell's poetry provides fertile ground for all manner of interpretation is a gross understatement, implying the first pitfall. His poetry is so complex and the levels of meaning so numerous and potential that no one slant is sufficient. That this is so can be realized by the extensive critical work that has been published on Marvell in recent years, which, however, exhibits a lack of critical agreement, a limited compass of the poems examined and a delimiting of level or approach, and an all-too-frequent drawing back from possible conclusions one might be led to. Few of the books on Marvell have proved to be acceptable as a basic statement for further studies to interact with or to amplify, as, for example, Rosemond Tuve's or Joseph Summer's books on George Herbert have. Marvell studies are there usually to argue with.

The second pitfall is our lack of biographical knowledge of Marvell. We do not have even fairly probable dates for many of the poems, and thus an uncertain chronology, and we know little of his personal life. To raise even vaguely psychological outlines is to court vigorous naysaying and even vituperation.

Related is the third pitfall: canon and text. Marvell's "complete" poems fill only a small volume, but if "Mary Marvell" had not devised a scheme of publication in 1681 to acquire some financial return for Marvell's alleged debts, we would have only a handful of poems from other sources, and these would include the authenticated satires. (The Popple MS, Bodleian English poetical MS d.49, corrects the 1681 Folio edition and amplifies it with the three Cromwell poems, which would have become available to modern scholars, almost completely, from other sources.) Clearly we cannot be sure that we have all the poems that Marvell wrote and might have printed, or that those we have are in every instance his; and we cannot be sure that the text is really always reliable, although the Popple MS emboldens us to be a lot surer than scholars could have been before its discovery in 1944. For example, "A Dialogue between Thyrsis and Dorinda" is probably not Marvell's, having been printed four times before 1681, being found in three manuscripts, and not being included in the Popple MS. The well-known *hue/glue, glue/dew,* and *gates/grates* cruxes in "To His Coy Mistress," or the alterations since Cooke's edition of 1726 of ll. 79–80 in "Daphnis and Chloe," illustrate textual problems. And so generally theories of a hidden or inferred self can reflect at best only those poems and those texts that we now have and now assign to Marvell.

As I read the criticism (what little there is) and annotation of "The Fair Singer," I infer that the "I" of the poem is often taken to be Marvell himself and the occasion a "courtly compliment paid to a lady to commend her skill in singing, playing an instrument, or dancing."[2] This suggests a real occasion and a real person. But the poem is not a commendation of a singer. The title is an epitome of the oppositions on which the poem is built: sight and sound. The woman assaults the reluctant "I" with her eyes, binding his heart, and with her voice, captivating his mind. From the reverse perspective his eyes see her fair beauty and his ears hear her lovely singing, and "both beauties," joined, create a fatal harmony, seeking his death. The oppositions resolve in a combination of nature and art. The military imagery is most commonplace; we remember it in Donne, Marino, Suckling, Lovelace, and Rochester, and it derives from the topos of Venus and Mars, who in coition meld Love and War into Joy and Peace. The woman is the poet's enemy and seeks his death (with the connotation of sexual intercourse); that is, she seeks the annihilation of his individual being. He says he could have escaped one kind of assault, but not both together. Though his heart might be bound with "the curlèd trammels of her hair" (with its obvious Freudian overtones), his soul would be free, except that the air carrying her voice has fettered him. The heart is engaged by the tangible; the soul by air. She has "gained both the wind and sun"; that is, both windward and leeward, thus surrounding him. The line completes the fusion of opposites, the wind relating to the song carried on the air, the sun lighting and making visible her physical beauty.[3]

The poem is so given over to playful intricacies of poetic expression using commonplace imagery and a basically "Petrarchan" situation that autobiography is nowhere in sight. For Ann E. Berthoff[4] the poem is not unmistakably Marvell's because "though Marvell here characteristically speaks of mind and soul as well as heart, yet the confrontation is not of fate or time but only of 'fatal Harmony'; and without the grand Marvellian theme, neither the tone nor the development of the imagery is typical." My disagreements with the premises upon which such indefensible statements are made should be evident. It is a typically well-made poem whose aim is to create a well-made poem to vie with others' poems on similar subjects, using similar language and imagery, and giving it similar treatment. And this occurs frequently with Marvell, as with others. The poet is outside his poem; the self here is a performing self, and the hidden self is only that which would set itself against other poets working in comparable material, stressing craft, stressing variety and differences from others, stressing reader effect, as to his "sincerity." Marvell has been most successful in reader effect, for it does seem to be read—erroneously—as having a reality quotient. The hidden self of this poem is a poet of ambition, and the craft of the poem attends to the viability of that ambition.

"Mourning," to turn to another poem, makes reference to Clora's eyes, and since the name is used in "An Elegy upon the Death of My Lord Francis Villiers"—not, however, certainly by Marvell—she has been identified with Mary Kirke, daughter of Aurelian Townshend, as noted in chapter 12. Mary Kirke would have mourned Villiers's death, and the Clora of "Mourning" is weeping. But the name appears also in "The Gallery," as we have seen, and is common for a female lover in the pastoral mode. The question the poem examines is why does Clora weep: "What mean the infants which of late / Spring from the stars of Clora's eyes?" It seems she cries because Strephon lies on the ground—apparently dead. But some in the poem suggest that she cries more for the sake of crying and would cry for anyone. Indeed, some even insinuate that she is really joyful and cries because she has a new lover. The "I" of the poem, however, is "sure as oft as women weep, / It is to be supposed they grieve." The last stanza moves the poem away from a specific occasion and a real person. (And need we remark amazement that anyone could think that Marvell would write a poem on a real person, Mary Kirke, mourning a lost friend, Villiers, and then say that she "casts abroad these donatives / At the installing of a new"?) Marvell's subject is woman's weeping, a characteristic element of seventeenth-century poetry, whether serious, as in Crashaw's "The Weeper," or merely Petrarchan stock. He looks at it as a serious result of loss, then antithetically as a ploy to hoodwink observers, then cynically as a result of gladness that her loss has allowed a desired replacement to be installed. An image commonplace in love poetry of the seventeenth century is examined in a kind of analysis of such poetry, leading the reader to recognize, if the reader has not before, that, typically, a poem like "Lucasta Weeping" (by Lovelace) is not to be taken so seriously and autobiographically as it usually is. The Lovelace poem and others, including Marvell's "Mourning," are poems written on a common theme in the coterie game of poetry writing.

The structure of Marvell's poem is two stanzas describing Clora's weeping, one stanza concerned with her weeping for Strephon, one stanza concerned with her false weeping, the central stanza to which we will return, one stanza concerned with her crying out of joy, one stanza concerned with her new lover, and two stanzas of rejection of such contemptuous distrust. The symmetry is noteworthy and implies authorial concern with art as a major intention. The first of the last two stanzas employs the image of Indian slaves diving for pearls, a rather outrageous metaphor here, leading one to suspect some tongue-in-cheek significance. The divers would find Clora's tear deeper than the seas in which they search, and thus they would not be able to reach the bottom of her tears. But the last line—"And not of one the bottom sound"—also may be read in restatement of the cynical preceding stanzas to mean that they would not find those tears to be valid or real pearls. The last stanza seems to plump for her honest weeping, but then we notice that the poet does not say, "It is in truth because they grieve"; he says, "it is to be supposed they grieve." We have to keep up their fiction. That is part of the game of love.

The central stanza suggests her vanity:

> And, while vain pomp does her restrain
> Within her solitary bower,
> She courts herself in amorous rain;
> Herself both Danaë and the shower.

Zeus, we remember, descended as a golden shower to make love to the beautiful mortal Danaë, and "bower" here recalls sexual bowers of bliss. The offspring of Zeus and Danaë was Perseus, who grew up to slay Medusa, whose look turned men to stone. Thomas Carew's "Song: Celia Singing" ("Hark how my Celia") might be compared for stock imagery of tears and stone, the antitype, as it were, being Niobe. The product of Clora's self-courting—remember the tears are called infants—would seem to be, in intention at least, the figure of herself as tragic being who would melt the emotional stones of others' hearts, eliciting compassion for herself. Is this perhaps what the "I" is really saying in his alleged "silent judgement"? Women cry to evoke sympathy for themselves.

Like "The Fair Singer," "Mourning" is a calculated poem to vie with others' poems on similar subjects, using similar language and imagery, and giving it similar treatment, for there are many weeping poems. But is the silent male chauvinism important to note? (Men, of course, do not cry.) Is there something here a bit more significant for the poet who is still outside the poem? Is the contrast with something like "Lucasta Weeping" particularly meaningful as an index to the respective poets' attitudes in the battle of the sexes? Have we a hint of a more deliberately hidden self?

Perhaps not too distant is the epitomizing of woman as nature's treasure

and man as the experiencer of great and sincere love in "The Match."
Twentieth-century readers must be reminded that for the Renaissance and
for the seventeenth century woman was the fickle sex, as we have noted
before: recall Hamlet's lines about his mother and the rumors about
Ophelia. "The Match" is a contest between woman and man, Celia and
"I," with each as the match for the other, but also it is the fuse to ignite the
nitre, naphtha, sulfur that Love has stored within the "I" of the poem.
(Donno's constant attempt to create autobiography in the poems suggests
implausibly that Celia here may be the Celia of "To His Worthy Friend
Doctor Witty.") Again the poet is outside his poem; he indulges in the
commonplace categorizing of woman as beauty and external and man as
heart, with its connotation of sincerity, and internal. To read into the poem
any psychological import is invalid: the hidden self is again the competing
poet. He is competing with poems like Carew's "The Tinder" and "Song: To
My Mistress, I Burning in Love," except that Carew's poems are seduction
poems with the desired end being sexual union. Marvell's poems in this
vein generally exist outside such standard intentions (feigned or actual)
despite the union that may conclude a poem, as in "The Match."

One of the best-known seduction poems and one using the *carpe diem*
argument, of course, is "To His Coy Mistress." But the literature is long
which indicates that this is not really a seduction poem. In place of
seduction the concern is time, and many have pointed this out. The
reference to the conversion of the Jews, however, would seem to result from
the press of time when this poem was probably written (late 1640s or early
1650s): the approaching millennium was to occur in 1657, or so some
thought, or at least so some writers made believe to achieve meaningful
metaphor. The millennium would be accompanied by the conversion of
the Jews to Christianity. With the end of the world as humans know it, the
poems takes on added meaning and anxiety:

> But at my back I always hear
> Time's winged chariot hurrying near:
> And yonder all before us lie
> Deserts of vast eternity.

One may be adjudged a sheep or a goat, and ascend or descend to one's
respective eternity. Since these are deserts and her honor will become dust
and his lust ashes, their eternity can be only the fire of hell. The things of
this world will disappear—like the woman's beauty and the poet's song, as
well as her physicality in terms of virginity and his emotionalism in terms
of lust. These—virginity and lust—are the extremes of the Petrarchan
attributes of ice and fire. The stock qualities of female and male are the
same ones that Marvell played on in "The Match." But since this world is

about to disappear (and substituting mortal time as simply aging agent does not change my point), the "I" of the poem argues that they should sport while they may; that is, they should make every second of time count without regard to moral futures rather than just let it more slowly move on. "Rage against the dying of the light," Dylan Thomas exhorted his father, even though he knew that death was inevitable.

The oral imagery of "birds of prey," "our time devour," "slow-chapped power" is decidedly sexual in that it follows close on "let us sport us while we may," implying some of the ways they will sport. Sport is sexual intercourse for its own sake, not for procreation. Of course progeny would be meaningless now that the millennium is imminent. Their strength (basically male) and their sweetness (basically female) he proposes they "roll . . . up into one ball," drawing a picture of the couple in coition. They will then "tear" their pleasures "with rough strife"—after all, she is supposed to be a virgin—"thorough the iron gates of life." As Dennis Davison finally said in print,[5] the last phrase connotes the woman's *labia*, through which birth would otherwise occur. ("Gates" indicates both a going-in and a coming-out.) The iron gates, besides, may be a pun on her virginity and resistance until this time. All the rejections I have read of these sexual annotations are prudish and plain obtuse. Pierre Legouis in the third edition of Margoliouth's Oxford text (1971) writes, for instance: "While the conclusion of the poem clearly aims at sexual consummation I see no evidence that the images are themselves sexual. And I cannot even make up my mind whether the human couple and the 'Pleasures' stand, until these are 'torn,' on the same or on different sides of the 'gates' . . . ," whatever that is supposed to mean.

We talk of the gates of life, but "iron" gates suggest the gates of death, for it is an iron gate in Hell opened by an iron key. Milton was to have Adam say,

> suffering for Truths sake
> Is fortitude to highest victorie,
> And to the faithful Death the Gate of Life.
> (*Paradise Lost* XII, 569–71)

That is, by dying the good and faithful achieve eternal life. Sexual connotations, not applicable for the lines from *Paradise Lost*, also arise in Marvell's poem: death (sexual intercourse) can bring forth life (birth). Here the couple of the poem will not bring forth life, nor, the millennium coming apace, do they want to. Marvell is playing on the same kind of imagery and philosophy that Milton is in *Paradise Lost* except that Marvell's lovers fly in the face of faith by succumbing to present needs, rejecting future hopes, and concluding that they will not be among the saved anyway. They will make the gates of life for humankind like hell-gate for themselves, first, because such promiscuity is not moral and will lead to their damning, and second, because woman as enticer of man leads him to destruction. The irony is that here it is man who is trying to lead woman to such destruction. Eve enticed Adam as humankind's journey through the wilderness of life was to begin, said the cliché; man now tries to entice woman as that journey is about to end. Their mutual fires are a metaphor for the conflagration that 2 Peter 3.10 tells us will end the world.

Philosophically the "I" of the poem has already disbelieved himself to be one of the elect; he is not a Joshua, who is a type of Jesus, and the best he can do is make the chariot of the sun, which in its race records the passage of time, hasten along to the approaching end. As seduction poem on the surface, the poem awaits evaluation in terms of other poets' essays into the theme, but it is more than this: it is a poem concerned with ontology, positing an author—and the reference to the Humber has even implied a biographical detail for some—who wonders like Milton momentarily considering whether it is

> not better don as others use,
> To sport with *Amaryllis* in the shade,
> Or with the tangles of *Neaera's* hair?
> ("Lycidas," 67–69)

For where will sound his echoing song? The personality that the poem seems to reveal is one concerned with his lack of achievement and the possibility of time's descent without hostages to fortune (whether human or intangible). The poem, in this way, is a product of despair and possible self-rejection; there is a tone of desperation beneath it that critics seem not to have felt. The hidden self is as he was before in "The Fair Singer" or "The Match," but he is also a more individualized self showing philosophic concerns and some depressive paranoia. Yet there is nothing in the poem that equates Marvell with an "I" who hopes to seduce some coy mistress. J. B. Leishman is so far from the mark in seeing this as a poem about love,[6] and Marvell's own sexuality makes that reading even worse than superficial.

A most different poem from those we have been looking at is "The Coronet." The poet and his work are posed against Christ and his achievement. The poet, attempting to write a poem in honor of his Savior, which he calls a coronet and which thus would supposedly offset the crown of thorns borne by Christ, finds himself filled with pride. He then realizes that his diadem proposes to debase Heaven's and asks God to untie the serpent's slippery knots making up his coronet or shatter the serpent and it. By Christ's treading on the serpent and the poem, it may crown Christ's feet though it could not his head.

Many have seen the poem as a rejection of his art by the poet, and the poet is then often identified as Marvell himself. Berthoff (46) in rebuttal answers that Marvell nowhere exhibits any degree of self-consciousness as an artist, but the interpretation is simply not worthy of any rebuttal. The poem argues the inferiority of all things to God, the insubstantiality of the belief that man can redress his wrongs by such an act as described, and the pride that may arise from any human achievement. There are superficial likenesses to Donne's "Batter my heart" sonnet and "Twicknam Garden," worth mentioning only because they indicate the lack of individuation in the theme. (Recall, too, Donne's "La Corona.") The individuation of the poem comes in the treatment, the entwined syntax, the involved metric and rhyme pattern, which generally moves from a more involved metric to ten pentameters and from a slightly more regular rhyme scheme to a slightly more involved one. The poem represents the coronet that would emerge from the poet's having summoned up all his store.[7]

The final couplet has caused some difficulty: "That they, while Thou on both their spoils dost tread, / May crown thy feet, that could not crown thy head." The plural pronoun should refer to the flowers, except for one of the pronomial occurrences Marvell has inserted *both* indicating both the flowers and the serpent, which he has recognized will be crushed together, in order to crush the one. It is clearly the flowers that "May crown thy feet, that could not crown thy head," for the serpent would not "crown" God's feet. The serpent trodden on is a common symbol of the defeat of evil, deriving from part of God's judgment on the serpent, the protevangelium "I will put enmity between thee and the woman, and between thy seed and her seed: it shall bruise thy head, and thou shalt bruise his heel" (Gen. 3.15). Thus the clause "while Thou on both their spoils dost tread" makes reference to both the flowers and the serpent. "Spoils" has brought forth the annotations "the sloughed-off skin of a snake" (which is rejected by Legouis) and "plundering." The word sets up a number of meanings and puns. First, despite Legouis's calling the meaning snake's skin "irrelevant," it is very revelant, for the devil as serpent will have escaped—his head is only bruised—and what will thus be ruined is but the useless carcass that housed evil, not the essence. Second, the pride that has been engendered in the poet constitutes the devil's "spoils" (that is, the plunder acquired by Satan as victor in the war of good and evil with humankind). Third, the poet's spoils are the coronet he has made through his special efforts (a basic meaning of the word in the plural, with a negative connotation hanging over it). Fourth, Marvell is indicating that the coronet as spoils is unnecessary: the word derives from the same word that *spill* comes from.

Spoils are always excessive, unnecessary, the result of succumbing to the devil's second temptation involving *concupiscentia ocularum.* The third temptation, *superbia vitae,* involves pride, the basic problem for the poet within the poem. And fifth, the etymology of *spoil* and *spill* is from the Latin *spolium,* from Greek σφαλλείη, a verb meaning to cause to fall. The etymology, whether in Marvell's knowledge or not, reinforces the pertinency of the citation of the temptations.

Where then does the self come in? First, I cannot read the "I" of the poem as Marvell; it is Marvell only in as much as it is anyone who attempts an equivalency to the coronet. Once one aggrandizes achievement to a balance for Christ's achievement, the poem is arguing, that person has fallen into pride. Next, the self is again the competitive poet; the poem as indicator of that self asks for evaluation in terms of its individuation. And finally the emergent self is one who has demonstrated religious concepts: the poet is a creator like God, but most inferior to him; the author of the poem is a creator who believes in the superiority of God; and the poet is perhaps one who on occasion has allowed pride to dominate, at least momentarily. None of these selves is specific; there are many like Marvell as far as these things are concerned. But that is just the point. The self is at times a performing self, and often enough one can infer a self from its relationship to that performing self in content and tone. In Marvell's poetry we have many—and mostly—performing selves, and we may be able to elicit some data for a psychological reading, spotty though such data are for Marvell.

I cannot possibly deal with many poems here—there are three more I shall look at—but the point should lead to different readings from some in print, when applied to other poems. There are the poems with the real Marvell: "Flecknoe, an English Priest at Rome," "To His Noble Friend Mr. Richard Lovelace," "An Elegy upon the Death of My Lord Francis Villiers," "Upon the Death of the Lord Hastings," "Tom May's Death," "To His Worthy Friend Doctor Witty," "A Letter to Doctor Ingelo," "Two Songs at the Marriage of the Lord Fauconberg and the Lady Mary Cromwell," and "On Mr. Milton's *Paradise Lost.*"[8] From these we can learn much of the personality, interests, thinking, and attitudes of Marvell. There are the poems with the performing self, and in spite of the argument against this one or that which might be made, I cite them: "Clorinda and Damon," "Ametas and Thestylis Making Hay-ropes," "A Dialogue, between the Resolved Soul and Created Pleasure," "The Gallery," "Daphnis and Chloe," "Eyes and Tears," "Young Love," "The Nymph Complaining for the Death of Her Fawn," "On a Drop of Dew," "A Dialogue between the Soul and Body," the Mower poems, "Music's Empire," "Bermudas," and "Upon an Eunuch."[9] These poems range from the apparently simple performing self, as in "The Fair Singer," to the more complex and inferential self, as in "To His Coy Mistress." Related to these poems are satires, working on different material, for different purposes and effects, but often suggesting a hidden self beyond the merely performing self. And then there are those like the Cromwell poems, "The Picture of Little *T. C.* in a Prospect of Flowers," "Upon the Hill and Grove at Bilbrough," and "Upon Appleton House," which have varying degrees of suggestion as to the real Marvell, the performing Marvell, and the inferred Marvell. Whatever the difficulties inherent in "Bermudas" and "The Nymph," the inferential Marvell is not so difficult of agreement. But these latter poems—the Cromwell poems and others—pose grave problems of psychological agreement, and this is true of the three poems I have not listed above: "The Garden," "The unfortunate Lover," and "The Definition of Love." While I would place these all into the performing-self category, I would also place them at the extreme of the inferential selves, hidden deliberately behind images and ambiguities and ideas.

Much has already been written on "The Garden," and I have remarked upon it in chapter 12. The focal couplet, "Annihilating all that's made / To a green thought in a green shade," should be read against the intertextual "source" of Sir Edward Herbert, Lord Cherbury's "Sonnet Made Upon the Groves Near Merlou Castle." This poem has much to comment on in Marvell's verse, and will thus suggest a performing self. This realization, coupled with my ensuing remarks as I turn to the last two poems, should lead to a different reading of "The Garden" from the rather ubiquitous one stressing a philosophic view of nature. Cherbury's sonnet reads:

> You well-compacted groves, whose light and shade,
>   Mix'd equally, produce nor heat nor cold,
>   Either to burn the young or freeze the old,
> But to one even temper being made,
> Upon a green embroidering through each glade
>   An airy silver and a sunny gold,
>   So clothe the poorest that they do behold
> Themselves in riches which can never fade;
>   While the wind whistles, and the birds do sing,
> While your twigs clip, and while the leaves do friss,
>   While the fruit ripens which those trunks do bring,
>   Senseless to all but love, do you not spring
> Pleasure of such a kind as truly is
> A self-renewing vegetable bliss?

We catch an underlying hint of doubt, a realization that all this depends on time and attitude, and that this too may pass. The doubt lies in beholding riches which can never fade, in the four "whiles," and in the question, for not only seasons will change the groves but so will the expectations or moods of those who experience them. The verb "spring" includes the rather common pun on "bring on the season of spring," which will yield "pleasure." The pleasure is the reproduction of kind, "a self-renewing vegetable bliss," which translates into human terms as undisguised sexuality, bliss resulting only from the bodily. The vegetable bliss (as in "To His Coy Mistress") implies fecundity: the kind of growth that the sonnet presents as a positive will, unchecked, become fecund. And its result is the negative emphasis only on self and self's gratification. Appearance rather than reality greets us as we reread the octave: "So clothe the poorest that they do behold / Themselves in riches which can never fade."

As we now reread "The Garden" we see the appearances offered up; we see the garden as the same kind of escape from reality that the groves near Merlou Castle proffered. "Senseless to all but love" are Marvell's "Fond lovers"; the fecundity has become a reality in stanza five (though the stanza at first appearance sounds paradisiacal). Cherbury had implied that the vegetable soul had subsumed the rational, which emerges as we read carefully those "whiles" and the question. Marvell, in the second half of his poem, calls such springing "pleasures less," and moves us into that subsumed rationality. While each glade of Cherbury's groves is clothed with a green embroidering of an airy silver and a sunny gold, Marvell, now withdrawn into the world of the mind, has taken us into the world Cherbury avoids entering, "Annihilating all that's made / To a green thought in a green shade." Part of what is annihilated is the self-renewing vegetable bliss, replaced by the lost Eden of Adam. Once woman enters the scene—the commonly iterated explanation by male Renaissance poets (whether believed or not) of man's "travail"—the "happy garden-state" will disappear. Such a paradise was double paradise; but all that is left is the contemplation of the garden as time moves on. We should not, I believe, force upon Marvell either philosophic concepts beyond the rather ordinary ones to be found in the received poetic attitudes or psychological explanations of his view that this was a "happy garden-state, / While man there walked without a mate." While the next two poems provide hints of a sexual orientation that may lead some people to want to read this poem as a product of a hidden self, too much of its substance lies in the performing self's world for it to be read only in that way.

Peter T. Schwenger[10] has shown a homosexual strain in the love being described in "The unfortunate Lover." As a foray into one area of love generally undescribed by other seventeenth-century poets, it can be treated as the product of a performing self playing witty poetry games by supplying this missing element in the range of love poetry. (Rochester's "Love a woman? You're an ass!" has sometimes been charged as revealing homosexualism in Rochester; see chapter 14.) "The unfortunate Lover," unlike the Rochester poem, which is playful, does suggest a hidden self, deliberately hidden, by its very serious tone. The point of view of homosexualism makes more sense of lines like

> A numerous fleet of cormorants black,
> That sailed insulting o'er the wrack,
> Receiv'd into their cruel care
> Th' unfortunate and abject heir.

Or, remembering the imagery of water as female and fire as male,

> And tyrant Love his breast does ply
> With all his winged artillery,
> Whilst he, betwixt the flames and waves,
> Like Ajax, the mad tempest braves.

The lover is unfortunate because he is homosexual in a world of heterosexuality, and more importantly because he does not accept that homosexuality overtly. The Ajax image corroborates this, since Ajax had offered to violate Cassandra (a representative of fate) only to be punished by Athena (goddess of wisdom), who destroyed his ship (a symbol of man's body traveling the sea of life). Ajax found refuge on a rock (the etymological meaning of his name being earth), here suggesting escape into nonemotionalism, only to have that rock split by Neptune, god of the sea. The split for the poem might suggest division of sexual relationships.[11]

Not only is the poem a contribution to the literature of seventeenth-century poetry of love and its various guises, it is a contribution to the psychological understanding of one kind of homosexual personality, that which resists its sexual orientation because of community pressures, and thus the poem seems to take on more personal tones. This lover thus is bloodied and granted a banneret by Love (the only banneret the tryant Love has created) because he has resisted all Love's winged artillery and been dressed in his own blood. The unfortunate lover, granted Love's only banneret, becomes thus a type, not a specific individual. The lover is "he" throughout the poem; the poet enters only as "my" in "my poor lover floating lay," but the meaning is simply the poet's subject in the poem. I do not think we should wrench this to some personal level.

A later literary use of the poem is provocative. T. S. Eliot recalled the lines "Yet dying leaves a perfume here, / And music within every ear" in the interior monologue "The Love Song of J. Alfred Prufrock," in which Prufrock rejects his amorous feelings for a young woman when human voices wake him, and he drowns:

> I know the voices dying with a dying fall
> Beneath the music from a farther room.
>   So how should I presume?

and

> Is it perfume from a dress
> That makes me so digress?
> Arms that lie along a table, or wrap about a shawl,
>   And should I then presume?
>   And how should I begin?

Or are the backgrounds of homosexualism in "The Waste Land" emerging earlier? For instance, "In the room the women come and go / Talking of Michelangelo," perhaps significantly for the poem an avowed homosexual. Despite the references to the girl who settles a pillow by her head, the hidden self may be deliberately hidden "senza tema d'infamia," not unlike Whitman's Calamus poems. At least the Phoenician sailor, Phlebas (from the Greek, meaning *blood*), in "The Waste Land" (in addition to so many other literary and mythic sources) may owe something to Marvell's unfortunate lover, who is "drest / In his own Blood" and who was by "the sea . . . lent those bitter tears / Which at his eyes he always wears."

"The lover here described is fated never to be born," Schwenger writes of "The unfortunate Lover"; "its very potential for existence is aborted"—which surely is a misreading of the poem. But he continues, "Its curious nature is best described in Marvell's own 'Definition of Love'" (368). This is the only hint of the homosexual nature of this latter poem. Most readings look at it as a platonic kind of love, a spiritual love that is superior to physical love.[12] Harold Toliver, supposedly writing of the poem "and Poetry of Self-Exploration,"[13] has nothing to say about any self. We cannot necessarily equate the "I" of the poem with its author, although further biographical study of Marvell may suggest a deliberately hidden self.

Once we recognize the sexual orientation of this love, the problems of "Definition of Love" move to solution (my italics):

> My love is of a birth as rare
> As 'tis for object strange and high:
> It was *begotten by Despair*
> *Upon Impossibility.* . . .

And therefore her decrees of steel
Us as the distant Poles have placed,
(Though Love's whole world on us doth wheel)
Not by themselves to be embraced. . . .

As lines (so loves) oblique may well
Themselves in every angle greet:
But *ours so truly parallel,*
Though infinite, can never meet.

Therefore the love which us doth bind,
But *Fate so enviously debars,*
Is the conjunction of the mind,
And opposition of the stars.

That is, to paraphrase, the persona of the poetic voice says his love is the sexual creation of *despair* (as male figure) upon *impossibility* (as female figure). The *despair* arises because the love object is "high" (sincere and worthy) but "strange" (socially unacceptable) and because the love cannot come to overt manifestation (in view of society's homophobia). It involves *impossibility* not only because of the strictures against overt homoerotic manifestation but because sexual creation will not result in any noticeable *birth.* The imagery of sexual intercourse and of resultant birth is clear; the lack of usual sexual fruition in the situation depicted here seems equally clear. The unchangeable decrees of Fate have placed these *Two perfect Loves* diametrically apart (like the North and the South Poles) though their love is the world about which their lives revolve. Their loves are parallel (being male and male rather than male and female—it was commonplace to believe that men and women experienced different kinds of emotions), but thus they cannot intersect, no matter how lasting their loves for each other may be. The only way of union, because Fate (the opposition of the stars) has debarred male/male sexual relationship, is through their minds.

Whether we allow a biographical substrate or not, the poem is a lyric as I have previously defined it: the poet is concerned with writing a poem, here most consciously and strikingly by using puns and double entendres, cosmic and universal imagery (to move it out of the only personal), and metaphoric statement for a topic seldom pursued in poetry of the period. The lyric is, indeed, a prime example of the performing self. "The Definition of Love" is another facet of the subject matter of love, just as Donne's "Loves growth" and "Loves diet" oppositely examine the unlimited capacity of loving ("No winter shall abate the springs encrease") and its potential "burdenous corpulence" ("to make it lesse, / And keepe it in proportion, / [I did] Give it a diet"). Or Donne's "The Autumnal," playing on love between a young man and an older woman, balanced by Rochester's "Song of a Young Lady to Her Ancient Lover." These are all examples of lyrics and of the performing self.

In Marvell's poems we have evidence of a hidden self as performing self, perhaps of a hidden self deliberately hidden, and of a hidden self inferred from its relationship with the performing self. The kind of examination of the self in poetry that we have made is obviously another, and different kind of, limen into a deeper and "new" reading of a poem. Such examination will furnish data for at least a tentative psychological analysis of Marvell and, ironically, for less complex readings of most of his poems.

Rochester's Poetry and
Its Seventeenth-Century Antecedents

C ertainly no period that can be characterized by a type of thinking, an ethic, or an artistic mode has a sharp beginning or a sharp end. But the last forty years of the seventeenth century have frequently been severed from what precedes by literary critics and teachers as if they were somehow totally distinct. Yet this period does continue and "complete" the literary movements of the immediate past while it also changes and develops. Now, what that means is that some things are lost or absorbed, some things are developed and expanded, and some things emerge that appear to be "new." Aside from the obvious links—Edmund Waller and Sir John Denham, Shakespeare and Milton—little is seen to unite the Restoration with the earlier seventeenth century in literary discussions. Earl Miner's study of poetic modes in the seventeenth century—the metaphysical mode, the cavalier mode, and the Restoration mode—moves to dispel this chronological dichotomy, but his underlying perception that the century engages various unities is rare indeed.[1]

The poets of the earlier seventeenth century were less ignored than many have apparently believed, and they influenced the poetry of the later seventeenth century—in certain ways at least. This view has been advanced elsewhere, but it is not commonplace.[2] The intertextuality of sources and influences provides another means into reading and understanding literature. But some of the intertextuality of the poetry immediately prior to 1660 has been overlooked in that of the Restoration, though it leads to awareness that much of that poetry falls into a coterie class, one less "sincere" and more purposefully "literary" than critics have usually allowed. Perhaps the mind-set that has led to this kind of inadequacy has been the domination of a satiric mode with its contemporary contexts and the neoclassical bias for the age (though it was stronger in the early eighteenth century) with dismissal of all but Shakespeare and Milton as "proper" mentors.[3] The poetry of John Wilmot, Earl of Rochester, whose accepted canon of poems seems to date from around 1665 through 1680, when he died, has thus been misrepresented in various ways, I believe, because of the frequent critical divorce of pre-1660 from post-1660 poetry.[4] He does not represent all the strands of seventeenth-century poetry, and I mean no reductionism of Rochester's work where I see it evolving from earlier authors. But only by recognition of its full context can we, I think, validly evaluate it. I use the edition of David Vieth (1968) and the canon as given there. I will not, therefore, raise the question of a poem like "A Session of the Poets," which Vieth would prefer assigning to Elkanah Settle, a poem clearly deriving from Suckling's verses of similar title.

While Vieth notes relationships of Rochester's poems with Malherbe, Petronius, Lucretius, Ovid, Anacreon, Ronsard, Boileau, Montaigne, Hobbes, Horace, Sir Carr Scroope, and other contemporary poets or poems being satirized, there is only one citation of any other literary influence, and that is for the earliest Rochester poem (" 'Twas a dispute 'twixt heaven and earth"). Vieth, showing his attitude basically to be that to which this chapter is opposed, writes: "The exact date of composition is unknown, although the old-fashioned style of the poem, reminiscent of Ben Jonson's lyrics, suggests an early work." Some allusions also occur (for example, to Suckling, Waller, and Falkland), but only in two instances are pertinent "sources" cited: one to Marlowe's "Come Live With Me" (of course, not a seventeenth-century poem) in "The Platonic Lady" and one to Lovelace's "To Lucasta" in a song beginning, "How happy, Chloris, were they free." Vieth sees the Restoration as an intellectual crossroads and is concerned to differentiate it from what preceded and what followed. But he casts most of Rochester's early poems as self-consciously conventional ones, "including pastoral dialogues, Ovidian imitations, and lyrics incorporating features of the general courtly love and Petrarchan traditions," and he remarks that "the best satires follow native traditions and are written in a native four-stress measure, either iambic tetrameter couplets resembling those of *Hudibras* or anapestic tetrameter that recalls the accentual, alliterative verse of Old English. It is almost as though Rochester, in order to make his contribution to the newly emerging literary sensibility, was condemned to relive the history of English prosody, as a human embryo is said to recaptiulate the stages of evolution prior to birth." In all, Vieth's introduction gives little hint that the immediately preceding poetry of the seventeenth century had existed as even the vaguest of influences on Rochester. I assume he includes it, however, in "the general courtly love and Petrarchan traditions" and perhaps in the "pastoral dialogues."

Even one of the few anthologies of seventeenth-century literature that cover the full century and one that has long been popular for college courses casts no earlier seventeenth-century poetic shadow over Rochester's poems. Witherspoon and Warnke[5] introduce Rochester by mentioning only "graceful lyrics and effective satires," "brittle but melodious love lyrics," and "pornographic verses." On the last point—the pornographic verse—which seems to be the most observable feature of Rochester's output for some people, we need only note the way paved by just two earlier poems: Suckling's "A Candle" (its phallicism will escape no one)[6] and Lovelace's "Lucasta Taking the Waters at Tunbridge." The latter interestingly is placed at the site of one of Rochester's major satires. Its last lines— "Through all the heavens you were brought / Of Virtue, Honour, Love and Bliss"—compress Lucasta's progression from virgin to satisfying sex partner; the waters that lap in and out of her vagina image her effect on the action with the "I" of the poem. Certainly Rochester's "pornography" had immediate respectable, though tamer, antecedents.

Rochester's alleged prosodic travails are without foundation. The image of a recapitulating poetic embryo does not even square with the chronological order of the poems. Rather, Rochester's prosody has obvious precedents (and one could even say "sources") in the popular poetry that preceded his. We can note that Lovelace's lyric just cited employs alternate rhyme and iambic tetrameters in quatrains, the specific meter or near meter of seven Rochester poems. The same meter is found in other earlier poems similar in theme to these of Rochester; for example, Carew's "Song: The Willing Prisoner to His Mistress" and again Lovelace's "Guileless Lady Imprisoned; After, Penanced." It is Donne's meter in "The Extasie." Similar to the previous prosodic form is Rochester's use of the quatrain with alternate rhyme and alternate tetrameters and truncated tetrameters or trimeters; there are fifteen poems in this meter. These patterns are found, typically, in Carew's "Pastoral Dialogue," in Suckling's "I prithee send me back my heart," and in Lovelace's "Lucasta Weeping." It was Donne's prosodic form in "The Undertaking." Rhyming couplets in tetrameters or truncated tetrameters is the meter, of course, of Milton's "L'Allegro" and "Il Penseroso," and Carew's "Parting, Celia Weeps," Suckling's "My Dearest Rival, Lest Our Love," and Lovelace's "Against the Love of Great Ones." Rochester employs it often, sometimes with stanzaic breaks (seven poems), which also occurs in Carew's "Lover, in the Disguise of an Amazon, Is Dearly Beloved of His Mistress," Suckling's "Love's World," and Lovelace's "Lucasta at the Bath."

Some poems fall into a category that "follow[s] native traditions . . . written in a native four-stress measure" in verse resembling "Hudibras"; yet one like "A Ramble in St. James's Park" should be compared with, among many others, Suckling's "Against Absence"—and we might also note Suckling's sneering tone and female persona, which incidentally are in generic descent from Donne's "Womans Constancy." The most frequent meter for Rochester is, expectedly, the pentameter couplet; it is the meter of twenty-two poems, and three others are similar. It is a glory of Jonson's verse, but also Donne's, and it is the standard meter of the verse satire from Edward Hake and Thomas Lodge onward.

The triplet called "Under King Charles II's Picture" gives varying line lengths, and triplet stanzas are used for "Upon Nothing." Among other poets, Edward Herbert, Lord Cherbury, used the same form in "The Idea," as did Lovelace in "Calling Lucasta from Her Retirement." "Rochester Extempore" is a double triplet. The stanza of varying line lengths and/or varying rhyme schemes, a major achievement of Donne, whose Songs and Sonets repeat only the alternating rhymed quatrain four times, also appears in Rochester ten times. We need note only Lovelace's poem "Sonnet," beginning "Depose your finger of the ring," which is in two six-line stanzas, rhyming, like Rochester's, *a b a b c c,* in tetrameters and trimeters conditioned by the rhyme scheme, as is Rochester's.

Remaining to be cited from Rochester's canon are those poems that I take Vieth to mean when he says "the best satires follow native traditions and are written in a native four-stress measure . . . [in] anapestic tetrameter that recalls the accentual, alliterative verse of Old English." There are only three: "The Submission," "Quoth the Duchess of Cleveland," and "Signior Dildo." All are in quatrain couplets with four accents per line; there are usually eleven or twelve syllables per line. Generally thus the lines can be scanned as anapestic tetrameters, although at times a syllable (or more) may be missing and at times a different kind of foot from the anapest emerges. Is there a precedent in earlier seventeenth-century poetry? Of course there is; Suckling's "Sessions of the Poets," which generally uses eleven-syllable lines, is clearly the most obvious example:

> He openly declar'd that it was the best sign
> Of good store of wit to have good store of coin;
> And without a syllable more or less said
> He put the laurel on the Alderman's head.

Besides, there is Charles Cotton's "Voyage to Ireland in Burlesque," written around 1670 in three cantos, which uses the same meter, though he does not break it into quatrains.

In all, Rochester's verse forms and prosody show clear affinities with what immediately preceded. And while he most frequently employs the iambic pentameter couplet, as do others of the Restoration period, he is not restricted to it any more than Dryden is, or Waller is, or Jonson was, or Donne was. Too easily, I think, critics have stressed this versification to the detriment of determining a clear view of Restoration poetry and its relationships with the past.

These comments on versification point the way to tackle subjects and

techniques, which will link up with others' poetry and which will thereby
provide avenues into reading Rochester's work and seeing his *literary*
achievements, achievements that are the result of intentionality of writing
rather than only sociological or philosophic precepts. For not only is the
prosody of Rochester's poems seen in earlier poems such as those cited, but
so is much of his subject matter, approach, and attitudes—and that will be
evident from comparison of Rochester's work with the poems of others
already noted. Rochester's "Woman's Honor" should be compared with
Donne's "The Dampe," with Carew's "A Rapture," and with Suckling's
"Love and Beloved," and particularly we should look at Suckling's " 'Tis
now, since I sate down before," with its common military imagery in an
assault on Honor. His "Platonic Lady," an adaptation of a poem by Petronius,
elicits the comment from Vieth that its title is inappropriate. But Platonic
love, the superficial view of nonsexual love, is lampooned frequently, just
as Rochester is doing here. I think immediately of four poems of that
title—"Platonic Love"—two by Cherbury, one by Cowley, and one by
Robert Fletcher. Some of the language of Cherbury's poems is similar to
Rochester's, but what Rochester is doing is turning Cherbury's kind of
argument around from the point of view of the lady. However, Suckling
had already done so in his own way. In one of his "Against Fruition" poems
he writes:

> Stay here, fond youth, and ask no more; be wise:
> Knowing too much long since lost paradise.
> The virtuous joys thou hast, thou wouldst should still
> Last in their pride; and wouldst not take it ill,
> If rudely from sweet dreams (and for a toy)
> Thou wert wak'd? he wakes himself, that does enjoy.

Suckling's female persona's view here that "Fruition adds no new wealth,
but destroys, / And while it pleaseth much the palate, cloys" could serve as
psychic rationalization for the impotence of Rochester's male in "The
Imperfect Enjoyment." Suckling's woman says that "They who know all
the wealth they have are poor; / He's only rich that cannot tell his store,"
but Rochester's woman asks, "Is there then no more? / . . . All this to love
and rapture's due; / Must we not pay a debt to pleasure too?" In Suckling's
"Song" not only are some of the words and attitudes the same as in "The
Platonic Lady," but the persona is also a woman:

> I prithee spare me, gentle boy,
> Press me no more for that slight toy,
> That foolish trifle of an heart;

> I swear it will not do its part,
> Though thou dost thine, employ'st thy power and art.

The point in all this is not specific debts that Rochester owes, not sources in any direct sense, but the fact that his themes have precedents in the poetry of Donne and the so-called Cavalier poets, like Carew, Suckling, Lovelace, and others too; his themes, his points of view, his personae have all been drawn from a popular form of poetizing on the questions concerning love. The man-woman mix is constantly shifted and reviewed and re-created with twists and changing circumstances. And this is as much a part of Donne's poetic as it is Suckling's and as it is Rochester's. All three exhibit poetizing, or as it often nowadays is called, coterie poetry. While Donne writes a poem to an older woman, "The Autumnal," Rochester writes "A Song of a Young Lady to Her Ancient Lover." While Donne uses the deformed mistress theme in "Marry, and love thy *Flavia,*" Rochester gives us "a proud bitch" with "savory scent of salt-swoln cunt," who, rather than picking out "some stiff-pricked clown or well-hung parson" "to rub her arse on," turns "damned abandoned jade" in "A Ramble in St. James's Park." He wishes "stinking vapors choke her womb" and a new lover "bluster in her cunt," for like the "I" of Donne's "The Apparition," wishing a cruel revenge on his former lover whom he envisions in a quicksilver sweat in bed with her new lover, Rochester wants "To plague this woman and undo her" with the same cruel revenge:

> But my revenge will best be timed
> When she is married that is limed.
> In that most lamentable state
> I'll make her feel my scorn and hate.

Rochester's "The Advice" seems almost a pastiche of such Donne elegies as "Going to Bed," "Change," and "Loves Progress" in language, image, situation, and the influence of the blazon, but I suspect few have seen this latter influence in Rochester's lines on the "gentle brooks" that can "swell with rage" and "ravage o'er the banks they kissed, the flowers they fed before." But the blazon does lie behind his poem.

And what of Rochester's alleged homosexuality, say in "Love a woman? You're an ass!"? The poem is a giant step past Donne's "Farewell to Love," where the poet acknowledges that shunning the heat of woman's loving is "but applying worme-seed to the Taile," but its stance is the same: the betrayed lover who rejects this "silliest part of God's creation." With a clear look at Donne's "Loves Alchymie," Rochester says, "let the porter and the groom . . . Drudge in fair Aurelia's womb / To get supplies for age and graves" (her name, of course, puns on the etymology *gold*, the hoped-for alchemical formula in Donne's laboratory). Part of Rochester's speaking voice's sex drive will be allayed (physically) by drinking, part (psychologically) by obscene jokes. But Rochester more thoroughly rejects fickle woman, for he ends unlike Donne, who always holds out the possibility of finally finding true love, with a complete put-down: he can get sexual relief more easily, without trial and deprivations and attachments and problems—the meaning of "forty" as symbol—with a "sweet, soft page" than he can with "forty wenches." No, it is not homosexual; it is a witty resolution for sexual drives that more usually lead a man into woman's alleged snares and take away his "freedom."

The interpretation of the last poem is central to our understanding of Rochester's poetry (as well as earlier poets') and to our understanding of a unity in seventeenth-century poetry. Scholars seem to read poetry like this only in terms of biography or serious, sociological themes. That is, Donne is supposed to be philosophically concerned about the relationship of soul and body even in his songs and sonnets. But Donne is having poetic and witty fun in things like "The good-morrow" when he talks about sucking on "cunt - ry pleasures."[7] Since sex is ever-present in life, since wittiness is often synonymous for some people with obscene connotations, and since poetizing was often the diversion of gentlemen and schoolboys, many poems of many poets should be viewed primarily as competitive "play." This is not to say that a good depth-psychological study could not be made of Rochester's seeming emphasis on phalluses and spermatic issue and impotence or that sociologically he did not recognize the evils of his times and see them epitomized by the licentious activities of the great and the small, but it does suggest that the death-bed conversion has been enhanced by an overreading of the poems that precede. (We do have "Rochester's Ghost," of course, as aid to such overreading.)[8]

Dryden's casting Donne's lyrics as love poems aiming at engaging the minds of the weaker sex (in his preface to Juvenal's satires) seems echoed very often in our own times. Such a comment alone should raise questions about Dryden's astuteness as a critic. But who has recognized Donne's twisting of the common symbol of "A Bracelet of bright haire about the bone" in "The Relique" as referring to vaginal hair surrounding a phallus? However, surely even Dryden did not read "Leave thy gaudy gilded stage" as Vieth does—that is, as a lyric possibly addressed to an actress like Elizabeth Barry. It is a version of Donne's "If our two loves be one, or, Thou and I / Love so alike, that none doe slacken, none can die," using a world-theater image. Certainly Rochester's contemporaries did not read his advice to Phyllis in "By all love's soft, yet mighty powers" to "take to cleanly sinning" as sociological or satiric. This was simply another situation to be described: the "fair nasty" whore who lies in foul linen and uses no paper behind or sponges before. She is still available on many streetcorners. These poems are to be evaluated as poetry, not as sociological, philosophical, biographical, or satirically critical documents. They partake of "play," not philosophy.

The preceding remarks also apply to Rochester's satires. Poems may be verse satires and they may be satiric, as we have seen in chapter 2. "Tunbridge Wells" is a verse satire; "A Very Heroical Epistle in Answer to Ephelia" is not. The verse satire goes back a long way, and for Rochester and his contemporaries people like Donne, Jonson, Cherbury, and Cleveland helped develop its form and substance as much as Horace and Juvenal. The use of specific people and events to give lively proof to the universal points being made was far from new in 1660. Such satiric works remain in the social mode, as Miner defines it, but the greater concentration on specific people and events in Restoration verse satires does indicate a change. The change depended largely on the interpretation of what poets like Horace and Juvenal were understood to be doing in their ("classical") poems and the concept of imitation or translation that stressed equating the *sense* of another's work by contemporary images and allusions. Too, it is another form of closure that can be seen throughout the intellectual currents of the Restoration world, which tended to formulize and generally restrict.[9]

In "A Satyr Against Reason and Mankind" we see that allusions to Ingelo, Patrick, Sibbes, and Meres are not in themselves important; they are not yet the butt of the satire as Dryden was to be in Rochester's "Allusion to Horace." It is not different from Donne's references in "Satyre IV" to Jovius, Surius, Calepine, Beza, and others, but the satirical verse epistle "A Very Heroical Epistle"—an obvious antecedent would be Suckling's "An Epistle," which lampoons theological controversy such as that over Socinianism—becomes pointed, here against John Sheffield, Earl of Mulgrave. A satiric lyric like "On Mrs. Willis" combines a universal type or subject and a specific person or context. In a way, but without the venom, this is what Suckling does in "Upon Tom Carew Having the Pox," and Lovelace does in "A Mock Song," and Jonson does in "An Epigram on the Court Pucell." Rochester's poems, typical of the more public mode of his age, sometimes move out of only the social mode, and in these poems—like "Quoth the Duchess of Cleveland"—his satire becomes critical about real public figures. We can remove Dryden from "An Allusion to Horace" and get much from the universal theme and observations, just as we can Shadwell from "MacFlecknoe," but we cannot remove Cary Frazier and her parents from the quatrain about her, though something is being said about parents who abet the eventual prostitution of their children for their personal gain.

The satire of the Restoration, Rochester's included, harks backward but makes greater strides forward than other kinds of poetic writing by alterations of the received forms and techniques. It is a rather logical development of what can be observed in the satires or satiric poems from Wyatt and Joseph Hall onward.

Part of what happens to Restoration poetry is that it stresses certain generic forms, thus generally casting out other generic forms, and sets up rules of prosody, language, and decorum that are greatly narrowed down from what had chronologically preceded the period. All of this can be related to the changes wrought by the influence of Ramus, as Walter Ong has argued,[10] or by the influence of a scientific and largely mechanistic spirit, or by the arguments about the ancients and moderns that relate in turn to the theories of the earth that the seventeenth century wrangled over. But in any case the heroic couplet came into prominence, we know, although someone like Rochester shows much more variety than that, and indeed more variety than most of the other poets of the period, who simply were inferior. Thomas Shipman commented in 1678 on Milton's error in using blank verse,[11] a typical attitude of the age, and noted that Thomas Rymer had promised a discussion of the matter. Rymer's half-sentence at the close of his *Tragedies of the Last Age Consider'd and Examin'd* (1678) is often alluded to in similar ways by others, including Dryden. Even though Milton's blank verse is damned—and the decision to use it almost surely was made no earlier than the very late 1650s—his epic is a generating force behind such varied heroic verse as Dryden's "Absalom and Achitophel" (1681), William Wollaston's "Design of Part of the Book of Ecclesiastes" (1691), Samuel Wesley's "Life of Our Blessed Lord and Saviour Jesus Christ" (1693), and Sir Richard Blackmore's "Prince Arthur" (1695) and "King Arthur" (1697). Rochester's most frequent prosodic mode is in conformity with his times, although it was common enough from the very beginning of the seventeenth century, but he also exhibits in a narrower range some of the varieties of the past. His narrower range is not narrower than Jonson's or Herrick's or Waller's, let alone people like Carew and Suckling and Lovelace, cited so frequently before.

Rochester's genres narrow themselves as well from the variety of the earlier age: the sonnet is gone, so is the ode, so are the larger forms, so is the impossibility poem and the advice-to-the-painter satire (common though it was in his own age), as well as the topographical poem, the topiary, and others. But this kind of narrowing and omission of some of the specific types is true of his age as well. Rochester gives us the pastoral, the dialogue, the lyric, the song (if we can make a differentiation from the lyric, as I have argued in chapter 6), the verse satire, the epitaph, the epigram, the verse epistle, and the Anacreontic, forms persistent from the past and of his present.

The themes are those of the Cavalier, remaining usually in what Miner calls the "social mode" and only in some of the satires moving into the "public mode," though never really into Dryden's public form. As Miner says, Rochester is given to disorder, but I do not really agree that he offers a thesis of what the *vita beata* is. The skepticism that pervades the seventeenth century emerges as it does in Donne's lyrics, and it may indicate a longing on the author's part for belief and for order, but it is not a proffered philosophy of life. Not enough attention is given to "play," too much to "seriousness."

Vieth epitomized Rochester's technique, particularly that of the verse satires, as a simultaneous manipulation of several conflicting levels or planes of experience. "The point at which two or more such planes intersect is the poem, and the name of the resulting effect is irony" (xxxv). But an example like that of "Upon His Leaving His Mistress," which interplays masculine "heroic" honor in war, feminine honor in love, and the fertility of nature, does not strongly enough evidence a "discovery of the way to limit discontinuous modes of experience" (xxxvi) to make it different from preceding poets' work. What Rochester does is achieve great lyric and satiric verse, in his own way better than most others before him and contemporary with him, and his style does have a quality. But to assign to him a kind of literary philosophy of composition is, I think, wrong. The interplay of war and love in "Upon His Leaving His Mistress" is commonplace—most of us think of Lovelace, although Donne's "Loves Warre" set a pattern for many to follow who did not have classical models at their minds' edges. The strand of the fertility of nature is different from what might be inferred, for the poet of Rochester's poem is using analogic reasoning to get rid of his mistress. He *says* he has not grown weary of her; he *says* she is too attractive to confine herself to one man as meaner spirits of her sex have to; but the point is he is tired of her and she has become a leech to him. He argues that since earth as womb receives and germinates all kinds of seed, why should not she (as a mere womb) do as much for many other men besides him? She is a possessive woman (if the reader will allow Rochester's male chauvinism) that the poet wants to get rid of. If she has not been a whore before, the poet makes clear that his attitude is the frequent enough male attitude that any chaste woman who has finally given him what he wants has become a "loose" woman in his eyes. Somewhere in the background is a poem like Donne's "Communitie," which tells us that "All may use All" women and that when a man has eaten the kernel, "who doth not fling away the shell?" And Donne's "Confin'd Love" is also in that background, with lines like "And thence a law did grow, / One should but one man know; / But are other creatures so?" and "Good is not good, unlesse / A thousand it possess, / But doth wast with greedinesse." Rochester's making his mistress "the mistress of mankind," of course, also makes her Eve, the meaning of the name in Hebrew, and males all know that it was through Eve that they "came to travaile" (to use Donne's words in "The Indifferent").

By seeing an author like Rochester within the poetic continuums of which he is a part, we can more validly evaluate his achievement—but not by assigning to him ideas and intentions he did not pursue, nor by obscuring *literary* contexts by inducing philosophy and sociology and moralities. The lack of attention to some of Rochester's sources and influences, as we have seen, not only has obviated the readings and literary qualities of his poetry we have examined, but it denies avenues into meaning and evaluation. If there are points of "typicality" for the age about Rochester's poetry, then perhaps we will understand that Restoration poetry is part of seventeenth-century poetry, that it continues earlier leads in prosody, subject, treatment, and technique, that it absorbs or changes or drops earlier leads, and that it develops "new" avenues for literary expression by such continuation, absorption, change, and rejection. Perhaps the words one should address to poetry from 1600 to 1700 can be summarized thus:

> The worst that I could write would be no more
> Than what thy very friends have said before.[12]

15

Summary Conclusion: Liminal Entries to Reading Literature

Briefly, the thesis of this book is that many literary works have been incompletely and even invalidly read because of the lack of attention to matters reflecting the writer writing. Included in such matters are genre, subgenres, and modes, which continue to have significance despite some blurring of their nature, and such devices as structure, numerological considerations, allusion or imitation, onomastics, and literary (poetic or narrative) voice or self. Such matters are thresholds into a reading—an interpretation, an understanding—of a work. Ignoring them may lead to incomplete reading, if not misreading; recognition of them should lead to valid reading. Certainly the writer writing wants to say something or communicate feeling or idea, and thus decides before writing or shortly thereafter to employ one or more of these thresholds: the pre-text or foreconceit. Rejecting a generic form or mode becomes a threshold, of course, and confusions of literary voice or of structures also yield avenues into an understanding of the writer writing. The reader reading is subject to many things, among them the work itself, which incorporates such limina and which encases the authorial presence as craftsperson. The reading may not be adequate to the writing because of the reader or because of the writer; it may be more than the author's intentionality for the text. But herein lie the factors of evaluation, and evaluation may perhaps be of the craft or of the substance or, better and more to be hoped, of the craft and the substance working together. A major detraction from the reader reading what the writer has written, of course, is an expectation, perhaps derived from another reader's misreading, that attention to such limina would avoid. Expectation, one often finds, is a cliché that collapses under examination. This thesis is arguing against the popular conception of the reader-response methodology that finds response reading linearly only and with blinders on as to contexts of the work in question. Contexts may range from associations with other literary works—as in a sequence or collection, as well as alongside a literary work of similar subject or type—to political, historical, biographical, ideological, and other worlds. It is arguing for a thorough reader response, while acknowledging that help from the critic-reader may be necessary from time to time. Thereby it denies that the seemingly disengaged approaches of new-critical theorists, poststructuralists, and others, useful though they are, can adequately read and appreciate and discriminate literature.

Brief discussions of two Colonial American seventeenth-century poets, one well known, the other generally unknown, supply additional examples of the importance of these limina to reading. Only Edward Taylor and Anne Bradstreet have received real literary treatment and general approbation as Early American poets. Much of the work on Bradstreet has attempted to reverse Moses Coit Tyler's opaque opinion that she was "sadly misguided by the poetic standards of her religious sect and of her literary period."[1] Some of her resurrection as a poet has been as a result of the rather recent women's movement: "Bradstreet, I believe, was the first woman poet who attempted to view women in some kind of historical perspective. . . . "[2] Jeannine Hensley, while commending Bradstreet's poetry, indicates the influence of this factor on her evaluation: "But we also see a charming and very human woman who loves her tables and trunks and chests, allows her sometimes excessive humility to turn into feministic irony, and through her dread of dying in childbirth lets us see that her deeper fear is a jealous one that her husband might remarry."[3] But all of Bradstreet's work should be given the meaningful scrutiny that some of it has received, and the liminal means that have been discussed will direct a revised reading of her poems.

"The Flesh and the Spirit" employs pictures, concepts, and language that derive from the New Testament, yet the poem is clearly an example of the medieval débat of Body and Soul, looked at previously. After eight lines of introduction, Flesh speaks—as is standard—through line 36. Next Spirit speaks in double that length, seventy-two lines. The balancing is obvious. But usually the balancing is the other way around: Body speaks, say, twelve lines and Soul but six, followed by repetitions of twelve and six, for Soul normally speaks last (as here), always wins the debate (as here), and needs fewer arguments to win. Bradstreet makes Flesh and Spirit sisters; that is, they come from the same generative source and thus represent a psychological duality. (The mythic concept of the double is pertinent and is made more significant than it is in the usual body/soul poem.) Spirit assigns Flesh's father as Adam and hers as God: clearly a psychomachia common to all humans is one background of the poem. Its genre leads us to read the poem as a variation of a form and a theme: a successful manipulation by the author. And we realize that such variation is purposeful to lead to ideas contrastive to those in the usual generic example. Its thesis is, thus, that things of this world are things that will know only a past, whereas the things of heaven are things to come where "there shall be no darksome night." The triumph of the Spirit's argument is not simply a moral one but a reminder of Christ's admonition to "lay up treasures for yourselves in heaven" (Matt. 6.20).

This poem is, of course, not a "confessional" poem of the type that some have come only to appreciate and to see only as the substance of a gem like "A Letter to Her Husband, Absent upon Publick Employment." Reexamination in terms of its imagery and structure suggests more than just a biographical/psychological emotion. A two-line catalogue is followed by a pun on head (the husband) and heart (the wife) separated by but a neck (the distance they are apart). A major image is the body, specifically their oneness in body as well as in spirit. The zodiacal imagery labels the husband the sun, who brings on Capricorn, the winter season, by having gone southward; his return northward will bring Cancer, the summer season. The ironic use of antithetic imagery is important: normally southerly movement suggests warmth, summer, and growth, and northerly movement cold, winter, and death. Usually Capricorn suggests sexual activity and Cancer something evil. But here, the dead time of winter presents to her view, ironically, only "those fruits which through [his] heat [she] bore"; the presence of him as sun within her heart (Cancer, in her glowing breast) is wished for to irradiate outward, apparently, through her whole being like a cancer or through the arteries leading from the heart. Coitional imagery appears throughout:

> I wish my Sun may never set, but burn
> Within the Cancer of my glowing breast,
> The welcome house of him my dearest guest.

It is capped by "Flesh of thy flesh, bone of thy bone, / I here, thou there, yet both but one." The allusion to Eve and Adam is, however, another reversal, for it is Adam who partakes of the forbidden fruit because of his love for Eve as flesh of his flesh and bone of his bone. Here it is Anne who assigns the sexual concept of original sin to herself through her love of Simon. The substance of the poem is more than just "confessional" or personal—as all good poetry should be: its imagery demands attention and its antitheses require close reading.

If one knows the poetry of Anne Bradstreet, one knows "Contemplations," a "nature poem on the transcience of man's life," as it has been epitomized. References to Eden and Adam, Cain and Abel, yield additional perspectives, but the authorial presence that persists in the poem's structuring has not been observed. This poem on the transience of life is in thirty-three stanzas, and immediately we should recognize an allusion to Christ, for he was crucified at age thirty-three and it has thus become a commonplace symbol. The point is clear: though the poem treats transience in this our life, it is really about resurrection. The last two lines, with an allusion to Revelation 2.17, are "But he whose name is grav'd in the white stone / Shall last and shine when all of these are gone." ("Shine" likewise suggests sun, thence, Son.) Yet there is more underscoring of the thesis of the poem by the poet's craft. Each stanza is in seven lines: six lines of iambic pentameter, rhyming *a b a b c c,* with a final line of iambic hexameter (that is, an alexandrine) with a *c* rhyme. The stanza is that used by John Milton in the proem to his ode "On the Morning of *Christs* Nativity," except that the rhyme scheme is slightly different. This antecedent helps stress the Christ figura beneath Bradstreet's poem, which can also be realized from the first stanza in the reference to Phoebus, from the fourth stanza, where the sun becomes a deity, and from stanza five, which begins with an allusion to the parable of the wise and foolish virgins (Matt. 25.1–10): "Thou as a Bridegroom from thy Chamber rushes." There are but three rhymes, a suggestion thus of Trinity, and seven is the number of creation, since it is a combination of three, the Trinity, and four, the number of nature and Man. Further, the alexandrine in this context effects a sense of continuance, as do the last two lines, with their concept of resurrection. It is the same effect one gets in Milton's stanza and in the stanza of the hymn in the "Nativity Ode," as well as in his "Fair Infant Elegy," its stanza being the same as the stanza of the proem of the "Nativity Ode."

And then we come to the first two lines of stanza 6: "Thy swift Annual, and diurnal Course, / Thy daily streight, and yearly oblique path," which sets up the chiasmus Annual:diurnal/daily:yearly. It was a common trick of poets writing about Christ to include his sign, *chi* (as in "Xmas"). Line 3 of Milton's proem gives us another example, which Bradstreet surely would have recognized: "Of wedded Maid, and Virgin Mother born"; wedded:Maid/Virgin:Mother, and it is placed in line 3. We can go further, however, with this arithmetic structuring. The golden section lies within stanza 20, which reads: "Nay, they [the things of nature] shall darken, perish, fade and dye, / And when unmade, so ever shall they lye, / But man was made for endless immortality." There are echoʋs there of the fourteenth stanza of Milton's hymn. The poem, as we can see from all these data, is resurrectional: it is not simply concerned with the transience of life, but with a human's contemplated afterlife, one's name having been graved in the white stone.

I suppose the major reason for people's lack of knowledge of a poet like Richard Steere is the general unavailability of the poems. His "Earths Felicities, Heavens Allowances" is in blank verse; it is a blank verse employing the line as unit, not the verse paragraph as we find in *Paradise*

Lost, despite a possible influence. Steere completes the 527-line poem with a couplet placed on three lines:[4]

> From Heav'n on Earth, to Heav'n in Heav'n ascend,
> Where our Felicities can know no
> > End.

It is a device employed by John Donne in a verse epistle to Sir Henry Wotton ("Sir, more than kisses"), and it is not unlike Herbert's devices in *The Temple.* It is actually a restatement of the thought of the central point of the poem, line 264: "And raise our Souls to God from whence they came." The poem has proceeded from discussion of the three felicities (Riches, Honours, Pleasures), to the contexts for enjoying those felicities, to the means to enjoy them, and then to God's commandment to enjoy and thereby "raise our Souls to God." The midpoint does not create a symmetric poem, but it does balance the subject matter and suggests the two halves as containers coming to the same ends. The second half of the poem moves from the dangers lying within the felicities, to the means for circumventing those dangers, to apostrophes to Heaven's allowances, and finally to a quick summary of the main point of the entire poem:

> If thus the Earths Felicities we use,
> Looking through them up to those joys beyond,
> And so Enjoy them with a heav'nly mind,
> We may in them feel heav'nly joys below,
> That when our days shall Terminate, we may
> From Heav'n on Earth, to Heav'n in Heav'n ascend,
> Where our Felicities can know no
> > End.

If there are such balances intended as I suggest, then the verse paragraph of the ending of the first half, lines 232–64, thirty-three lines, and the verse paragraph of the ending of the second half (above), lines 521–27, seven lines, should be contrasted and may have been controlled to achieve significant numbers, whose mystic understanding was noted before. The contrast of the two passages is led by the concept of using the felicities "In their true use and moderate Enjoyance"; that is, use and "Enjoy them with a heav'nly mind." The poem has not just been written line after line to the end: it was planned and executed with artistic as well as didactic purpose.

Such artistic planning—the writer writing—has been the burden of this book. It cannot be dismissed, and it does direct the reader reading, whether the standard authors and works often mentioned here or the expanded canon of popular authors or of those little-known ones who appear in these pages. These limina may—should—cause us to rethink canon, reevaluating more highly the familiar and positively evaluating at least some of the new.

Notes

Chapter 1

1. See William Coward, *Licentia Poetica Discuss'd* (London, 1709), copy owned by William Andrews Clark Library.

2. Ernst Fischer, *The Necessity of Art: A Marxist Approach*, trans. Anna Bostock (London: Penguin, 1970).

3. Published discussions pertinent to various remarks in this chapter have become numerous but will not generally be referenced. Recent studies have often been in disagreement with the particular statement here; however, the reader might compare one investigation that supports the tenor of the statement, Barbara Herrnstein Smith's examination of "The Speaker: Utterances as Acts" and "The Listener: Utterances as Events" in *On the Margins of Discourse: The Relation of Literature to Language* (Chicago: University of Chicago Press, 1978).

For a review of some of the matters taken up in this chapter see Gary F. Waller, "Author, Text, Reading Ideology: Towards a Revisionist Literary History of the Renaissance," *Dalhousie Review* 61 (1981): 405–25. While there is much in this discussion that I agree with, I cannot accept the lack of attention to what made the text what it is. I concur that there is no external textual point of meaning, but some of Waller's statements are so extreme (and absolute) that one sees him doing that which he objects to.

4. Quotations from Milton are taken from my edition of *The Complete Poetry of John Milton* (Garden City, N.Y.: Doubleday Anchor, 1971).

5. The importance of establishment of a text is manifest. If in William Butler Yeats's "Lapis Lazuli," line 5, we read "That if nothing drastic can be done" as the version in the *New Republic*, 13 April 1938, has it (rather than "That if nothing drastic is done"), we are subject to two different readings. If in John Donne's "The Flea" we read in line 3 "It suckt me," as do the first editions of 1633–54 and various manuscripts and most modern editions, or "Me it suckt," as in the edition of 1669 and some manuscripts and in an important modern edition, we are subject to two different tones, two different linguistic affects, two different prosodic understandings.

6. See the note to the line in my edition.

7. Quotations come from *Three Short Novels by Joseph Conrad*, ed. Edward Weeks (New York: Bantam, 1960); see 11, 7, 2, 5, 94, 29, 58, 83, 93.

8. Quotations come from my edition of *The Complete Poetry of John Donne* (Garden City, N.Y.: Doubleday Anchor, 1970).

9. Quotations of Carew's poems are from *Minor Poets of the Seventeenth Century*, ed. R. G. Howarth (London: Dent, 1963), the source also for quotations from Cherbury, Suckling, and Lovelace. "Secrecy Protested" appears on 72.

10. See *Poems/Third Edition/Wadsworth Handbook and Anthology* (Delmont, Calif.: Wadsworth, 1973), 86–87.

11. I would agree with E. M. Forster "That all literature tends towards a condition of anonymity, and that, so far as words are creative, a signature merely distracts from their true significance" (82), but we must always remember that the author "dips a bucket

down into" his personality, even while we discount his surface life (87)—"Anonymity: An Enquiry," 77–88 in E. M. Forster, *Two Cheers for Democracy* (New York: Harcourt, Brace, 1951).

The "ideal" reader's text may equate that which I have called the author's text. But my experience with various readings of a text (various readers' texts, that is) little suggests that "ideal" readers are generally existent without help from a critic-reader. That critic-reader may supply historically oriented information or aesthetically oriented reactions. The reader may thus be an "ideal" reader and we can, perhaps, omit mention of the author and what I have called the author's text (calling it instead the "ideal reader's text"?). However, such omission seems merely perverse and calculated only to avoid being accused of indulging in intentional fallacy. The "implied" reader of Wolfgang Iser is simply an obfuscation of the problem. The text cannot refer only to itself; no referents would then exist for the reader implied.

For a discussion of evaluation of literature, see chapter 6 of John Reichert's *Making Sense of Literature* (Chicago: University of Chicago Press, 1977), 173–203. Note also his view of reader response ("to assign to the reader only so much knowledge as is necessary to understand what he reads correctly, in which case the critic's search for a true understanding of the nature and shape of the passage or text is itself a search for the response the reader ought to have to it," 84) in chapter 3, 59–95. Compare David Bleich's *Subjective Criticism* (Baltimore, Md.: Johns Hopkins Press, 1978). Bleich argues that in much current criticism "knowledge is constructed rather than discovered" (213) and that largely this occurs through the difference between presenting models of the reader (such as critics like Roman Ingarden and Iser do) without studying specific responses of specific readers and their own mental processes as readers (101, n. 5).

12. See Jacques Derrida, "La Loi Du Genre/The Law of Genre," trans. Avital Ronell, *Glyph* 7 (1980): 176–232, for a deconstructing of "laws" of genre. He says, "Making genre its mark, a text demarcates itself," with an implication that although any text exhibits genre, it is nonetheless unique generically. I think this is not the conclusive statement to be drawn from a recognition that the text "enfolds within itself the condition for the possibility and the impossibility of taxonomy." Each text is unique, yes, but while a text may stay "at the edgeless boundary of itself," it is still within a frame, an arena. Its intertextuality does not allow generic uniqueness. Perhaps my difficulty with Derridean thought on this issue is that I do not see form, characteristics, or authorial attitude as "law"; I see this as descriptive means of placing a literary work within a certain family of literary works (or families, at times). Unfortunately, one of the origins of modern critical theory has been the prescriptive attitudes of teachers and critics and inferior writers.

W. R. Johnson in *The Idea of Lyric: Lyric Modes in Ancient and Modern Poetry* (Berkeley: University of California Press, 1982) does not accept the morphological dimension of genre: "The idea of genre is defined not by its accidents or representation, its material causes (meter, music, dance) but by its substance, that is, by its contents, its agents, objects, and purposes of mimesis" (178). His stress on content to define genre is, for me, almost totally wrong.

13. An important way of looking at genre involves "recognition," which "is the informal authority genre assumes as it collects and separates information . . . ; in this sense, recognition is an activity generated by the relationship between reading and genre." See William H. Epstein, "Recognizing the Life-Text: Towards a Poetics of Biography," *Biography* 6 (1983): 301, n. 1. Compare also my remarks throughout this book (particularly those concerned with various Renaissance authors) with M. Thomas Hester's comment about the coterie poet and the issue of genre: genre should be looked at "not just as sets

of rules and conventions which must be literally fulfilled, but . . . as metaphors for social/ethical actions"—"'All are players': Guilpin and 'Prester Iohn' Donne," *South Atlantic Review* 49 (1984): 14.

14. Adrian Marino, "Toward a Definition of Literary Genres," in *Theories of Literary Genre*, ed. Joseph P. Strelka (University Park: Pennsylvania State University Press, 1978), vol. 8 of the Yearbook of Contemporary Criticism, 47. For Costanzo Di Girolamo, "The literary genre is generally defined as a set of rules and restrictions presiding over the production of a text" (*A Critical Theory of Literature* [Madison: University of Wisconsin Press, 1981], 70).

15. A recent book, accepting the nonviability of genre for today's criticism, proposes that genre is the figural deployment of symbolic power, working through three diverse genres. See John Snyder, *Prospects of Power: Tragedy, Satire, the Essay, and the Theory of Genre* (Lexington: University Press of Kentucky, 1991). He views aesthetic language deployed as power organizing itself as generic intervention: tragedy becomes political through mimesis; satire, rational through rhetoric; and the essay, textual through "constative" rhetoric.

16. A good review of genre and the history of genre theory is Heather Dubrow's *Genre* (London: Methuen, 1982). She does not approach definition as I do, nor does she consider the third element that I propose. Thus she writes, understandably enough,

> Even after attempting to delimit the idea of genre in these ways, we are confronted with a large range of literary kinds whose claims to the title remain viable but debatable, depending as they do on exactly what we think a genre is and hence what characteristics we take into account when deciding whether to grant that label to a given literary type. (5)

She makes no distinction for mode.

According to Thomas L. Kent, genres may be classified on the basis of ten assumptions, some of which may be "synchronic," that is, staying within the bounds of definition, and some of which may be "diachronic," that is, repeatedly changing their boundaries. See *Genre* 16 (1983): 1–20.

One of the most important recent books on the subject opposes definition grounded in content or necessary elements or essential characteristics; see Alastair Fowler, *Kinds of Literature: An Introduction to the Theory of Genres and Modes* (Cambridge, Mass.: Harvard University Press, 1982). Fowler adds, "A very few necessary elements exist . . . , but not nearly enough to supply a theory of genres" (39). He sees genres as families rather than as classes (41), with an overlapping and crisscrossing of family relations. He is concerned primarily with demonstrating that an original generic state has altered diachronically through changes within the critic's own time. "Mode" is seen as adjectival, a position I heartily endorse, but attached to "kinds."

17. Edward Stankiewicz, "Structural Poetics and Linguistics," *Current Trends in Linguistics*, ed. Thomas A. Sebeok, vol. 12, part 3, "Linguistics and Adjacent Arts and Sciences" (The Hague: Mouton, 1974), 640.

18. See, for example, Paul Hernadi, *Beyond Genre: New Directions in Literary Classification* (Ithaca, N.Y.: Cornell University Press, 1972), who uses the term *mode* to indicate the form that the literary piece may take (e.g., "narrative mode," "thematic mode," "dramatic mode," "lyric mode"). He would seem to use "mood" to imply what I call "mode," although "mood" is simply the prevailing tone, not the total effect of a work. He basically follows Northrop Frye in *Anatomy of Criticism: Four Essays* (Princeton, N.J.: Princeton University Press, 1957), although Frye's modal vocabulary is not related to form.

19. James H. Druff, Jr., indicates some of the problems in the concept of "the dissolution of genres" (quoting Robert Langbaum, *The Poetry of Experience: The Dramatic Monologue in Modern Literary Tradition* [rpt., New York: Norton, 1963], 232) in "Genre and Mode: The Formal Dynamics of Doubt," *Genre* 14 (1981): 296ff. From my remarks elsewhere in this book, it is clear that I would more strongly stress that variations are possible within any genre without the loss of generic category and indeed that an aim of many authors is to achieve variety while remaining within the general and some specific parameters of a genre. This may lead to development of other aspects of genre from the traditional (even ultimately to a "new" genre) or to the obscuring and/or deletion of a traditional aspect. I am in agreement with Druff's thrust in this essay, although I consider his working definition of genre inadequate because it is too general and his discussion of mode still too accepting of certain proffered ideas. He does not reexamine the definition of mode or offer a definition himself. That "mode defines the artist's attitude in relation to his subject" (300), following Frye, is quite correct, but that Frye's labels cover all modes or supply definition I question. (Definition should indicate what is included and what is excluded; the problem is easily seen in trying to call "mythic" a mode.) Druff is right in rejecting Robert Scholes's argument that a theory of modes is a "theory of ideal types," which fails to distinguish mode from genre (see Robert Scholes, *Structuralism in Literature: An Introduction* [New Haven, Conn.: Yale University Press, 1974], 132). Druff is concerned with the novel without realizing that the novel, as often a kind of prose-epic form, may partake of *genera mixta* (and therefore also mixed modes), as does the epic.

20. John Crowe Ransom, "Piazza Piece," *Selected Poems* (New York: Knopf, 1969), 3d ed., 9.

21. Stankiewicz, 648. Compare my previous remarks on the sestina and its possible variations.

22. Many of my ideas and readings will be seen to be in agreement with John Reichert's views, which also argue against exclusively reader-oriented criticism, and with Denis Donoghue's in *Ferocious Alphabets* (Boston: Little, Brown, 1981). Donoghue looks favorably upon "epireading" (that is, the reflection of a speaker in a work of literature) and argues against "graphireading" (that is, literature read as devoid of voice).

Chapter 2

1. A most instructive study of genre is Rosalie Colie's *Resources of Kind: Genre-Theory in the Renaissance,* ed. Barbara K. Lewalski (Berkeley: University of California Press, 1974). See also Hernadi, *Beyond Genre;* Fowler, *Kinds of Literature;* and Norman K. Farmer, Jr., "A Theory of Genre for Seventeenth-Century Poetry," *Genre* 3 (1970): 293–317. The usual understanding of some generic terms lies in the definitions found in Marjorie Donker and George M. Muldrow's *Dictionary of Literary-Rhetorical Conventions of the English Renaissance* (Westport, Conn.: Greenwood Press, 1982), which also gives significant bibliography for each term.

2. Among numerous studies the reader should consult *The Philosophy of Literary Form: Studies in Symbolic Action* (Baton Rouge: Louisiana State University Press, 1967, 2d ed.), *The Grammar of Motives* (Berkeley: University of California Press, 1969), and *The Rhetoric of Motives* (Berkeley: University of California Press, 1969).

3. Many practitioners will absolutely deny this premise. A piece of writing may evolve from unplanned composition, but either the emotion or thought is recognized and under-

stood well before completion (which may take numerous writing periods) or the piece of "free" writing remains—inept. Unfortunately some of this "free" writing has seen print.

4. Denise Levertov, "Obsessions," *Collected Earlier Poems, 1940–1960* (New York: New Directions, 1979), 93.

5. Quoted from *Tottel's Miscellany (1557–1587)*, ed. Hyder Edward Rollins (Cambridge, Mass.: Harvard University Press, 1966), rev. ed., I, 87.

6. Donald Hall, "Six Poets in Search of a Lawyer," *Exiles and Marriages* (New York: Viking Press, 1955), 61–62.

7. e. e. cummings, "Poem, or Beauty Hurts Mr. Vinal," *Poems, 1923–1954* (New York: Harcourt, Brace, 1954), 167–68.

8. Compare my essay "Form and Content in Milton's Latin Elegies," *Huntington Library Quarterly* 33 (1970): 331–50.

9. *Andrew Marvell: The Complete Poems*, ed. Elizabeth Story Donno (Harmondsworth: Penguin, 1972), 222. Quotations from Marvell come from this edition.

Chapter 3

1. William E. Gruber, in "The Polarization of Tragedy and Comedy," *Genre* 13 (1980): 259–74, argues that "In opposition to tragedy, then, all comedy can be said to be concerned with time's successful redemption" (264) and that "Comedy, then, in contrast to tragedy, suspends the rule of organic future succession" (265). These concepts seem to oppose themselves and imply, quite erroneously I think, that tragedy produces a sense of organic future succession. Is there not conflict when Gruber remarks that "The rhythm of these comedies [Shakespeare's] is always open—never, like tragedy's, closed and final"? In his further remarks he confuses "open/closed" and "closure": "For marriage is really the only important ceremony in which the closed curve of the individual's Destiny coincides with the generic, open-ended functions of the entire race. Once comedy adopted the closed form of serious drama, marriage was the only practical event the comic dramatist had at his disposal to pretend to the illusion of drama—individual destiny—at the same time he subverted it." While the marriage "closes" or ends the work, it does not create a closed form: it implies, if nothing else, "they lived happily ever after," and time moves into some kind of implied future succession. Closure does not imply of necessity either openness or closedness.

2. Gruber postulates that the orientation of comedy is not social but aesthetic on the basis of Francisco Andrados's *Festival, Comedy and Tragedy*, trans. Christopher Holme (Leiden: E.J. Brill, 1975).

3. James P. Driscoll delineates the difference between the two genres, on the basis of a main character's real, social, conscious, and ideal identities, thus: "If the quest for ideal identity generates sharp conflicts with the needs or demands of the first three identities, then tragedy can ensue. But when the obstacles to harmony among the four primary identities are successfully surmounted, the final outcome will be unqualifiedly comic." See *Identity in Shakespearean Drama* (Lewisburg, Pa.: Bucknell University Press, 1983), 22. This way of analyzing the action and outcome of the play fits well into the concepts I have expressed, as the contrast between Hamlet and Prince Hal demonstrates, except that it defines, for me, mode rather than genre. Note, as well, Driscoll's "unqualifiedly comic"; he does not say "an unqualified comedy."

4. I do not read Hamlet's offstage arrangement to have Rosencrantz and Guildenstern

killed to be the climax for the hero; that action is a result both of Hamlet's discovery of the plot against him and of his resolution that "from this time forth, / My thoughts be bloody, or be nothing worth!" (IV, iv, 65–66). The offstage action, which occurs between Scenes iv and vi of Act IV, does not involve anagnorisis but is an external continuation of peripeteia. This "night sea-journey," which has reversed mythic movement from east to west, is the galvanizing of Hamlet to death, the manifestation then and in Act V of his now-bloody thoughts.

5. This does not deny psychological interpretation (which has often, however, been marred by inadequate attention to the play's sources—where the sexual issues are encased as archetypes—and to the theatrical context); rather it suggests that a source of the tragic mode is Hamlet's lack of individuation in his sexual being (witness his treatment of Ophelia more than of his mother and compare Laertes's hypermasculine attitudes and activities). Hamlet is divided between activism and passivity, unsure of the reality and the illusion, in his sexual being, and what is more modally tragic is that he seems not to realize it. The psychosexual reading of the play is, in other words, a metaphoric substratum raising the questions that exist within the tragedy of the play itself: (1) disorder—the sexual disorientation in the "adultery" of his mother, the seeming possibility of Ophelia's lack of chastity; (2) sin—ideal love versus carnal desire; and (3) anagnorisis—recognition and acceptance of one's own sexuality in relationship to others', the need for a kind of Lacanian mirror image.

6. Clayton Koelb (" 'Tragedy' and 'The Tragic': The Shakespearean Connection," *Genre* 13 [1980]: 275–86) is not concerned with mode but with August Wilhelm von Schlegel's concept that " 'the tragic' is a pre-condition for the existence of 'tragedy' " (277), that is, with that which "every mind not closed to feeling" must experience. His examination concludes that a work of literature may be tragic without being a tragedy, and a tragedy without being tragic. Koelb contends that tragedy no longer constitutes a literary genre; see "The Problem of Tragedy as a Genre," *Genre* 8 (1975): 248–66.

7. *Princeton Encyclopedia of Poetry and Poetics*, ed. Alex Preminger, Frank J. Warnke, and O. B. Hardison, Jr. (Princeton, N.J.: Princeton University Press, 1974), enlarged edition. G. N. G. Orsini's historically oriented entry is on 307–9; R. J. Dorius's discussion is on 860–64.

8. Harry Levin, "Form and Formality in *Romeo and Juliet*," *Shakespeare Quarterly* 11 (1960): 1–11; reprinted in *Shakespeare and the Revolution of the Times* (New York: Oxford University Press, 1976).

9. See Henri Bergson, *Laughter: An Essay on the Meaning of the Comic*, trans. Cloudesley Brereton and Fred Rothwell (New York: Macmillan, 1911).

10. Significantly contributing to the circumstances of the tragedy are the Capulets' marriage demands for their daughter. The sociopolitical dimension of the play, beyond the feud, has not often enough been attended to, partially perhaps because Shakespeare obliterated its significance.

11. Susan Snyder's concerns in *The Comic Matrix of Shakespeare's Tragedies* (Princeton, N.J.: Princeton University Press, 1979) are dissimilar to mine, and conclusions on which we both seem to agree are derived from dissimilar approaches but similar definitions. "Tragedy is usually characterized in terms of emotional effect," she writes (8), and "tragedy expresses the two sides of the paradoxical attitudes I have been exploring— recognition of necessity and resistance to the cutting off of human possibility—through plot and character, respectively" (11). Comedy (of the early 1590s) presents "a love story with a happy ending," despite threatened disaster, "the obstacles to the marriage of true minds . . . [being] removed by providential chance and human ingenuity" (36). She explores in discussions of *Romeo and Juliet, Othello, Hamlet,* and *King Lear* the way in

which traditional comic structures and assumptions shape tragedy.

12. See Barbara C. Vincent's "Shakespeare's *Antony and Cleopatra* and the Rise of Comedy," *English Literary Renaissance* 12 (1982): 53–86 for the view that "the Roman play, and particularly the Roman world of *Antony and Cleopatra*, should be regarded as Shakespeare's attempt to portray the archetype of tragedy" (54) and, on the other hand, that "The theory of art embodied in *Antony and Cleopatra* could be characterized as comic because desire plays a greater role in creating the reality of the play than allegiance to an objectively realistic vision" (83). Vincent sees the genres of the play unified on an epic scale, with movement from a dominance of tragedy (largely Roman) to a dominance of comedy (largely Egyptian), culminating in Cleopatra's death as transcendence over tragedy.

13. See note 16, chapter 4, for definitional discussion.

Chapter 4

1. See *Concluding Unscientific Postscript*, trans. David F. Swenson and Walter Lowrie (Princeton, N.J.: Princeton University Press, 1968), 459.

2. James Joyce, *Ulysses* (New York: Modern Library, 1961), 2–3.

3. Observe their literally similar and opposed names: single *l*, double *o*, small *m* —double *l*, single *o*, large *M* (*L–M–O* lying at the center of the alphabet, with perhaps "and" equating *N*), beginning with the consonant *B* (second letter of the alphabet) and ending with the vowel *Y* (second letter from the end of the alphabet): B–L–OO–M/M–O–LL–Y.

4. The quotations come from Robert D. Hume's *Development of English Drama in the Late Seventeenth Century* (Oxford: Clarendon Press, 1976), 37.

5. Compare Northrop Frye's important essay "The Argument of Comedy," *English Institute Essays* for 1948 (New York: Columbia University Press, 1949), 58–73.

6. See Bergson, cited in note 9, chapter 3.

7. *Lectures on Rhetoric and Belles Lettres* (London, 1783), II, 531.

8. Hume, 56–57.

9. Blair, II, 532.

10. See *Poetica* vi.2–3, in *Aristotle, The Poetics; "Longinus," On the Sublime; Demetrius, On Style*, ed. W. Hamilton Fyfe, Loeb Classical Library (London: William Heinemann, 1932), 22–23 (Greek and English).

11. Albert Cook, in *The Dark Voyage and the Golden Mean* (Cambridge, Mass.: Harvard University Press, 1949), considers some novels as comedy, as does Richard B. Sewall in *The Vision of Tragedy* (New Haven, Conn.: Yale University Press, 1959). A number of critics have examined such "comic" novels as Henry Fielding's *Tom Jones* and Saul Bellow's *Adventures of Augie March*. Hernadi in *Beyond Genre* indicates an acceptance of my point (see 178–79), but he does not explore the idea. While this study is an excellent examination of genre theories (note the plural), it does not itself come to grips with definition. See Elder Olsen's *Tragedy and the Theory of Drama* (Detroit, Mich.: Wayne State University Press, 1966), 169, for the view that tragedy must be a drama. The difficulty in generic definition can also be observed in Percy G. Adams's brilliant discussion of the novel as genre in *Travel Literature and the Evolution of the Novel* (Lexington: University Press of Kentucky, 1983); see especially 1–23.

12. An excellent discussion of genre will be found in Claudio Guillén's "Essay 4: On

the Uses of Literary Genre," *Literature as System: Essays toward the Theory of Literary History* (Princeton, N.J.: Princeton University Press, 1971), 107–34. For a discussion of mode, compare Karl Viëtor, "Die Geschichte literarischer Gattungen," in *Geist und Form* (Bern: A. Francke, 1952).

13. I would distinguish these terms by employing "comedic" to refer to the mode created by the structure of the work and its pervasive characteristics and "comic" to refer to the mode experienced by the reader as overall effect or as effect here and there as a result of content and treatment.

14. Delivered as a lecture in 1877 and published in 1897.

15. See my fuller discussion in "Shaw's Early Plays: Beyond Apprenticeship," *Greyfriar: Siena Studies in Literature* 17 (1976): 20–32. One example of the importance of the point being argued is the interpretation of *Mrs. Warren's Profession,* which has erroneously been read and produced as a play concerned with prostitution and its acceptance rather than correctly as being concerned with the viciousness of economics and businessmen.

16. The approach to tragicomedy has been that it is a mixed genre, the purpose of which is to purge the mind of melancholy, thus emphasizing audience effect. From tragedy, in this view, come great persons, though great action is eschewed, and a verisimilar plot involving danger and delight but not death and sadness; from comedy comes modest laughter built on a feigned complication with a happy reversal. See the discussion and demonstration by Joan Hartwig in *Shakespeare's Tragicomic Vision* (Baton Rouge: Louisiana State University Press, 1972). Building upon that, what I suggest is that tragicomedy, approached as a genre in its own right, evidences certain forms and characteristics and authorial intention toward the literary work: it courts the potentially undesirable as a pattern for society, which undesirable aspect arises from the characters or personalities of the persons of the work, one or more of whom reverse character or personality (or are forced to reverse it), thereby averting the undesirable; such persons are ordinary or at least within the action of the work operate as only representative types; the action is contrived to display the persons or types, neither action nor persons being skewed by angle of vision or distinctiveness of being. While the effect on the audience is firmly at the forefront of the author's mind as he or she writes, the concern is not to rebuke or nullify vice except that a moralistic judgment may enter by implication: all those in the audience whose characters or personalities are like those of the persons of the work and could be reversed like theirs, it is implied, should follow the example. The movement of the work does not involve cyclic myth as does comedy, but it does indicate that life goes on; it does not lead the reader or auditor to feel a finality has been reached, but it does suggest a finality to the actions within the work, though the persons go on. It is not clearly modal in Northrop Frye's paradigm. Its potential moralism creates what has been called the sentimental mask (as in Sir Richard Steele's *Conscious Lovers*) or mere sentimentalism of the brave-soul variety (as in Henry Mackenzie's *Man of Feeling*). For further discussion see my "Tragicomedy as Genre, Past and Present" in *Renaissance Tragicomedy: Exploration in Genre and Politics,* ed. Nancy Klein Maguire (New York: AMS Press, 1987), 13–32.

17. Jean Giono, *Le Chant du Monde* (Paris: Gallimard, 1934), 9 (*The Song of the World,* trans. Henri Fluchère and Geoffrey Myers [New York: Viking, 1937], 3).

> Night. The river shouldered its way through the forest. Antonio walked out to the far end of the island. On one side, the deep water, sleek as a cat's fur; on the other side, the whinnying of the ford. Antonio felt the oak. He listened through his hand to the shiverings of the tree. It was an aged oak, more sinewy than a man of the mountains. It stood at the very tip of the

isle of jays, right in the rush of the stream, and already half its roots emerged from the water.

18. Ibid., 316–18 (ibid., 310–12).

The stream carried hard. Stumps and shallows were no longer to be feared. They were on the swell of the water. All that had to be done was from time to time to pull slightly at the rudder. In the depth of the night, they heard the gorges blowing.
"We'll reach the isle of jays at dawn." . . .
He was thinking that now, Clara and he, all the time together . . .
Antonio was thinking that he would be free and that he would keep her close to him, on the island. Very gently. Step by step. . . .
He was thinking that he was going to take Clara in his arms and lie down with her on the earth.

19. Günter Grass, *Hundejahre* (Berlin: Lucterhand, 1963), 682 (*Dog Years* [Greenwich, Conn.: Fawcett, 1966], 569).

And this man and that man — who now will call them Brauxel and Matern? — I and he, we stride with doused lamps to the changehouse, where the changehouse attendant takes our hard hats and carbide lamps. I and he are led to cabins where Matern's and Brauxel's clothes are in keeping. He and I strip off our mine outfits. For me and him bathtubs have been filled. I hear Eddi splashing next door. Now I too step into my bath. The water soaks me clean. Eddi whistles something indeterminate. I try to whistle something similar. But it's difficult. We're both naked. Each of us bathes by himself.

Note too the intermixture of nouns and pronouns: Brauxel/Matern; I/he; I/he; Matern's/Brauxel's; He/I; me/him.
20. Quotations are from Henry Roth, *Call It Sleep* (New York: Avon Books, 1964), 419, 429, 441, and 431.

Chapter 5

1. I am aware of such "spontaneous" writing as that of Sue Lenier, who boasts of never altering a line after it has been put down, and of some critical assessments that have been quoted to increase sales. I rest my case on the reader's evaluation of her work. Jonson's jibe at Shakespeare in *Timber; or Discoveries* (1641) corroborates the truism of the need for planning and revision: "The players have often mentioned it as an honor to Shakespeare that in his writing . . . he never blotted out a line. My answer hath been, 'Would he had blotted a thousand!' " ("De Shakespeare nostrati" in Herschel Baker, ed., *The Later Renaissance in England* [Boston: Houghton Mifflin, 1975], 700).
2. The reductionism in John Carey's reading of Donne's poems is a well-known excursion into this kind of unjustified biographical and basically anticreative approach to literature; see *John Donne: Life, Mind and Art* (New York: Oxford University Press, 1981).
3. A wonderful example of what I mean is Robert Pack's account of a reaction to a

poem about his brother's dying. After having read the poem to a popular audience, he was greeted by a commiserating member of the audience, who was moved by his eloquent expression of loss and hurt. The listener's attitude quickly changed to a kind of contempt when he told her he never had a brother. "The intimacy of lyric poetry," he writes,

> seems to invite a response that assumes an autobiographical revelation has been made, that the poet has offered a confession to his reader. And no doubt he has, even though the historical facts have been selected, rearranged or altered. A convincing illusion of a human speaker. This fidelity to creating a convincing illusion marks the poet's seriousness about his art.

See "Lyric Narration: The Chameleon Poet," *Hudson Review* (Spring 1984): 54.

4. See chapter 8 for discussion of this poem.

5. The lines allude to the parable of the sower (Matthew 13 3–23) and the legend of Cadmus, who sowed dragon's teeth that sprang up as armed warriors who then fought to found Thebes.

6. Quotations come from J. Max Patrick's edition, *The Complete Poetry of Robert Herrick* (Garden City, N.Y.: Doubleday Anchor, 1963).

7. Quotations come from William B. Hunter's edition, *The Complete Poetry of Ben Jonson* (Garden City, N.Y.: Doubleday Anchor, 1963).

8. From Weever's *Epigrams in the Oldest Cut and Newest Fashion* (London, 1599).

9. Quotations are from George Walton Williams, ed., *The Complete Poetry of Richard Crashaw* (Garden City, N.Y.: Doubleday Anchor, 1970).

10. Carmela Pinto [McIntyre]'s discussion in "Understanding Ben Jonson's Book: The Reader as Critic," an unpublished paper drawn from her dissertation, "Style and the Reader: Dialectic in Ben Jonson's *Epigrammes,*" argues that "On the Famous Voyage" engages the same "processes of scrutiny, comparison, selection and synthesis necessary to read the *Epigrammes* as a book." Since the poem offers the negative of the "models on which a virtuous society is founded," its inclusion makes good sense. See *Dissertation Abstracts* 42 [12] (1982): 5130A.

Chapter 6

1. In his influential discussion *Grundbegriffe der Poetik* (Zurich: Atlantis Verlag, 1946), Emil Staiger equates these broad poetic genres with recollection, tension, and representation. I agree that a key to the lyrical mode is recollection and that the genre lyric involves purported recollection. I think, however, that more has to be entailed for generic definition.

2. A continuing example is Käte Hamburger's study *The Logic of Literature* (Bloomington: Indiana University Press, 1973), second, revised edition, trans. Marilynn J. Rose. While she talks of genre, Hamburger seems to mean mode ("fictional [epical] genre," "lyrical genre"), and she places all literature into the realm of statement-subject, the lyric, with the only exception being narration, a statement-object (31). Thus she concludes with the chapter "Special Forms," in which, typically, she remarks that "the ballad's special form as an epic-fictional work within the lyrical genre is one which is not immediately evident" (293). The dramatic genre or mode is subsumed for the most part under the category "fictional genre." Statement is the statement of a subject about

an object. "Statement-subject" is, roughly, the context (involving speaker or circumstance) out of which the statement is made; the "statement-object" is, roughly, the content.

3. Edward Manwaring in *An Historical and Critical Account of the Eminent Classical Authors in Poetry and History* (London, 1737) excludes the bucolic, elegies, epitaphs, and epigrams from his discussion of the lyric (344–46).

My position is not different from what Isvetan Todorov has explained: "Some genres have never had a name; others have been confused under a single name despite their different properties" ("Genres litteraires," *Dictionnaire encyclopédique des sciences du language* [Paris: Edition du Seuil, 1972], ed. Oswald Ducrot and Tzvetan Todorov, 193).

4. Hamburger's approach places a great stress upon that which involves intention, for the statement-subject falls into one of three categories, the historical, the theoretical, or the pragmatic. She gives examples of a church hymn, which as pragmatic statement-subject is not in the realm of the lyric as a literary genre or which as theoretical statement-subject is a lyric. "Pragmatic" covers the statement-subject that is not individualized or that gives a command or asks a question; "theoretical" covers the statement-subject that is individualized when the subject (speaker) is "identifiable" and declarative.

She discounts form: "The fictional genre consists of several different forms in which it can manifest itself," but "the lyrical genre is not differentiated" (291). "[I]t is of utmost importance that we stringently separate the *lyrical statement-subject*—which constitutes the lyric—from the *form* of lyric poetry. Because the lyric is located within the statement-system of language, its own characteristic form can be transferred onto any statement; conversely, where a lyrical statement-subject is present, the form in which it 'is speaking' by no means must meet the aesthetic claims of a lyric form as a work of art" (241). "In the lyric poem form and meaning are identical" (249).

On the other hand, Walther Killy in *Elemente der Lyrik* (Munich: C.H. Beck, 1972) discusses form as essential in relation to repetition, inflection, and suitability, but divorced from prosody: "Denn wenn sich elementare Formen, Bilder, Verfahren der Poesie über lange Zeiträume hinweg zwar nicht gleich, so doch ähnlich bleiben, so kommt ihren Wandlungen oder gar ihren Schwinden das höchste Interesse zu" (3).

5. It should be clear that my (incomplete) schema for creative literature as outlined here reads something like:

1. prose (each division here and below may have possible
   subdivisions and interrelationships; e.g., novel, short
   story, "nonfictional" novel)
2. play
3. poem
   A. epic
   B. dramatic poem
   C. lyric
      a. sonnet
      b. ode
      c. hymn
      d. encomium
      e. song
      f. verse epistle
      g. lyric (that is, the undifferentiated lyric)
      h. other subgenres
   D. epigram (each genre following may be compounded into some
      other kind of grouping, but none strictly belongs to *epic,*

> *dramatic poem*, or *lyric*)
> E. verse satire
> F. elegy
> G. pastoral
> H. prose poem
> I. other genres

At times, of course, something like a verse satire takes on the form of a verse epistle, but its characteristics and authorial intention remove it from the classifications verse epistle and lyric.

6. Joseph Trapp, *Lectures on Poetry Read in the Schools of Natural Philosophy at Oxford* (London, 1742), 204.

7. For example, see Thomas Twining, *Aristotle's Treatise on Poetry, Translated* (London, 1789): "The general character of Lyric Poetry is enthusiasm; and enthusiasm, says M. Batteux [Principes de la Lit. Traite, 6, ch. 1], 'n'est autre chose *qu'un sentiment quel qu'il soit*—amour, colere, joie, admiration, tristesse, &c.—produit par une idee' " (Notes, 140).

8. Hugh Blair, *Lectures on Rhetoric and Belles Lettres* (London, 1783), II, 353–54.

9. Twining, 140.

10. Frye, 250.

11. See *Roots of Lyric: Primitive Poetry and Modern Practice* (Princeton, N.J.: Princeton University Press, 1978). He finds its roots in *melopoeia* (that is, primitive charms that often took the form of dance or song and speech) and *phanopoeia* (that is, the riddle). In turn *logopoeia* (the resonant word) becomes the lexis of poetry. Further sidestepping of the issue can be found in the essays comprising *Forms of Lyric*, ed. Reuben A. Brower (New York: Columbia University Press, 1970).

12. Welsh, 242.

13. *The Poet in the Poem* (Berkeley: University of California Press, 1960), 16.

14. Stephen Manning, *Wisdom and Number: Toward a Critical Appraisal of the Middle English Religious Lyric* (Lincoln: University of Nebraska Press, 1962), vii, and see chapter 1, "The Lyrics as Songs."

15. Manning, viii.

16. The words quoted are Catherine Ing's in *Elizabethan Lyrics: A Study in the Development of English Metres and Their Relation to Poetic Effect* (London: Chatto & Windus, 1951), 20. See also her description of lyric on 15–17.

17. Manning, 35. For Frye the lyric poet (apparently of "dramatic lyric") turns his back on his audience. Similar are T. S. Eliot's first voice, which presents "his own thoughts and sentiments to himself or to no one," and W. R. Johnson's "meditative poem," *Idea of Lyric*, 3ff., which developed in the nineteenth century through a shift from the "I–You" poem that defines classical lyric.

18. Friedrich Nietzsche, *The Birth of Tragedy*, Section 5, trans. Clifton P. Fadiman, in *The Philosophy of Nietzsche* (New York: Modern Library, n.d.); see especially 372.

19. For Sharon Cameron in *Lyric Time: Dickinson and the Limits of Genre* (Baltimore, Md.: Johns Hopkins University Press, 1979), "no sense of subjective or interior time [is] substantially different from objective or exterior time" (118). Cameron and I are in much agreement when she writes, "The lyric finds its meaning not through individual interpretations of experience . . . but rather in its ability to isolate meaning from time, to spatialize it" (197). Working through a model of lyric, William Elford Rogers, who is particularly concerned with interpretation and less with definition, remarks, "The relational concept associated with the lyric mode in this scheme is *community* or

reciprocity. The interpreted mind of the work, that is, finds itself in a relationship with its world such that it seems that either is determining the other" (*The Three Genres and the Interpretation of Lyric* [Princeton, N.J.: Princeton University Press, 1983], 67–68).

20. *Transformations in the Renaissance English Lyric* (Ithaca, N.Y.: Cornell University Press, 1970).

21. Compare also Gemino H. Abad, *A Formal Approach to Lyric Poetry* (Quezon City: University of Philippines Press, 1978), and Barbara Hardy, *The Advantages of Lyric* (Bloomington: Indiana University Press, 1977), as well as Rogers.

22. Joseph A. Wittriech's analysis of Milton's "Lycidas" in *Visionary Poetics: Milton's Tradition and His Legacy* (San Marino, Calif.: Huntington Library, 1979) demonstrates that it is a prophetic poem; though the term "lyric" weaves in and out of the discussion (for example, on 138 in a quotation from E. S. Shaffer's *Kubla Khan and the Fall of Jerusalem* [Cambridge: Cambridge University Press, 1975], 177), "Lycidas" is not strictly of the genre lyric. It is a hybrid of an elegy and a pastoral, neither of which is a lyric. See note 24, below.

23. William Flint Thrall and Addison Hibbard, *A Handbook to Literature* (Indianapolis, Ind.: Bobbs-Merrill, 1972), revised and enlarged by C. Hugh Holman, 269.

24. "Lycidas" is a problem. Poems like William Mason's "Musaeus" and Shelley's "Adonais," which both employ "Lycidas" as surtext, are elegies and not lyrics. But Milton's poem, developed out of Theocritus, Vergil, and Spenser's nonlyric "Astrophel," is less an elegy for a dead person than a lyrical utterance of its author. Milton called it a monody, thus separating it from the genre *elegy* and suggesting its generic *lyric* association. While it is not strictly lyric by genre, it certainly is lyric in effect, that is, by mode. In "Milton's 'Unexpressive Nuptial Song': A Reading of *Lycidas*" (*Renaissance Papers, 1982* [Raleigh, N.C.: Southeastern Renaissance Conference, 1983], 15–26), Michael Lieb reads the poem as Milton's epithalamic celebration of the immortal wedding that can never be dissolved. This nuptial song is thus indebted to the amatory tradition of classical bucolic verse, indicating a lyric proportion within the pastoral.

25. Compare note 3, chapter 5, above.

26. Surely the author or the reader may experience a cathartic effect; surely the author may psychologically put down a statement for such catharsis, but such an unobjectified poem is a less effective and to my mind a poor lyric, if lyric it be. Examples abound: for me, William Henley's "Invictus," Alan Seeger's "I Have a Rendezvous with Death," and the self-indulgent verse found everywhere in recent years.

27. John T. Shawcross, "The Poet as Orator: One Phase of His Judicial Pose," in *The Rhetoric of Renaissance Poetry From Wyatt to Milton*, ed. Thomas O. Sloan and Raymond B. Waddington (Berkeley: University of California Press, 1974), 35.

28. "Once a poet begins thinking in terms of sincerity," remarks C. Day-Lewis, discussing lyric, "he lays himself open to that self-consciousness which clogs the springs of the lyric impulse" (*The Lyric Impulse* [Cambridge, Mass.: Harvard University Press, 1965], 21). He continues, "the lyric impulse, when it possesses a poet, asks one thing of him above all, a pure commitment without reserve or circumspection to the creature of his love" (25).

29. This is not in disagreement with Charles Altieri's view about sonnets, which, "perhaps like most literary works, develop a distinctive space of rhetorical performance that employs the freedom of rhetorical play in order to suggest certain *possible* attitudes toward the nature of language and the play of desire" (see "Rhetorics, Rhetoricity and the Sonnet as Performance," *Tennessee Studies in Literature* 25 [1980]: 4).

Chapter 7

1. George B. Johnston, *Ben Jonson: Poet* (New York: Columbia University Press, 1945); Wesley Trimpi, *Ben Jonson's Poems: A Study of the Plain Style* (Palo Alto, Calif.: Stanford University Press, 1962). Among more recent studies on Jonson or those significantly including him are J. G. Nichols, *The Poetry of Ben Jonson* (New York: Barnes and Noble, 1969); Joseph H. Summers, *The Heirs of Donne and Jonson* (New York: Oxford University Press, 1970); Earl Miner, *The Cavalier Mode from Jonson to Cotton* (Princeton, N.J.: Princeton University Press, 1971); Anne Ferry, *All in War with Time: Love Poetry of Shakespeare, Donne, Jonson, Marvell* (Cambridge, Mass.: Harvard University Press, 1975); Judith K. Gardiner, *Craftsmanship in Context: The Development of Ben Jonson* (The Hague: Mouton, 1975); George Parfitt, *Ben Jonson: Public Poet and Private Man* (London: Dent, 1976); Claude J. Summers and Ted-Larry Pebworth, *Ben Jonson* (Boston: Twayne, 1979); and Richard S. Peterson, *Imitation and Praise in the Poems of Ben Jonson* (New Haven, Conn.: Yale University Press, 1981).

An early study is particularly pertinent to this chapter, Ralph S. Walker's "Ben Jonson's Lyric Poetry," *Criterion* 13 (1933–34): 430–48. While Walker recognizes that the poems "represent a . . . sustained current of experimentation," he believed that "success is occasional and spasmodic" and that "it has to be admitted that the supreme lyric success of Ben Jonson, as far as bulk goes, is small. . . . He very seldom attains to the poise between endeavour and achievement which allows an unimpeded precipitation of artistic emotion." I accept such ideas as "His lyric . . . possesses a peculiar integrity of its own, it seems to express nothing beyond or behind itself, but in its final state, to be itself the idea which it expresses," but I strongly reject Walker's obvious prejudice against such poetry. He is too much a product of a romantic and moral sensitivity to appreciate Jonson's lyrics. See also the three articles cited in notes 7 through 9, below.

2. Critical books devoted individually to these authors are few: Edward I. Selig, *The Flourishing Wreath* [Carew] (New Haven, Conn.: Yale University Press, 1958); Lynn Sadler, *Thomas Carew* (Boston: Twayne, 1979); Charles L. Squier, *Sir John Suckling* (Boston: Twayne, 1978); Cyril H. Hartmann, *The Cavalier Spirit and Its Influence on the Life and Work of Richard Lovelace* (London: George Routledge & Sons, 1925); Manfred Weidhorn, *Richard Lovelace* (New York: Twayne, 1970); Alexander W. Allison, *Toward an Augustan Poetic: Edmund Waller's "Reform" of English Poetry* (Lexington: University of Kentucky Press, 1962); and Warren L. Cherniak, *The Poetry of Limitation: A Study of Edmund Waller* (New Haven, Conn.: Yale University Press, 1968).

3. Algernon Charles Swinburne, *A Study of Ben Jonson*, ed. Howard B. Norland (Lincoln: University of Nebraska Press, 1969), 5.

4. *Personae: The Collected Poems of Ezra Pound* (New York: New Directions, 1926), 89.

5. The printed version gives ninety-two and a half lines; the remainder, found in Bodleian Library Rawlinson MS 31 (fol. 20), was canceled because it referred to the Earl of Rutland's impotence.

6. Volumes like Barnabe Googe's *Epitaphs, Eglogs, and Epigrams* (1560) exhibit partial attention to composite order. Spenser's "Shepheardes Calender" is a carefully organized volume of poems, with an overlying development and structure. Jonson's achievement is discussed by Richard C. Newton in "Jonson and the (Re-)Invention of the Book," *Classic and Cavalier: Essays on Jonson and the Sons of Ben*, ed. Claude J. Summers and Ted-Larry Pebworth (Pittsburgh, Pa.: University of Pittsburgh Press, 1982), 31–55.

7. "Ben Jonson's Green World: Structure and Imaginative Clarity in *The Forrest*,"

Studies in Philology 78 (1981): 170–93. Quotations are from 171 and 193.

8. "Why Jonson Wrote Not of Love," *Journal of Medieval and Renaissance Studies* 12 (1982): 195–220. Quotations are from 197 and 219.

9. "The Silva Tradition in Jonson's *The Forrest*" in *Poetic Traditions of the English Renaissance,* ed. Maynard Mack and George deForest Lord (New Haven, Conn.: Yale University Press, 1982), 163–80.

10. The text of the poem may be helpful:

VIII. To Sicknesse

Why, *Disease,* dost thou molest
Ladies? and of them the best?
Doe not men, ynow of rites
To thy altars, by their nights
Spent in surfets: and their dayes,
And nights too, in worser wayes?
    Take heed, *Sicknesse,* what you doe,
    I shall feare, you'll surfet too.
Live not we, as, all thy stalls,
Spittles, pest-house, hospitalls,
Scarce will take our present store?
    And this age will build no more:
'Pray thee, feed contented, then,
Sickness; onely on us men.
    Or if needs thy lust will tast
    Woman-kinde; devoure the wast
    Livers, round about the towne.
But, forgive me, with thy crowne
They maintayne the truest trade,
And have more diseases made.
    What should, yet, thy pallat please?
    Daintinesse, and softer ease,
    Sleeked limmes, and finest blood?
    If thy leanenesse love such food,
    There are those, that, for thy sake,
    Doe enough; and who would take
    Any paines; yea, thinke it price,
    To become thy sacrifice.
    That distill their husbands land
    In decoctions; and are mann'd
    With ten Emp'ricks, in their chamber,
    Lying for the spirit of amber.
    That for th'oyle of *Talke,* dare spend
    More then citizens dare lend
    Them, and all their officers.
    That, to make all pleasure theirs,
    Will by coach, and water goe,
    Every stew in towne to know;
    Dare entayle their loves on any,
    Bald, or blinde, or nere so many:
    And, for thee, at common game,

> Play away, health, wealth, and fame.
> These, *disease,* will thee deserve:
> And will, long ere thou should'st starve
> On their beds, most prostitute,
> Move it, as their humbles sute,
> In thy justice to molest
> None but them, and leave the rest.

11. Hunter, ed., *Complete Poetry of Ben Jonson,* 76.

12. The same may be said for John Donne's Holy Sonnets, which are generally critically misread as only *documents* of the poet's wrestling with self and ontological concerns.

13. *Cataline* of 1611 was also dedicated to him.

14. Hunter's note, "The Lady who speaks this dramatic monologue has not been identified" (84), misunderstands the poem and the sequence.

15. "Enter ye in at the strait gate: for wide is the gate, and broad is the way, that leadeth to destruction, and many there by which go in thereat: because strait is the gate, and narrow is the way, which leadeth unto life, and few there be that find it."

16. As implied in chapter 6, I believe that Frye's remarks about the lyric and lyricism are often quite astute, but because they do not really consider the author's relationship *to the poem being written* they fall short of complete definition and understanding of the lyric impulse.

17. Jonson pushes the point into even more meaningful but more difficult recognition when, in poem 9 of *A Celebration of Charis,* "Her man described by her owne Dictamen," he has the poetic voice begin, "Of your Trouble, *Ben,* to ease me, / I will tell what Man would please me." A reading of this sequence as "true experience" with the "Ben" here being fully congruent with Ben Jonson, author, misreads the sequence and every poem in it. The "internal mimesis" is only apparent, not real.

18. The lines "But we propose a person like our Dove, / Grac'd with a Phoenix love" (91–92) also, of course, play on two aspects of the godhead.

Chapter 8

1. But see M. L. Rosenthal's "Modern British and American Poetic Sequences," *Contemporary Literature* 18 (1977): 416–21, and M. L. Rosenthal and Sally M. Gall, *The Modern Poetic Sequence: The Genius of Modern Poetry* (New York: Oxford University Press, 1983).

2. See Marilla's "Secular and Religious Poetry of Henry Vaughan," *Modern Language Quarterly* 9 (1948): 394–411, and *The Secular Poems of Henry Vaughan,* Essays and Studies on English Language and Literature, vol. 21 (Uppsala: University of Uppsala Press, 1958).

3. Marilla, "Secular and Religious Poetry," 395.

4. (Pittsburgh, Pa.: University of Pittsburgh Press, 1972), 82. See also Jonathan F. S. Post, *Henry Vaughan: The Unfolding Vision* (Princeton, N.J.: Princeton University Press, 1982), 7–19 and passim.

5. Thomas O. Calhoun has discussed *Poems* (1646) as a lyric sequence, seeing two personalities and voices in the poems, much satire, and a conventional process in its content. He seems to assume that it is a sequence rather than demonstrate that it is. See *Henry Vaughan: The Achievement of Silex Scintillans* (Newark: University of Delaware Press, 1981), chapter 1, "The Lyric Sequence: *Poems* (1646)"; but the sequence is discussed only briefly on 32–36. I quote from French Fogle's edition

The Complete Poetry of Henry Vaughan (Garden City, N.Y.: Doubleday Anchor, 1964).

Other poems in the Jonson canon also tend toward sequence like those in *The Forrest* (discussed in chapter 7) and the *"Poems* of Devotion" in *Under-wood* (No. 1 in three poems); see particularly the discussion of Elegies Nos. 38, 40, and 41 in Summers and Pebworth, *Ben Jonson,* 184–87.

6. Raymond B. Waddington in " 'A Celebration of Charis': Socratic Lover and Silenic Speaker" in *Classic and Cavalier,* ed. Summers and Pebworth, 121–38, comments importantly on the songs and their placement in that sequence, on the fusion of public and private modes, and on the tetrameter-couplet form, particularly in its influence from the Anacreontic odes. One should compare Anacreontics with Vaughan's poem No. 10, "A Rhapsodis"; see 109–10.

7. For example, Joan Bennett believes,

> there are two peculiarities in these early poems. The first is that Vaughan never appears to be interested in his subject. He plays lovingly with an image and delays its application which is finally huddled into a last stanza. The other is that he prefers to draw his images from the countryside even when his model was Donne, who seldom looked in that direction. The result is often that his own experience, which finds an outlet in the image, has no inevitable connection with the situation to which he applies it with a logic more painstaking than convincing.

See *Five Metaphysical Poets* (Cambridge: Cambridge University Press, 1964), 72.

8. The pattern, with poems that specifically cite Amoret italicized, is 1, 2, 3; 4, 5, 6, 7, *8, 9,* 10; and *11, 12,* 13. The individual poems are 1, "To my Ingenuous Friend, *R. W.";* 2, "Les Amours"; 3, "To *Amoret.* The Sigh"; 4, "To his Friend Being in Love"; 5, "Song"; 6, "To *Amoret.* Walking in a Starry Evening"; 7, "To *Amoret* gone from him"; 8, "A Song to *Amoret";* 9, "An Elegy"; 10, "A Rhapsodis"; 11, *"To* Amoret, *of the difference 'twixt him, and other Lovers, and what true Love is";* 12, "To *Amoret* WEEPING"; and 13 "Upon the PRIORIE GROVE, His usuall Retyrement."

9. The tavern setting of this poem suggests a story told of Jonson and Randolph: Randolph came to a "Club" of wits, centering around Jonson, at the Devil Tavern near Temple-Bar. Being without money and looking shabby, he only peeped into the room, but was spied by Jonson, who called him in. The wits composed verses on his ill-condition on the spot, and these prompted a quatrain from Randolph, which Jonson so approved that he said, "I believe this is my Son *Randolph,"* and thereafter Jonson always called him his son. See Giles Jacob, *An Historical Account of the Lives and Writings of our Most Considerable English Poets, Whether Epick, Lyrĭck, Elegiack, Epigrammatists, &c.* (London, 1720), 169–70, under "Randolph."

10. This has been read only as a drinking song and has thus suggested to critics the poet's complete withdrawal from the world into a limited society; see Marilla, *Secular Poems of Henry Vaughan,* 126, and Simmonds, 126. The world of the tavern does imply a buffer against the violent world outside, a kind of satiric paradise. But it is not really desirable to the poet, as we see on careful reading.

11. See Marilla, *Secular Poems of Henry Vaughan,* 135, and Simmonds, 64.

12. The poet has moved from the cynical Donne (implied in the "other Lovers") to the Donne of the second classification under which Helen Gardner prints the "Songs and Sonets," the author of poems of mutual love. Vaughan has certainly engaged in derivativeness here, indicating continued role playing: he now plays upon the philosophic to plumb the success of the emotional role playing of the three previous poems

where he first admits his fault, where he then becomes her champion, and where he finally envisions for Amoret his life without her.

13. That is, of the thirty-five lines, .618 lie before this point and .382 after it.

14. See Simmonds, appendix II, 204–7, for a discussion of the identification of Amoret and for disassociation with Etesia, who figures in seven poems in *Thalia Rediviva* (1678).

15. See *Secular Poems of Henry Vaughan*, 140.

16. The only repeated rhymes in this poem are couplets found in the third verse paragraph and in this section of the fourth verse paragraph. The structure can be seen best in this way:

	Lines 21–36	Lines 53–58	
	k		
	k		
4	l		
	l		
	m	p	
	m	p	
	n		
	n	aa	2
4	o	aa	
	o		
	p	m	
	p	m	
	q		
	q		
4	r		
	r		

17. While I have spoken of the Donnean form of love poem, since so many of the specific phrases can be traced to his poems, and many of the attitudes and images, I have intended the wide corpus of love poetry and sonnet sequence developed by the Elizabethan Petrarchan poets and their heirs. Among them are certainly Sir Philip Sidney, Giles Fletcher (the Elder), Lord Cherbury, and William Alexander. The reactions of Donne to the Spenserian mold are carried on by such "Cavaliers" as Carew and Suckling; but Vaughan goes them one better by rejecting all of that for the poems of the plain style that emerge, Nos. 12 and 13, "sincere" love poems that do not worry the mind of the addressee as Dryden thought Donne's did.

18. Simmonds, 135–36.

19. F. E. Hutchinson had commented that there is "little enough in it [*Poems*, 1646] to employ his time" except for Vaughan's version of Juvenal's tenth satire (*Henry Vaughan: A Life and Interpretation* [Oxford: Clarendon Press, 1947], 50).

Chapter 9

1. Compare Harry Levin's "Title as a Literary Genre," *Modern Language Review* 72 (1977): xxiii–xxxvi. I extend significance to the genre-title the author gives a work.

2. I do not wish to fall into the presumption of many critics, who, not understanding

the text—and not trying to—presume to remark what is wrong in language, image, thought, meter, rhythm, device, and so forth. Yet Pound's title "Villanelle" is not cogent. His explanation of the title suggests that he did not really know what a villanelle is beyond its repetitions and their effect. Christine Froula writes,

> Pound's poem is obviously a metaphorical villanelle, in which the obsessive repetitions of the form are abstracted into thematic obsession with middle age, the absent friends, the things he wants to share with them. As he wrote elsewhere of the villanelle form, "the refrains are an emotional fact, which the intellect, in the various gyrations of the poem, tries in vain and in vain to escape" (LE, 369n). Pound was dissatisfied with the poem, and explained to his father, "I wanted the effect of a recurrence of a theme and meant 'Villanelle' to mean generally the feel of the villanelle form in a modern subject. . . . I wanted to convey the sense—the 'feel' that something critical is happening to some-one else at a distance. . . . I have however only succeeded in giving the impression that *I* was disappointed by their absence" (L, 18 December 1915). (*A Guide to Ezra Pound's* Selected Poems [New York: New Directions, 1983], 61.)

LE is *Literary Essays of Ezra Pound*, ed. T. S. Eliot (London: Faber and Faber, 1954); L is *Letters of Ezra Pound Transcribed by D. D. Paige* (New York: Harcourt, Brace, 1950).

3. Let it be noted that my approach to reading literature is to believe (until it is disproved) that the author knows what he or she is doing and wants to say and how to say it.

4. I am aware, of course, that some people allege that any and all words put together constitute "writing" (even creative forms) and that some believe in never blotting a line. (Ben Jonson's criticism of Shakespeare echoes here.) Such lack of sensitivity to literature and such lack of appreciation of literature do not lead to evaluation but to indiscriminate apologiae, usually in psychological terms of the cathartic significance for the writer or the reader. It has helped lead to poststructuralism, which is not concerned with literature but with the effect of words only. The same may be said of some popular endeavors in music and art and film.

5. Carol Maddison in *Apollo and the Nine: A History of the Ode* (London: Routledge & Kegan Paul, 1960), 20, allows that the modern "Anacreontic just falls inside our definition of the ode" on the basis of its being a public utterance.

6. *Poetry and Its Conventions*, ed. Frederick R. Lapides and John T. Shawcross (New York: Free Press, 1972), 33–34. Note the structure of the poem: 5 lines, 1 line, 4 lines, 1 line, 6 lines.

Chapter 10

1. Fortunately one venture has been published. *The Latin Poetry of English Poets* (London: Routledge & Kegan Paul, 1974), ed. J. W. Binns, considers the Latin poetry of Thomas Campion, George Herbert, John Milton, Richard Crashaw, Vincent Bourne, and Walter Savage Landor. Kenneth J. Larsen's "Richard Crashaw's *Epigrammata Sacra,*" 93–120, does not look at the epigrams that I discuss here, nor does it have the same interests or concerns as my remarks. See also Fred J. Nichols's introduction to his edition of *An Anthology of Neo-Latin Poetry* (New Haven, Conn.: Yale University Press, 1979).

2.   *In beatae Virginis verecundiam*

In gremio, quaeris, cur six sua lumina Virgo
   Ponat? ubi meliùs poneret illa, precor?

O ubi, quàm coelo, meliùs sua lumina ponat?
   Despicit, *at coelum sic tamen illa videt.*

              On the Blessed Virgins bashfulnesse

That on her lap she casts her humble Eye,
'Tis the sweet pride of her Humility.
The faire starre is well fixt, for where, o where
Could she have fixt it on a fairer Spheare?
'Tis Heav'n 'tis Heaven she sees, Heavens God there lyes,
She can see heaven, and ne're lift up her eyes:
This new Guest to her Eyes new Lawes hath given,
'Twas once *looke up,* 'tis now *looke down* to Heaven.

3.   *In Beatae Virginis verecundiam*

Non est hoc matris, sed (crede) modestia nati,
   Quòd virgo in gremium dejicit ora suum.

Illic jam Deus est. Oculus jam Virginis ergò,
   Ut caelum videat, dejiciendus erit.

[Translation by Phyllis S. Bowman: "This is (believe it) the modesty not of the mother but of the Son, / that the virgin casts her eyes down at her lap. // There now God is. Now therefore the eye of the Virgin / in order to see heaven must be cast down."]

4. Among these are, from *Olor Iscanus* (1651), "Ad Posteros" (elegiacs), "Ad fluvium Iscam" (alternate hexameter and iambic dimeter), "Venerabili viro, praeceptori suo olim & semper Colendissimo M^{ro}. Mathaeo Herbert" (elegiacs), "Praestantissimo viro, Thomae Poëllo in suum de Elementis opticae libellum" (elegiacs), "Servilii Fatum, sive Vindicata divina" (elegiacs), and "De Salmone" (elegiacs). There are also some miscellaneous poems or fragments in Latin.

5. See *Masques of God,* 78. The text of the poem is (italics reversed)

O Dulcis luctus, risuque potentior omni!
   Quem decorant lachrymis Sydera tanta suis.
Quam tacitae spirant aurae! vultusque nitentes
   Contristant veneres, collachrymantque suae!
Ornat gutta genas, oculisque simillima gemma:
   Et tepido vivas irrigat imbre rosas.
Dicite *Chaldaei!* quae me fortuna fatigat,
   Cum formosa dies & sine nube perit?

6. See also Jonathan F. S. Post's discussion of the importance of the civil wars to *Olor Iscanus,* whose unity as a collection is demonstrated in *The Unfolding Vision.* Many of the Latin poems are discussed passim.

7. Translation by John Carey: "If you fear God, seek to know no more. Let the wise man go from here having heard enough: as for fools, I do not write for them." The dedication of *Silex Scintillans* II uses the dedication of *Silex Scintillans* I and extends it, with references to a broken heart and his "sad failings," "secret faults," and "wilde murmurings" against God.

8. Translation by John Carey: "Always shining, and saturated with the sacred elixir of eternal spring. . . . Then may the musk and cinnamon breathe forth. . . . "

9. Instead there is "The Authors Preface To the following Hymns" (in prose), a dedicatory poem to Jesus Christ, and a twelve-line verse beginning "Vain Wits and eyes."

10. Translation by John Carey: "You launch your attack and shatter that boulder, my stony heart. What was stone, becomes flesh. Look at it, broken in pieces! Look, its fragments are flashing at last to heaven and to you, and my cheeks are wet with tears wrung from flint."

11. Claude J. Summers and Ted-Larry Pebworth, in a most perceptive article ("Vaughan's Temple in Nature and the Context of 'Regeneration,' " *Journal of English and Germanic Philology* 74 [1975]: 351–60) argue that " 'Regeneration' develops as a traditional spiritual quest" (354); it is

> an account of the poet's own personal pilgrimage from a false spring of worldly pursuits to a genuine springtime of the soul. . . . Vaughan describes this temple of nature in terms that remind the reader of Anglican architecture and ritual, the earthly church denied to Vaughan by the Parliamentary triumph. As a result of that triumph, Vaughan apprehends in nature the enduring Church, the spouse of God, which is safe from the vicissitudes of the religiopolitical strife of his immediate experience. In this sense, 'Regeneration' is a public poem as well as a personal one. (359–60)

This kind of "biographical" context—that is, the contemporaneous world out of which a piece of literature arises—is essential for a defensible reading of a collection like *Silex Scintillans,* but it does not imply as impetus "conversion" or dire personal tragedy.

12. *T* sounds twenty-one and twenty-eight times respectively. *M* sounds fourteen times in the second section, maintaining fluidity but not dominating.

Chapter 11

1. *A Variorum Commentary on the Poems of John Milton,* vol. 2: *The Minor English Poems,* by A. S. P. Woodhouse and Douglas Bush (New York: Columbia University Press, 1972), part 1, 119–35.

2. Hugh N. Maclean, "Milton's *Fair Infant,*" *ELH* 24 (1957): 296–305; rpt., Arthur Barker, ed., *Milton: Essays in Criticism* (New York: Oxford University Press, 1965); Jackson I. Cope, "Fortunate Falls as Form in Milton's 'Fair Infant,' " *Journal of English and Germanic Philology* 63 (1964): 660–74. See also John T. Shawcross, "Milton's *Nectar:* Symbol of Immortality," *English Miscellany* 16 (1965): 131–41.

3. Cleanth Brooks and John E. Hardy, eds., *Poems of Mr. John Milton: The 1645 Edition with Essays in Analysis* (New York: Harcourt Brace, 1951), 243.

4. "Aureate": James Holly Hanford, ed., *Poems of John Milton* (New York: Ronald Press, 1953); "commanding": E. M. W. Tillyard, *Milton* (London: Chatto & Windus, 1930), 56; "exhibitionist": David Daiches, *Milton* (London: Hutchinson, 1957), 21.

5. See Joseph A. Wittreich, Jr., *Milton and the Line of Vision* (Madison: University of Wisconsin Press, 1975), 117–19, and Michael Lieb, " 'Yet Once More': The Formulaic Opening of *Lycidas,*" *Milton Quarterly* 12 (1978): 23–28.

6. Milton was sent down from Christ's for some uncertain difficulty with his tutor, William Chappell; he is said by later seventeenth-century antagonists to have been whipped. He returned to the college, as the ending of the elegy indicates, for the Easter term under the tutorship of Nathaniel Tovey. For a full discussion see Leo Miller, "Milton's Clash with Chappell: A Suggested Reconstruction," *Milton Quarterly* 14 (1980): 77–87.

7. Ralph W. Condee, "Ovid's Exile and Milton's Rustication," *Philological Quarterly* 37 (1958): 498–502.

8. See Stanley Stewart's discussion in *The Enclosed Garden: The Tradition and the Image in Seventeenth-Century Poetry* (Madison: University of Wisconsin Press, 1966).

9. Compare my "Form and Content in Milton's Latin Elegies," *Huntington Library Quarterly* 33 (1970): 331–50.

10. See "Milton's Decision to Become a Poet," *Modern Language Quarterly* 24 (1963): 21–30.

11. *Princeton Encyclopedia of Poetry*, 585.

12. The usual attitude toward these poems is given by Condee, in "The Latin Poetry of John Milton," in *Latin Poetry of English Poets*, 58–92, when he writes of "In obitum Praesulis Eliensis," "But the poem has little to distinguish it beyond its slight biographical interest" (65).

13. Condee points out ("Latin Poetry of John Milton," 91, n. 13) that the last line of Elegia tertia ("Talia contingant somnia saepe mihi") echoes a line from Ovid's *Amores* (I.5.26). He comments that it "is a most un-Miltonic howler. . . . [W]hile Milton's vision is of the saintly Bishop of Winchester in Heaven, Ovid's was of Corinna in the nude." Clearly Condee has not observed the point that I am making here: Elegia tertia, written October(?) 1626, with the poem on Ely also in October(?) 1626 and that on Gostlin in October-November 1626, presents an intellectual joke that Milton could expect some of the "mourners" to recognize. All three poems should be reread with this understanding at the fore. The periodic position of the line for Elegia tertia acts like the gagline of a joke based on some kind of double entendre. The line immediately preceding, for example, takes on new meaning: "Flebam turbatos Cephaleiâ pellice somnos" ("I wept for the dreams disturbed by the mistress of Cephalus"). While it is Aurora, the dawn, who was Cephalus's mistress, and the poet here is forced to awaken from his dreams, two subtle smirks are being implied: (1) As a result of Aurora's jealousy, Cephalus accidentally killed his wife Procris, whom he had accused of infidelity, with an infallible spear given him by Procris, who had obtained it as a gift from Diana, goddess of chastity and the hunt. It suggests that the poet's golden sleep ("aurea quies") had turned to a sexual dream and that it "pulsa," not only in being "banished" or "disturbed," but it took on "pulsating" or "violent motion." The "somnos turbatos" by Aurora likewise suggests that these dreams were "thrown into disorder" by Aurora, were "made excited" by her. (2) The etymology of Cephalus, significantly the only person cited in these last two lines of the elegy, is *head*. Aurora, a manifestation of Venus, of course, has banished the golden sleep and the visions the poet recounts, and so he says, "May such dreams often befall me!"—but remembering the Ovid, we know that though he wishes for cerebral dreams, it will be sexual dreams that take over. And is the liquid imagery therefore

significant for more than just sadness, perhaps seminal emission? I think Milton's schoolmates schooled in Latin and in Ovid would have heard the "dirty" puns, though latter-day critics do not.

14. *The Intellectual Development of John Milton* (Urbana: University of Illinois Press, 1961), II, 436.

15. "Milton as a Latin Poet" in *Neo-Latin Poetry of the Sixteenth and Seventeenth Centuries* (Los Angeles: William Andrews Clark Library, 1965).

16. See "Notes on Milton's Early Development," *University of Toronto Quarterly* 13 (1943–44): 66–101.

17. "My sorrows loud / Had got a race of mourners on som pregnant cloud" is called "The worst line he ever wrote"; see Martz, *The Poetry of Meditation: A Study in English Religious Literature of the Seventeenth Century* (New Haven, Conn.: Yale University Press, 1954; rev. 1962), 168.

18. He appended a note: "This Subject the Author finding to be above the years he had, when he wrote it, and nothing satisfi'd with what was begun, left it unfinisht."

19. See *Milton: The Critical Heritage* (vol. I), ed. John T. Shawcross (London: Routledge & Kegan Paul, 1970), 98.

20. See William B. Hunter, Jr., "The Date and Occasion of *Arcades,*" *English Language Notes* 11 (1973): 46–47.

21. See Hilaire Belloc, *Milton* (Philadelphia: J. B. Lippincott, 1935), 213ff., and George Saintsbury, *A History of English Prosody from the Twelfth Century to the Present Day* (London: Macmillan, 1908), II, 215–18, for discussion of the so-called Miltonic sonnet.

Chapter 12

1. In "An Elegy upon the Death of My Lord Francis Villiers," if this poem is indeed by Marvell, the name seems to be a mask for a real person, possibly Mary Kirke, daughter of Aurelian Townshend.

2. It is obvious that I do not read the mower as Death. This identification arises from the idea most explicitly expressed in "The Mower's Song" that he cuts down the "meadows fresh and gay" and from the final lines of "Damon the Mower":

> "Only for him no cure is found,
> Whom Juliana's eyes do wound.
> 'Tis death alone that this must do;
> For Death thou art a Mower too."

But the point in mowing grass is to make it stronger and more luxuriant, not to kill it. Indeed, poetic critics whenever they move to pruning images (even those who talk of George Herbert's "Paradise") seem ignorant of the basic agricultural fact that reduction of overgrowth produces stronger, more beautiful, larger, and more delicious flowers, fruits, or vegetables. What Juliana does to Damon's thoughts and him, in "The Mower's Song," is cause them to be more intense and stronger in their love for her by spurning his love. The analogy with the mowing of the grass can only be a cutting back of his thoughts and him by her, not their extirpation. And though Death is a mower, logic does not say that one who mows is Death. The lines, appropriate for the "Petrarchan" poem, say first that the lover (Damon, the mower) can envision only his death as end to the torment he feels from his cold mistress, and second, with traditional pun, only sexual intercourse (death) can end his smart. As sexual image, mow is not far from the bawdy meanings of plow, crop, and deflower. And according to Eric Partridge "mow" is Northern dialect for "copulate with" from around the sixteenth century through the eighteenth.

Chapter 13

1. Richard Poirier, *The Performing Self: Compositions and Decompositions in the Languages of Contemporary Life* (New York: Oxford University Press, 1971). See also Stephen Greenblatt, *Renaissance Self-Fashioning: From More to Shakespeare* (Chicago: University of Chicago Press, 1980) for a summary and expansion of the concept of the performing self.

2. Donno's note in her Penguin edition. For a discussion of "A Fair Singer," "Mourning," "The Gallery," and "Daphnis and Chloe," examining the poet's awareness of multiple perspectives that affect his ability to define his subject accurately, see Michael H. Markel, "Perception and Expression in Marvell's Cavalier Poetry," *Classic and Cavalier,* ed. Summers and Pebworth, 243–53.

3. What is involved is the traditional question over which sense enabled the mind to perceive beauty most readily; see David O. Frantz's discussion "The Union of Florimell and Marinell: The Triumph of Hearing," *Spenser Studies* 6 (1985): 115–27. Frantz cites Erwin Panofsky's *Problems in Titian: Mostly Iconographic* (New York: New York University Press, 1969), 119.

4. *The Resolved Soul: A Study of Marvell's Major Poems* (Princeton, N.J.: Princeton University Press, 1970), 117.

5. Dennis Davison, ed., *Selected Poetry and Prose* (London: Harrap, 1952).

6. J. B. Leishman, *The Art of Marvell's Poetry* (London: Hutchinson, 1966), 77.

7. In the background is George Herbert's "A Wreath" with its device of lines linked by repeated phrase, interlacing the wreath:

> A wreathed garland of deserved praise,
> Of praise deserved, unto thee I give,
> I give to thee, who knowest all my wayes,
> My crooked winding wayes, wherein I live,
> Wherein I die, not live: for life is straight,
> Straight as a line, and ever tends to thee,
> To thee, who art more farre above deceit,
> Then deceit seems above simplicitie.
> Give me simplicitie, that I may live,
> So live and like, that I may know, thy wayes,
> Know them and practise them: Then shall I give
> For this poore wreath, give thee a crown of praise.

And the poet's admonition to himself is like that of Herbert's "Jordan (I)": present direct heartfelt statement, plainly said, not fictions and enchanted groves.

8. "The Second Song" at the marriage of the Lord Fauconberg and the Lady Mary Cromwell is discussed in chapter 12.

9. "Clorinda and Damon" is discussed in chapter 2, and "Ametas and Thes ylis Making Hay-ropes," "Daphnis and Chloe," and "The Mower to the Glowworms" are examined in chapter 12. "The Bermudas" is referenced in chapter 12, as well.

10. "Marvell's 'Unfortunate Lover' as Device," *Modern Language Quarterly* 35 (1974): 364–75.

11. See also remarks in chapter 12.

12. See, for example, Angela G. Dorenkamp's "Marvell's Geometry of Love," *English Language Notes* 9 (1971): 111–15.

13. In *Bucknell Review* 10 (1962): 263–74; rpt. in *Marvell's Ironic Vision* (New Haven, Conn.: Yale University Press, 1965) and in *Andrew Marvell: A Collection of Critical Essays*, ed. George de F. Lord (Englewood Cliffs, N.J.: Prentice-Hall, 1968).

Chapter 14

1. See Earl Miner, *Metaphysical Mode from Donne to Cowley* (Princeton, N.J.: Princeton University Press, 1969), *Cavalier Mode from Jonson to Cotton* (Princeton, N.J.: Princeton University Press, 1971), and *Restoration Mode from Milton to Dryden* (Princeton, N.J.: Princeton University Press, 1974).

2. See, for example, George H. Gretton, *John Donne. Seine Beziehung zu seiner Zeit und sein Einfluss auf seine 'nicht-metaphysischen' Nachfolger: Carew, Suckling, Marvell und Rochester* (Düsseldorf: G.H. Nolte, 1938). Some specific debts of Rochester are indicated in a few incidental places; see Fredell Bruser, "Disproportion: A Study of the Works of John Wilmot, Earl of Rochester," *University of Toronto Quarterly* 15 (1946): 391, and Anne Righter, "John Wilmot, Earl of Rochester," *Proceedings of the British Academy* 53 (1969 for 1967): 47–69.

3. Editions of Donne (1669), Cherbury (1665), Herbert (1660, 1667, 1674, 1678, 1695), and Jonson (1692) appear after 1660. Perhaps their influence has been dismissed by modern critics partially because they accept as representative Dryden's often inept reading. Fulsomeness aside, Dryden's preference of Dorset over Donne (Dedication, iii, to *The Satires of Decimus Junius Juvenalis. Translated into English Verse* [London, 1693]), as well as his "tagging" of *Paradise Lost*, which Marvell and Miltonists have recognized as symptomatic of a prejudiced inadequacy, gives one little confidence in Dryden's full appreciation. Waller, Denham, Cowley, Vaughan, and Marvell, of course, continue to live into the Restoration and receive publication then.

4. But David Farley-Hills, *Rochester's Poetry* (Totowa, N.J.: Rowman and Littlefield; London: Bell and Hyman, 1978), views Rochester's poetry in relationship to some of the seventeenth-century love lyrics, including Donne's, Suckling's, and Carew's. See also Jeremy Treglown, "The Satirical Inversion of Some English Sources in Rochester's Poetry," *Review of English Studies* 24 (1973): 42–48.

5. Alexander Witherspoon and Frank J. Warnke, eds., *Seventeenth-Century Prose and Poetry* (New York: Harcourt, Brace, and World, 1956).

6.   A Candle

> There is a thing which in the light
> Is seldom us'd; but in the night
> It serves the maiden female crew,
> The ladies, and the good-wives too:
> They use to take it in their hand,

> And then it will uprightly stand;
> And to a hole they it apply,
> Where by its goodwill it would die;
> It spends, goes out, and still within
> It leaves its moisture thick and thin.

Herrick's verse also supplies examples, such as "The Vine."

7. Miner's comment on Suckling, typically, I think, arises from this same kind of blindness to "play." He writes, "Once again we may see how far the love poetry was concerned with the psychology of love, or with the motivations of passion, whether in observations of the lady, in compliment, or in consideration of the physical side of love" (*Cavalier Mode*, 239).

8. See also the anonymous "Rochester's Farewell" for his alleged moral crusade, for example, ll. 6–7, "Long I with charitable malice strove, / Lashing the Court these vermin to remove," in *Poems on Affairs of State* (New Haven, Conn.: Yale University Press, 1965), II, 218–19, ed. Elias F. Mengel, Jr.

9. See Walter V. Ong's discussion "Logic and the Epic Muse: Reflections on Poetic Structures in Milton's Milieu," in *Achievements of the Left Hand: Essays on the Prose of John Milton*, ed. Michael Lieb and John T. Shawcross (Amherst: University of Massachusetts Press, 1974), 239–68.

10. Ibid.

11. See *Henry the Third of France, Stabb'd by a Fryer* (London, 1678), A4v–*1r.

12. "On the Poet Ninny," ll. 27–28.

Chapter 15

1. Moses Coit Tyler, *A History of American Literature During the Colonial Period, 1607–1765* (New York: G.P. Putnam's, 1898), I, 292.

2. Emily Stipes Watts, *The Poetry of American Women from 1632 to 1945* (Austin: University of Texas Press, 1977), 10.

3. *The Works of Anne Bradstreet*, ed. Jeannine Hensley (Cambridge, Mass.: Belknap Press of Harvard University Press, 1967), xxiii. Quotations come from this edition.

4. Quotations are taken from Harrison T. Meserole, ed., *Seventeenth-Century American Poetry* (New York: W.W. Norton, 1968), 252–65.

Index

DATE DUE